THE
INTIMIDATOR

THE INTIMIDATOR: Dale Earnhardt

THE INTIMIDATOR

The Dale Earnhardt Story
An Unauthorized Biography

FRANK VEHORN

Ninth Printing, December, 1994

Publisher's Cataloging-in-Publication Data
(Prepared by Quality Books Inc.)

Vehorn, Frank. E.
    The intimidator: the Dale Earnhardt story, an unauthorized
biography / Frank Vehorn.
p. ill. cm.
ISBN 1-878086-09-X

1. Earnhardt, Dale, 1951-. 2. Stock car racing–Biography. 3.
Biography–20th century. I. Title. II. Title: The Dale Earnhardt
story: an unauthorized biography.

GV1029.9.S74   796.72
                                               QBI91-1444

Printed in the United States of America

Cover design by Harry Blair
Cover photo by Dozier Mobley
Book design by Elizabeth House

Down Home Press
P.O. Box 4126
Asheboro, N.C. 27204

Dedicated in memory of some heroes and friends: Joe Littlejohn, Tiny Lund, LeeRoy Yarbrough, Bobby Isaac, Tim Richmond, Joe Whitlock, and Ralph Earnhardt.

Contents

Introduction

Great race drivers are good fast. They are not great fast, but they are good fast.

You look at Dale Earnhardt, Richard Petty and Curtis Turner, and they are, or were, good fast, not great fast.

At Charlotte Motor Speedway, we have done all kinds of tests to determine what makes a good race driver, and we have never come up with anything physical, other than eyesight. I think it might just boil down to the seat of the pants. While Curtis Turner did not win a lot of races, most people will probably tell you he was one of the five greatest pure drivers we ever had in racing. He had the ability to run and feel a car by the seat of the pants like no one else in racing today. It is just a certain gift that only a few people have – and Dale Earnhardt is one of them.

Of course, Dale has tremendous desire, too, and that is something he was born with. I don't think you can develop desire. Dale takes cars into gray areas of the track where angels fear to tread and great race drivers are born. A lot of drivers won't take the chances he does, and he does it so well that he wins a lot of races that way.

Dale has got what I call a Rocky Marciano mentality. He likes a good fight. He likes conflict. Some drivers don't like conflict. Some drivers are even good because they don't like conflict. Bill Elliott doesn't like conflict, for instance, but he is a tremendous race driver. He will do things not to get in conflict with people. Dale likes it, and that is something you are born with. It is part of that tremendous desire and it comes out in the heat of battle.

Dale's dad, Ralph, was a good friend of mine. He was our dirt-track test driver when I was with Firestone. Ralph was a driver who beat you by out-thinking you, and he also was great at intimidating you.

I began to notice Dale and to think he had a lot of talent when he started running on what is now the Busch Grand National circuit, and he did pretty good on asphalt. That is always a big test for drivers who start out on dirt. But I think one of the reasons Dale is so good right now has much to do with that early dirt-track experience. He could do things on dirt that very few drivers could do and then he transferred that talent to slick race tracks, which most of them were when he moved to asphalt racing during that period.

Dale did not have it easy coming up through the ranks, and he went through some periods when things got pretty rough. He had gone through a divorce, and he lost his father, and that was just devastating to him, because he idolized his father. I didn't lose my father until I was thirty years old but it had a tremendous effect on me, and it took a long time for me to get over that.

I thought Dale probably needed some guidance during that period, and I tried to help him when I could. One thing I was noticing him doing a lot was over-driving his race car, and we used to talk about that a lot. He just had so much desire and aggression. Those things make great race drivers, but they also can cause a lot of wrecks, such as the one Dale had down in Atlanta in 1976 when he flipped his car eight or nine times.

I think through the years he has settled down a lot. After he won the Winston Cup Championship in 1980, in only his second season on the circuit, he was really having problems figuring out who he was. He knows who he is now. That is just maturing, and learning to do the right things. I think marrying Teresa had a real beneficial influence on him and helped to calm him down.

He has had considerable success, but he has retained a lot of humility, and in that regard, he is a little like Arnold Palmer. That is one of the reasons he still is able to run up front. While he has got a lot of confidence that might wind up making him appear cocky, you have got to have that confidence to be a great driver. On the other hand, the great race drivers who retain some humility tend to stay great longer.

In terms of greatness, Dale Earnhardt rates right up there with Richard Petty and Curtis Turner, and to an extent, even though he is not a great multi-dimensional driver – you can't be any more – I would put him right up there with A.J. Foyt, who may be the greatest race driver we ever had. Earnhardt has a lot of the attributes that Foyt has, such as the great seat-of-the-pants driving and that great desire to become one with the car.

Dale Earnhardt right now might be going through what John Jerome wrote about in a book called *The Sweet Spot in Time*. It is an interesting book because the author studied athletes when they were at the peak of their careers. They all had one peak that Jerome called "the sweet spot in time," when everything worked together – physically and mentally – for that one great year. You only have it once. That is what Jerome maintains and he puts up a serious argument on it.

Dale had a great year in 1990, but the interesting thing about him is that he may not have reached his sweet spot in time yet. That may be something we can look forward to seeing, and if he stays around long enough, we might be calling him the greatest race driver we ever had.

– H.A. "Humpy" Wheeler,
President, Charlotte Motor Speedway

Foreword

When I first started watching Ralph Earnhardt run, I was in high school in Charleston, and I used to go up to Columbia and watch him, Bobby Isaac, and Ned Jarrett. Man, I am telling you, those were my heroes. And Earnhardt was tough. I mean tough.

He built some of my early race cars. When I was a kid, I learned to go to him right off and get good stuff. He was as good a car builder as he was a driver.

I would carry all of the cars that I bought from him down to Georgia and win all the races. That was back when I was about nineteen years old.

Ralph had this move he used to put on people to win races. I saw him one night at Myrtle Beach. They had what they called the Sun Fun 101, and they said before the race they would not finish under caution. So they had a big wreck and it was a lap to go. They stopped the race. A guy named Earl Moss was leading, and a guy named Ken Rush was running second. Ralph – and I will never forget this – he had broke down, and he told Ken Rush that if he let him in that car that he would win the race for him. Ralph had an old pair of overalls on. He crawled up in that car and he passed Earl Moss coming off the corner on the last lap.

The guy was a racer. I can remember in Daytona, when he had never seen the race track before in his life, and he jumped into Cotton Owens' car, I think, and run fifth. Had never seen the race track before and didn't have any time on it. He was a racer.

Ralph used to stick that wheel up against your left rear tire, and man, it didn't take but just a little budge.

I spent a lot of time around him and he taught me a lot of stuff. He parked me a couple of times on purpose, and he made me mean, man. I learned, though, that there was only one way to beat him, and that was to stay away from him. That is what I did. I worked hard until my car got a little superior to his, because there was no such thing as actually out-driving Ralph.

It is kind of like Dale now. I mean, how could you out-drive him? And that is the way his dad was.

I guess at the height of his career, Ralph Earnhardt was one of the toughest people I have ever seen drive a race car. That is where Dale gets it.

If I had to race against Dale, I'd have to race him just like we used to have to race Ralph. There wouldn't be but one way to race him, and that would be to stay away from him. It is just that simple.

The intimidation thing, yeah, he does it. There is no question about that. And his dad, he was an intimidator. I mean, he convinced me to stay the hell away from him. And he had a lot of other people convinced of that, too. I mean, if he got close, it was too late. If he got close, it was over. That sounds funny now. But the difference is you go to Martinsville, and when two cars touch coming down the straightaway, everybody in the grandstands jumps up and makes a big deal out of it. But I can remember when they came together every lap, twice a lap in each corner, and both straightaways.

I used to love to go off into the corner and watch Ralph. I learned a lot by watching him. I'd see him run lap after lap and then I would see him take that one, long hard shove off into the first turn, just to see if the car would do it. And I used to always say, "Wow!"

Dale has got all of that in him.

Back in the early 1970s, I went to Metrolina Speedway near Charlotte. I had not seen Dale for years. Somebody told me about him, what kind of racer they thought he was going to be. I was there with Gene Petty, a guy who worked for Firestone, and I watched Dale come off the corner and I told Petty, "That man you are watching now will be the biggest superstar NASCAR has ever had."

He said, "How do you figure that?" and I said, "I see it in him."

There was never any question in my mind where Dale Earnhardt was headed.

He had that in him. It was just there. You could see it. He was a racer. Born in him, I guess.

— "Little" Bud Moore

1

'You gonna starve to death, boy'

Dale Earnhardt knew what he wanted in life from the time he was big enough to crawl through the window of his daddy's race cars, which were built and maintained in a shop out behind his family's two-story white house near the intersection of Coach and Sedan streets in Kannapolis, North Carolina, a cotton mill town north of Charlotte.

"Being a race driver is all I ever wanted to be," he says.

Many nights as a boy he fell asleep to the sweet sounds created by his daddy fine tuning an engine in the shop out back. It may have been noise to others, but it was music to him. He dreamed of growing up and following in the tire tracks his daddy, Ralph, left behind on visits to hundreds of victory lanes and a national championship on the old NASCAR Sportsman circuit.

"I had a lot of fun growing up," says Dale, who has two younger brothers and two older sisters. "We didn't have all the finer things in life, but we still had a good time. I can't ever remember wanting anything that I didn't have.

"There were lots of good times. I remember Daddy going

1

racing during the week, and I couldn't wait until I got home from school the next day to find out everything that happened. I wanted to hear it all. The only things I remember doing much as a kid was helping Daddy with the race cars, doing whatever he'd let me do, and being around racing people. I couldn't wait until I got old enough to drive race cars myself."

It was not long after growing old enough to get a race car of his own, however, that the good-time dreams faded and were replaced by the harsh realities of trying to make a living from stock car racing.

Worst of all, Dale was left to pursue his distant goal without his father, who suffered a fatal heart attack while working in his race shop on a September day in 1973.

Dale, who was born on April 29, 1951, already had experienced some of life's hard times before his father's untimely death. Against the wishes of his parents, he quit school in the ninth grade when he was sixteen. A year later, he was married and soon had a son, Kerry, who was born on December 8, 1969. The marriage didn't last.

He married again and fathered a daughter, Kelly King, born on August 28, 1972, and a son, Ralph Dale, Jr., born on October 10, 1974. But the second marriage didn't last either.

Although his marriages didn't survive the hard times of working long hours and living in trailers and small apartments, his dreams of being a race car driver did, although he had to keep them alive by going deep into debt and taking odd jobs. He built trailers. He became a certified welder.

"It was tough going through all of that, but I never thought it was going to be easy. I just knew that whatever it took for me to race, I was going to do it," he recalls. "I always thought I would make it as a race driver. I just kept wondering when I was going to get the break I needed to do it."

One of the jobs Earnhardt had in those turbulent days was installing insulation at a textile mill in Denton, N.C. It made him even more determined to make it as a race driver.

"I was insulating some pipe and working over the weave room in the mill. I would look down at those people, shake my head, and say, 'Boy, there ain't no way.' I watched those people working in that mill, and I knew I could never do that.

"I don't mean there is anything wrong with working in a mill, if that is what what you want to do. It just wasn't what I wanted to do. I wanted to race."

Dale's last job before going racing full time, was at Whitaker's Wheel Alignment shop in Concord only a few miles from Kannapolis, just up the road from Charlotte Motor Speedway, where he spent many exciting afternoons as a youngster watching Winston Cup races with his daddy.

"I just finally decided the only way I was going to get to where I wanted in racing was to do it full time," he recalls.

So in 1974, a year after his father's death, he told his supervisor he was quitting.

"What you going to do?" the supervisor asked.

"I'm going racing," Dale replied.

"You gonna to starve to death, boy."

Dale had raced on dirt tracks for about a year and a half before his father's death, and the only previous racing education he had gotten was from watching his father run on short-tracks in the Carolinas.

"You look at all the greats, and you work hard to be a little like all of them, I guess," he says when asked where he got his hard-driving, aggressive style. "But in racing you don't really pattern yourself after this one or that one. I think your personality and drive patterns itself. You might be a sly fox type like David Pearson was. You might be a Richard Petty type. But I think, really, it is just your personality that dictates how you are going to be in racing.

"I watched my daddy race for so many years that I believe I am more like him than anyone else. He raced against guys like Tiny Lund, Bobby Isaac, Rex White, all of those guys, and I learned some things from them, too. I stood on the back of the truck, or on a stack of tires, and watched Daddy race. That is how I learned to race. The first time I sat down in a race car, no one had to tell me what to do. I knew what was going on and what I was supposed to do."

Dub Coleman, one of Earnhardt's uncles, once told writer Tom Cotter that Dale's relationship with his father continued to develop after Ralph Earnhardt's death. "I think they are closer now, if that makes any sense," Coleman said.

"Ralph never encouraged Dale one way or another about getting into racing. He could easily have given Dale one of his cars to race, but he didn't do it. If Dale was going to race, Ralph wanted him to work for it."

Coleman remembered one of the few races in which Ralph ran against his son, but in a different division.

"Ralph would actually push Dale down the backstraight," Coleman said. "It was like a father helping his son with a special project. He was teaching his son the trade."

Dale agrees that he developed a stronger appreciation for his father when faced with having to continue his budding career without his guidance, encouragement, and advice.

"My racing was going pretty good on the dirt tracks and I was looking forward to Daddy and me being together as a team. Then, all of a sudden, he was gone. He taught me a lot, but after his death I started wishing that I had paid closer attention and learned more from him."

Dale's mother, Martha, always seemed to accept the fact her oldest son would take after his father and drive race cars.

"I can't remember Dale ever wanting to do anything else," she says. "He and his brothers spent a lot of time building models and racing slot cars when they were little. Dale won his first trophy with slot cars."

Dale and his mother never discussed his aspirations to race.

"I don't know if she was in favor or against me racing, really" he says. "She knew it was inevitable that I was going to race, and her concern and support were always there for me."

From the start, Dale was never one to sit back and take things easy. He grew up watching his daddy drive at the front of the field. That was the way he wanted to drive, too, and it didn't seem to matter who or what he had to run over to take the car to the front.

In one of his first victories, Dale found himself locked in a tight duel with veteran short-track driver "Stick" Elliott at one of the bullrings. After deciding there was only one way to make the pass, Dale smoothly gave Elliott a strategic nudge in the rear fender.

Elliott took a spin while Dale took the checkered flag. Dale didn't know what to expect when he saw Elliott climb from his bruised car and head straight for him in the pits.

He nervously stood his ground as Elliott walked up to him. Instead of being angry, the crusty Elliott grinned, stuck out his hand, and said, "Nice race, boy."

Richard Childress, who later would give Dale his ride of a lifetime, remembers the first time he ever heard about the young driver who was stirring up a fuss on the short-track circuit.

"My brother had been to a race down at Asheboro. When he got back home, he told me about this wild, young driver he had seen," Childress recalls with a smile. "I asked him what was his name, and he says 'Dale Earnhardt, I think it is Ralph's boy.' "

Veteran driver Red Farmer also remembers his introduction to the young charger, who once won a race by crossing the finish line with his car on top of another race car.

Farmer, who was running for the national Sportsman championship, ventured up from Alabama to race at one of the North Carolina tracks. He went back home shaking his xead and talking about "that Earnhardt boy, who hit everyone and everything at the track except the people in the grandstands."

After deciding to become a full-time racer, Dale switched from dirt tracks to asphalt. "I was doing good on dirt and I could have made a living from it," he recalls. "But I knew I had to make the switch to get to where I wanted to go, which was NASCAR racing."

He bought one of Harry Gant's old asphalt race cars and found the transition less difficult than he expected. Before the end of the 1974 season he had beaten veterans Tommy Houston at Metrolina Speedway and Bob Pressley at Hickory Speedway.

His biggest adjustment was learning to be a smoother driver. He couldn't beat and bang as much. Nor could he broadslide through the turns like he enjoyed doing on dirt tracks.

"There was a whole lot of difference driving asphalt, but I was always glad that I started out racing on dirt," he said later. "I learned some things that helped me out when I got on the Winston Cup circuit and began racing on the big tracks. You learn the feel of a car and sharpen your reflexes by racing on dirt. It bothers some guys when their cars gets loose on the big tracks and they can feel air coming in through the side window. But not me."

Dale made his debut on a high-banked track in the World Service Life 300 Sportsman race at Charlotte Motor Speedway in October, 1974. He started twelfth in a five-year-old Dodge and finished thirteenth.

He returned to Charlotte Motor Speedway in May, 1975, to compete in the World 600, which was his first appearance in a Winston Cup race. Driving a 1973 Dodge, he started thirty-third and finished 22nd.

He began attracting notice from some of the established Winston Cup stars, such as David Pearson and Bobby Allison, when he finished sixth in the Sportsman race at Charlotte in October, 1975, and 13th in a Sportsman race on his first trip to Daytona in February, 1976.

Dale talked his way into a couple of other rides for Winston Cup races in 1976, including the race at Atlanta in which he flipped several times on the backstretch while driving a car owned by John Ray, but he ran only one Winston Cup race the following season.

Instead of getting better, things started getting worse for Dale in the summer of 1978.

He was having to borrow money to buy tires and engines and even to buy gasoline to haul his race car to the tracks. "I never thought about quitting or giving up," he recalls of that period. "I kept racing, getting deeper and deeper in debt, and really didn't know just how far in debt I was.

"I was asking myself what I should do. I still believed that somehow I was going to make it, and a lot of people were trying to help me and were saying they knew I could do it. But my money was gone and I knew I couldn't keep on borrowing and borrowing.

"Right then, I wasn't looking for a bigger or better ride, I was just looking for a sponsor who could help get me out of debt. I wasn't the only one out there in that situation, either."

At Hickory Speedway, Metrolina in Charlotte, and even the outlaw track in Concord, near his home, Dale saw other drivers who had the ability but never the opportunities to realize their own dreams of reaching the Winston Cup circuit.

"You learn real quick in racing that you can't do it without money," he says. "All the way up the ranks I saw drivers who were really good and who probably could have made it if they had the sponsorship money to do it. I was just hoping that I wasn't going to end up like they did, without ever getting the chance to prove what I could do. That was one thing that was in the back of my mind, and it really scared me. What if I never got that chance?"

Finally, in the fall of 1978, when things were at their bleakest and Dale was being forced to consider selling some his racing equipment to pay the mounting bills, the break he had been seeking finally presented itself.

He had been buying used parts from Osterlund Racing, a new Winston Cup team that had appeared on the circuit in 1977 and was owned by Rod Osterlund, a West Coast businessman. Osterlund had met Dale at the shop, had seen him run a few

7

Winston Cup races earlier in the year for Will Cronkite, and admired his determination and desire.

In October of 1978, Dale wanted to run in the Sportsman race at Charlotte Motor Speedway but didn't have the money to get good parts for an engine. His beat-up race car wasn't all that healthy, either. Roland Wlodyka, the Osterlund team manager, suggested to Osterlund that they field a car for Dale to drive.

"The only problem was they really didn't have a car to put me in," Dale recalls. "But I had got to be friends with several of the guys in the shop, such as Jim Delaney, Doug Richert, Lou Larosa, and Ducky Newman, and they told Osterlund that they would fix a car and build an engine for me if it was all right with him. Osterlund said they could do it.

"So they took a car from out back of the shop that had the front end tore off and rebuilt the whole car. It was a Chevrolet Monte Carlo. They built the engine and we went over to the race track and started practicing. The car didn't really handle all that great, but when the race started, it was real consistent and I took it to the front of the field. I was outrunning Bobby Allison and Dave Marcis, who was Osterlund's Winston Cup driver at the time, and it made an impression on them.

"We were using basically used stuff and the transmission tore up with 10 laps to go and me leading the race. They told me to stay out on the track because with the transmission trouble they were worried about me getting in and out of the pits. I stayed out and Bobby Allison, Marcis, Harry Gant, and some of the other guys pitted for tires. When they restarted, I got going pretty good and the only guy that got by me in those final laps was Allison, so I ran second. We were pretty impressive, and everyone seemed pleased with the way things turned out."

Marcis and Wlodyka had been feuding for awhile, and Marcis told Osterlund after the Charlotte Winston Cup race that he was not going to be back in 1979. Pleased with Dale's performance in the Sportsman race, Osterlund decided to put him in a Winston Cup car for the Atlanta race.

Dale gave another sizzling performance as he finished fourth, behind Donnie Allison, Richard Petty and Marcis. "It would have been better, but I ran over an air hose in the pits and got penalized a lap for it," Dale remembers.

It was still good enough that Osterlund told Dale he was looking for an experienced driver to take Marcis's place, but that he would consider running Dale in a second car in about 15 races in 1979.

Osterlund also asked Dale to drive for him in the season-ending race at Ontario, California.

"I had gotten my hopes up a little bit that finally someone was going to help me out and give me a break, and when they flew me all the way to California and gave me a car to drive, man, I figured they must be serious about wanting me to drive for them," Dale remembers.

Although he'd never seen the Ontario track before, Dale finished 11th. A few weeks later, he learned that Osterlund was serious about wanting him as a driver.

"In December, Rod called and asks, 'You want to drive the car the full schedule in 1979?' " Dale recalls.

"Man, I couldn't believe it. I was going Winston Cup racing, and I didn't have to worry about paying for tires or engines or beating out dents in the fenders no more. The dream I'd had ever since I was a boy was coming true. It was like my daddy had told me once, 'If you work hard enough, your dream will come true.' "

2

Good ol' boy from North Carolina

Winston Cup stock car racing was approaching an era of enormous change when Dale Earnhardt slid behind the steering wheel of the blue and yellow Osterlund Team Chevrolet in 1979 to begin his first full season on the NASCAR Winston Cup circuit. It was a season in which Richard Petty would win the last of his seven Winston Cup championships, ending a three-year title streak by Cale Yarborough, and David Pearson would walk away from a seven-year victory tour on the superspeedways with the Wood Brothers.

With the leadership of tour sponsor R. J. Reynolds Tobacco Company, the circuit was recovering splendidly from the withdrawal of direct sponsorship from the automobile factories earlier in the decade. No longer were only a few select teams being pipe-lined the best equipment. Most high performance parts could be purchased over-the-counter by anyone, and that encouraged the participation in the sport of businessmen like Osterlund, who felt they had a chance to compete equally on the circuit.

The Old Guard, the teams of Junior Johnson, the Pettys,

10

Bud Moore, and the Wood Brothers, suddenly found themselves challenged by this fresh wind of competition blowing through the sport. Among the new owners were Harry Ranier, a Kentucky coal miner, whose team won the 1978 Talladega 500 with Lennie Pond in its first season. The Ranier team was even more optimistic of success with veteran Buddy Baker taking over the steering wheel in 1979.

The new wave was best represented by Bill Gardner's DiGard team, which featured rising superstar Darrell Waltrip, who was outspoken, controversial, and highly talented. Waltrip won six races in each of the 1977 and 1978 seasons and now he was ready to challenge King Richard Petty for the '79 championship.

Waltrip, a native of Owensboro, Ky., had sharpened his racing talents on the short-track at Nashville, Tenn., where he became a local celebrity, rubbing shoulders with the country music crowd, before advancing to the Winston Cup circuit for a handful of races with his own team in 1972. He did not begin running the full schedule until joining the DiGard team midway in the 1975 season, shortly after winning his first Winston Cup race on the Nashville track.

Waltrip was a smooth talker and a stylish dresser and he presented a polished image that some observers predicted would be characteristic of race drivers in the future.

But while Waltrip was taking Petty down to the wire before losing one of racing's tightest championship battles, Dale Earnhardt, whose hard-driving style and rugged features were reminiscent of a fading era, quickly emerged as the other new star on the Winston Cup circuit.

"Dale was a good, young driver who got the breaks he needed and had the talent and determination to make the most of them," says Benny Parsons, a former driver who later became a radio and television commentator.

"The Osterlund team was very good and ready to win races when Dale got the ride, and after only a couple of races that first season the team signed Jake Elder as its crew chief. That was a big, big advantage, because Jake is just super with young drivers who have not quite figured out which way is straight ahead.

"I know, because I floundered around as a race car driver for four or five years and I had no success until Jake Elder came in as my crew chief. It was like I had been going in circles and he put his hand on top of my head and said, 'That way, boy.' It was a lot easier for me after that."

Ironically, Elder also was the first Winston Cup crew chief for Darrell Waltrip and guided him to his first victory on the circuit.

Elder, who began the 1979 season with the Ranier team, switched to Osterlund's team right before the Atlanta race in March. He liked what he saw in his young driver.

"I could see from the start that Dale Earnhardt was going to win races," Elder says. "He had learned a lot when he was driving those Sportsman cars on dirt. Sometimes when he is running asphalt, he will pull them tricks like he's running dirt. And Dale is good enough to get away with it. He is willing to take that extra chance that a driver needs to win a lot of races."

Elder remembers that Dale made a strong run in the Atlanta race despite not having a competitive car.

"Some of the other mechanics asked me where I thought I would win my first race with Dale. I told them that we were going to win wherever the next race was run at. Well, it was at Bristol and at that time Darrell Waltrip was King Kong at Bristol.

"But I say I think we will win at Bristol, and they say, 'Man, you must be crazy. How can you go there and dominate and beat Darrell?' I told them that he could be beat and I had the driver to do it."

Elder, seldom wrong, wasn't this time, either.

"Sure enough, we went there and beat Waltrip," he recalls. "When Darrell put on fresh tires during his pit stops, he could outrun us for about 12 to 15 laps. After our tires got hot, we were more consistent and better than Darrell was.

"After the final pit stops, Dale just pulled out about three-tenths of a second ahead of Darrell and stayed there. He did not try to run real hard and punish the tires. Darrell was not gaining on us, and we were not losing nothing. That's how we won that first race, and we came back to Bristol the next year and did it again."

Dale completed his rookie season with only that one victory, but there may have been more if not for a violent crash at Pocono in July. He fractured both of his collar bones and missed four races in which David Pearson, who had not taken another ride since splitting with the Woods in April, filled in for him.

Pearson drove the Osterlund car to victory in the Southern 500 at Darlington in September and Earnhardt returned the next week to win pole position at Richmond.

Despite the pain, the most difficult thing about his injuries, Dale later recalled, was missing the four races. "I was on top of the world, and then, just like that, I was back listening to races on the radio.

"I was hurt in a lot of places, but the broken bones and the concussion and the headaches did not hurt as much as the frustration. I didn't know what was going to happen. I was worried that Pearson might do so well in the car that Osterlund would keep him and let me go. I have always appreciated the fact that Pearson did a great job while I was out and never once did he try to steal my ride from me."

Dale completed the season with a seventh-place finish at Ontario, California, to beat Joe Millikan for rookie-of-the-year honors.

In most other seasons, Millikan's accomplishments (no victories but five top-five and 20 top-10 finishes) would have been more than enough to win the title. The likable young man from Richard Petty's hometown, Randleman, just had the misfortune of making a run for the rookie title the same year that Dale Earnhardt came on the circuit with a rich car owner and a veteran mechanic, Elder.

"Most people kept comparing Dale and me that whole season because I stayed close to him in the rookie points," Millikan says. "But most people didn't remember that it was my first time on the Grand National circuit. Dale already had run a few races, although not enough that he was ineligible for the rookie award. He had gotten the feel of the competition and was a lot more comfortable. But the thing that probably helped him the most was getting Jake Elder when he did."

Dale's season was the best ever on the NASCAR circuit by a rookie driver. It included four pole victories and purse winnings of $264,085. He also became the first NASCAR rookie ever selected to compete in the International Race of Champions series.

He had only one major regret.

"I just wish Dad could have been here to see me," he said. "I think he would have been proud of me. He also could appreciate how far I have come. Dad had it tough all his life. I know he would not have liked the way I went in debt the four years before I finally got the break from Osterlund. But I think he would be proud of me now.

"The thing I am really happy about is that my Winston Cup career is off to such a great start. I am Ralph Earnhardt's boy, but I couldn't ride my daddy's reputation forever. My daddy's name opened a lot of doors for me along the way, and sometimes I was ashamed I had to use his name. It seemed I was taking advantage and it wasn't fair to do things that way. But I am a whole lot like him. All he ever wanted, all I have ever wanted, was to be a race driver."

Not only did Dale's great rookie season bail him out of debt, it permitted him to purchase a $145,000 house on Lake Norman near Charlotte.

"When I first started out, I worried about making it from

week to week," he said then. "I worried about ever owning my own home. Now I've got a nice place on the lake. I am comfortable and I am building security."

It had been less than 15 months since Dale had wondered if he would go broke before anyone gave him a break. In one magical season he had been swept into the fast lane and was being called a future superstar.

"I think about how fast things have changed and it scares me a little," he admitted at the time. "But I will take it. I am always in a hurry. There is always something else to do. That hasn't changed. But I will take it. I don't want to go back to where I was, but I don't ever want to forget where I came from either."

It seemed almost certain that the long, dreary days of struggle and financial insecurity were behind him, indeed. After the rookie season, Junior Johnson asked Dale what commitments he had for 1980. Dale replied that he was going to drive for Osterlund. Shortly afterward, he told team manager Wlodyka of Johnson's interest, and Wlodyka immediately informed Osterlund, who soon signed his young driver to a five-year contract.

Dale was delighted with the security such a contract supposedly represented, but others questioned his business judgment. Some of the sport's top stars were getting old enough to think about retirement and Dale would have the opportunity to inherit one of those rides, he was told.

"If I got out of the Osterlund car, I would be getting out of the best car on the circuit," he argued back. "Man, we have got four complete Chevrolet Monte Carlos ready to race right now. What more could I ask for? We have a great team, and it is getting to be a lot like the Pettys', a close-knit operation."

Dale felt both he and Osterlund could live comfortably with the agreement they had reached. "If I asked for more, it would hurt the operation. If I got less, it would hurt me," he rationalized. "I think it is an ideal contract. Rod told me that if

I was going to be competing against the Pettys, the Yarboroughs, and the Allisons, I should be making what they are making. Now I will be."

Dale received only a small percentage of the money that he won for the team in 1978, but he thought he gained in other ways as well.

"Rod took care of me when I got hurt in that wreck at Pocono," he said after his first season. "He helped me a lot in public relations, too. He coached me and he didn't get upset with me when I acted like a hot-headed punk.

"I am a much smarter driver now and that should make a big difference. I have a lot of drivers to thank for that, too. Last year, after I came back from being hurt, I felt I was behind and had to catch up. Richard sat down and talked to me at Rockingham, really gave me some good advice, and that settled me down for the rest of the season."

Dale also had reason to thank another member of the Petty clan, Richard's brother Maurice, the champion engine-builder.

"I don't want to get big-headed, and I can't afford to," Dale said. "When we were at Ontario, California, for the last race of the season, I was on a radio talk show. Maurice was listening to the show and later he came up to me and said that I had sounded just like a good ol' boy from North Carolina, and if I ever changed he was going to get a hold of me."

Dale smiled.

"I respect that. Besides, you don't ever want Maurice Petty to get a hold of you."

3

Move over, Darrell, here comes Dale

Anyone paying casual attention during the 1979 Winston Cup season could suspect it was only a matter of time before the sport's two young stars, Dale Earnhardt and Darrell Waltrip, would be battling to rule the front of the pack.

They didn't have to wait long.

In the 1980 season-opener at Riverside, California, Dale finished a close second to Waltrip, and from there they went to Daytona to wage a more furious battle in the Busch Clash, a 50-mile sprint race for the previous season's 12 pole winners.

Dale rode most of that race in second or third place, while Waltrip pushed his green Number 88 Oldsmobile to the front and held the lead for 11 of 19 laps before guiding a string of cars under the white-flag for the final, high-speed trip around the 2 1/2-mile high-banked oval.

Waltrip was still in the lead when he drove off the second turn and steered his car to the low lane on the long backstretch. He apparently was thinking that Dale wanted to make his move for victory on the inside lane.

When Waltrip left the outside door open, however, Dale

was more than willing to take that route. He positioned his car between Waltrip and the wall and pushed a little harder on the accelerator. Before Waltrip could recover, Bobby Allison drove under him and Neil Bonnett followed Dale around on the outside.

Dale roared off the fourth turn unchallenged while Bonnett held on for second place. Cale Yarborough drove by Allison for third, and Waltrip was drop-kicked to fifth place.

Dale collected a $50,000 paycheck in a race that lasted less than 16 minutes, and he led only in the final lap. He and the Osterlund crew staged a wild celebration in Victory Lane.

"I am not even thinking about the money," insisted Dale. "The thrill of winning this race just means so much more right now. It is a super feeling. A big high for me."

Indeed, it was another monumental moment for Dale and his crew. The young driver who showed he knew how to use his foot in his rookie season had proved he could use his head, too.

"The race was just like a game of checkers," Yarborough said. "You had to make the right move at the right time. The race just wasn't long enough for me to make my moves, but Earnhardt sure did everything he was supposed to do."

Dale revealed that his strategy came from watching films of the dramatic last-lap wreck involving Yarborough and Donnie Allison in the 1979 Daytona 500, which ended with the Allison boys, Bobby and Donnie, engaging Yarborough in a round of fisticuffs in the third turn.

"I remembered when Cale tried to go inside of Donnie on the backstretch of the last lap that Donnie pulled down on him," Dale said. "I didn't want Darrell and me to wreck like they did. I also remembered thinking that if I had been running behind Cale and Donnie last year that the place I would have wanted to go was the outside. When Darrell moved to the inside, that left plenty of room for me on the outside."

Waltrip had little to say about the finish, other than to contend he was "trapped between a rock and a hard place" when

Dale made his move on the outside. "When he went by, it just pulled everyone else on around me," Waltrip said.

After the race, Dale added an interesting footnote to his victory.

"A few days after I finished second to Darrell at Riverside, I dreamed that Darrell and I were racing for a victory and that I spun him out to win it. There were a couple of times out there today that I had the chance to spin him out, and I thought maybe that was what I should do, because of the dream. I am glad I didn't have to do that."

Others suggested the dream might have had a different meaning. Perhaps it was a revelation that Dale would wreck Waltrip's prediction that some day he would take over the circuit and dominate as Petty and Pearson had before him. Waltrip had made the statement a couple of years earlier, while Dale was struggling on the Carolinas' short-tracks.

It seemed a fair evaluation at that time. Waltrip already had established himself a winner on the circuit. He had enormous talent, a rich sponsor, and no one else seemed to be coming up through the ranks to offer him a serious challenge.

Now there was Earnhardt, only 29 years old, who had already proved himself a winner and had a solid team behind him. Dale expected people to begin comparing him to Waltrip and didn't mind when they did.

"I guess it is only natural that is going to happen," he said. "A couple of years ago, Darrell might have thought he would have the sport to himself when the older drivers retired or slowed down. But you can't afford to think that way. You won't ever be there by yourself. The door is open, and there always will be someone coming in it. That's what makes racing so competitive."

A week later, in the Daytona 500, Dale came close to pulling off an even more impressive triumph. He followed leader Buddy Baker through most of the race while again planning to make a last-lap charge to victory. But he never got the opportunity. During Dale's final pit stop, his crew put on a set of tires that caused the car to vibrate and he finished fourth behind Baker, Bobby Allison, and Neil Bonnett.

"I had stayed behind Buddy most of the day because it was more comfortable for me," Dale explained. "I wanted to wait until the last lap to put my move on him. But after we changed tires on the last lap, I couldn't run the car wide open because it was vibrating so badly. If we had only taken on gas that last pit stop, I really feel like I had a good chance of winning the race."

Baker complimented Earnhardt on driving a smart race but did not have much sympathy for his last-lap problems. He remembered days when he had come within a few laps of winning other Daytona 500s and was a victim of misfortune. It had taken him 18 years to win his first Daytona 500, and the only tears he shed in victory lane were ones of joy and relief.

"Dale has proved he is a great driver, and one of these days he will be sitting up here in the press box after winning his first Daytona 500," Baker predicted. "I can tell him right now that it is worth waiting for, too."

It wasn't as if Dale was leaving Daytona empty-handed, though. He jumped past Waltrip, whose car blew an engine after only 20 laps, to take the lead in the Winston Cup championship standings. He had a video, too, of his exciting last-lap victory over Waltrip in the Busch Clash. The video was well worn by season's end.

"The guys on the team would come up to my house on the lake during weekends off and the tape of the Clash was the first thing they plugged into the video machine," Dale recalls. "They watched me win that race a hundred times, and each time they would hoot and holler when the checkered flag fell."

Dale kept giving his crew and fans more to cheer, too. He finished fifth at Richmond, third at Rockingham, and rolled to back-to-back victories at Atlanta and Bristol, where he cockily told crew chief Elder during the post-race ceremony, "Jake, stick with me and we'll have diamonds as big as horse chips."

When the circuit arrived in North Wilkesboro, N.C., for the Northwestern Bank 400 in April, Dale was packing a 93-point lead over Bobby Allison in the championship standings and only Waltrip was refusing to accept him as a legitimate favorite to claim it.

No one ever had won rookie-of-the-year honors one season and the championship the next. Besides, there was a new theory in racing that a driver had to lose a championship, as Waltrip had done the previous year, before he could win one.

In his outspoken manner, Waltrip didn't hold back anything when asked about Earnhardt's chances to win the title.

"I would say it is durn near impossible, unless everyone else quits. I certainly wouldn't put any money on his chances of winning the title this year. That is because the worst is yet to come, and this is the voice of experience speaking."

Waltrip had six years experience on the circuit when he took on Petty in 1979. He seemed to have the championship in his grasp when he held a 229-point lead over Petty in early August.

But Petty won the title by 11 points in the final race.

"The going starts getting tough in June, because we will have five straight races, beginning at Charlotte, and taking us across the country and back, to Texas, California, and Michigan, and then to Daytona two weeks later," Waltrip explained.

"You are away from home all the time. It is hot and the men on the crews begin getting aggravated with each other. That is the first test of a team's worthiness to win the championship. But the critical month is September, when we have five straight races and the championship race begins exerting pressure. If a driver can hold his own and excel in September, he can really do some good."

Waltrip, who entered the North Wilkesboro race third in the championship standings and 104 points behind Earnhardt, claimed he had no desire to build a huge lead, as he had the previous year.

"I don't care about getting far ahead in the points. I love to lay down footsteps, but I hate to hear them. So I am really not going to worry about the points. If I win the championship, I win it. I would just hate to go through another agonizing affair like Richard and I went through at the end of last year. It is just so hard to race under those conditions."

Meanwhile, Earnhardt was getting serious attention from Petty, who was hoping to win his eighth championship.

"Here's the deal," Petty said. "Dale has finished in the top five consistently so far this season and that is what you have to do to win the thing. But the championship eventually will go to the driver who has the best luck all year long. The top seven or eight cars are so equal, any of those drivers could win the title if he had the best luck."

Petty admitted he had more than luck going for him to win the title the previous season. "Waltrip lost that championship. We didn't win it," he said. "We just kept on doing what we had been doing, but Darrell and his bunch changed what they had been doing. You know what I mean? They started counting the points, and figuring wasn't what got them there. Darrell got to figuring around and changing things."

Petty said Earnhardt would be a tougher man to beat down the stretch than was Waltrip. "Dale is serious about winning the championship, just as much as Darrell was last year. But Dale's outlook is different. He is as determined as Darrell, but he doesn't think he has anything to prove. I guess what it comes back to is there is a big difference in personality between Dale and Darrell."

Dale didn't take kindly to Waltrip's comments about him not having a chance to win the championship. "What gives him the right to say that I can't do it?" he demanded.

It didn't take long for Dale to discover how quickly things could change in stock car racing. Just as Waltrip predicted, the going started getting tough for for him just as the team was preparing to make the western swing in June.

Crew Chief Elder, the man credited with Dale's emergence on the Winston Cup circuit, abruptly resigned from the Osterlund team shortly after the World 600 at Charlotte Motor Speedway, where Dale finished 20th.

Elder, who had gotten the nickname "Suitcase Jake" because of his frequent team changes, said he no longer could work for Roland Wlodyka and did not feel he was getting solid support from all members of the crew.

"People told me there was no way I could get along with Roland, and they were exactly right," said Elder. "I had about three guys who wanted to win races and about five who couldn't care if the car won or if it blew up."

About his driver, Elder said, "Dale knew the problems I was having, but he never called." Later, Elder admitted that Dale wasn't a factor in his leaving the team.

"Dale was having some personal problems during that time I worked with him," he says, "but, don't get me wrong. I understood him. I knew Dale and my wife, Debbie, went to school with Dale and grew up with Dale. I knew his daddy real good. So, I knew the circumstances when I went to work with Dale.

"He had bad moods some days, you know, which I've got the same problem, and I guess that is why we hit it off so good. He understood me and I understood him. When he had a bad day, I didn't bother him, and he didn't bother me much. He knew I would tell him what I thought, and he could take it the wrong way or the right way. Later on, I would explain to him why I would say what I did. I think Dale took it into consideration that I was doing all I could to help him. I really believe he appreciated everything I ever done for him, too."

Elder said before walking out on the Osterlund team he tried to boost Earnhardt's confidence for the run at the championship.

"I told Dale the reason I was leaving had nothing to do with him. I just had to leave that mess I was in. And I told him that he was good enough that he could go on and win the championship without me. I told him it didn't matter who worked on the car, that he was good enough that he could tell them how he wanted the car to feel. I believed he would go on and win the championship, too. I knew his driving ability. That was going to play the biggest role."

Dale was not pleased with Elder's departure, and he became moody and irritable when questioned about it. "I don't hire or fire. I just drive the car. That is what I've been told to say," was his stock reply to questions.

Elder was replaced by 21-year-old Doug Richert, who had been a member of the Osterlund crew the last two years. Dale went from having one of the most experienced crew chiefs to the least experienced on the circuit.

The western tour to Texas, California, and Michigan was another draining experience for the Osterlund team. Cale Yarborough, emerging as another championship contender, won the NASCAR 400 at Texas World Speedway while Earnhardt finished ninth, two laps down.

Waltrip drove to his second victory of the season at Riverside International Raceway in the Hodgdon 400 and Earnhardt finished fifth at the tail end of the lead lap. Benny Parsons won the Gabriel 400 at Michigan International Speedway and Earnhardt finished 12th, three laps down.

Dale returned to North Carolina clinging to a 13-point lead over Richard Petty, who wasn't sure that Elder's departure was the reason for Earnhardt's recent slump.

"Dale has finished ninth, fifth, and 12th since Jake quit, but his problem has been with engines, and Jake was a chassis man. He didn't have anything to do with engines," Petty reminded.

Elder's departure did take one unexpected turn. When he left Osterlund, he was headed for Terry Labonte's team. Instead, he wound up working for Waltrip, who considered his hiring a psychological victory over Earnhardt.

"Everyone wants the best, and I have always considered Jake the best. He is the man you want in your pits when you are trying to win your first national championship," Waltrip said, a big smile breaking across his face.

Doug Richert was no Jake Elder. But he was a bright student who had learned many tricks from the master mechanic during the past year and would learn more from Earnhardt, who knew almost as much about preparing race cars as about driving them.

Richert, a native of San Jose, California, was only 16 when he first met Osterlund.

He tells the story:

"A lot of older guys in my neighborhood were into racing, both motorcycles and stock cars. I started hanging out with one guy in particular, tinkering with his cars and going to the local dirt tracks. Rod owned one of the tracks, and I got to know him, just when he was getting really interested in racing. Then the NASCAR deal came together for him in 1977, when he signed Dave Marcis to drive the car."

Richert, whose father was a carpenter and had no interest in racing, graduated from high school in June, 1978, and immediately set out across the country to join Osterlund's race team. Two years later, he found himself the crew chief for a team on the front end of a sizzling race for the Winston Cup championship.

"Except for working for Jake, I never had any real teachers in racing. Most of what I learned was picked up on my own," he says. "I did feel some pressure because the older crew chiefs knew so much more than I did. I thought Mr. Osterlund and Dale both had confidence in me. I just hoped we could keep it going and win the championship."

The next race was the July 4th Firecracker 400 at Daytona Beach, where the team had won the confidence-boosting Busch Clash and had made a strong run in the Daytona 500 in February. Both Dale and Richert thought it was a good place to recharge the team's championship hopes.

Dale was in the lead with 28 laps remaining when Bobby

Allison steered his Mercury around him to take the point position. Dale seemed content to ride in Allison's draft for the next 27 laps before making his move just as the leaders took the white flag.

But Dale was facing a challenge himself from David Pearson, and when the two locked up side-by-side, Allison scooted into a five-car-length lead that seemed ever larger because of the knot of traffic that separated him from the other two.

Pearson, who had waited until near the end before moving up from fourth place to make his challenge, barely cracked the throttle on his Oldsmobile as he drove into the first turn.

"Dale was underneath me when we went into the turn, and it pushed me up toward the wall. Once I backed off, I couldn't catch up to Bobby again. I was planning to make a a move at getting by Allison whenever I had the chance on the last lap. Once I backed off as we went into the corner, that was it," Pearson explained.

Dale, who led 38 laps, also was left to second-guess his decision to make his move around Allison at the beginning of the last lap instead of waiting to do it off the second turn, on the long backstretch, where he had passed Waltrip in February to win the Clash.

"I made it early because I was worried that if I waited I might get blocked by the traffic between me and Allison," he explained. "Maybe it was a mistake. I just felt if I waited until later that I would have really got messed up by the slower traffic."

Allison admitted he was playing the slower traffic to his advantage during the final four laps. "There was a string of slower cars that I figured would be right where we were on the final lap," Allison said. "In that kind of situation, I was not surprised that Dale made his move so early. If he had got around me, I don't think I could have passed him again because of the traffic. I knew, too, if he did not make it, he would not have another chance to beat me."

Dale finished third as Pearson slipped under him for second-place.

But just as Earnhardt and Richert had hoped, the race was a major boost for their championship hopes. They had been in the hunt for victory up to the final lap, and maybe they could have pulled it off if not for the slower traffic that forced the early move. Still, Earnhardt picked up 15 points on Petty, who finished fifth and did not lead a lap.

Yarborough's recent hot streak was cooled considerably when his Oldsmobile blew an engine on only the fifth lap and was the first car out. Waltrip left the race with engine failure after leading 36 of the first 110 laps.

Revived by the Firecracker effort, Dale went to Nashville and won the Busch 420 in a heated battle with Yarborough and Benny Parsons. He picked up another 20 points on Petty, who was thought to be his toughest challenger for the championship.

Those expectations were erased two weeks later, in the next race at Pocono, Pennsylvania, when Petty was involved in a serious crash during the Coca-Cola 500 and was hospitalized for two days.

Ironically, Petty's crash occurred at about the same spot as the one put Dale on the sidelines for four weeks the year before. Petty was leading when the right front wheel on his Chevrolet collapsed on the 57th lap. The car slid into the wall, bolted about 10 feet into the air and almost cleared the outside retaining barrier before crashing down on the track and sliding sixty feet before stopping.

"Everything is sore," Petty said the next day, "my neck, legs, and shoulders. When the car hit the wall, it stopped but I didn't, and everything got stretched. I hit at almost the same spot as Dale did last year, but Dale's car hit backwards, and mine went in frontwards. I saw the wall coming at me and I thought, 'Oh, man, this is going to hurt a bunch.' "

As battered as he was, Petty refused to say he would miss the next week's race at Talladega, Alabama. If he did not at least start the race to claim championship points, his bid for an eighth title almost certainly would be ended.

"It will depend on how I feel. I'm hoping that I will be able to start the car and let someone else drive the rest of the race so I can get the points," Petty said.

When the Talladega 500 began, Petty was in the car to start the ignition and steer it around the track for one lap before being replaced by Joe Millikan, the driver Dale had beaten for the rookie title the year before.

Petty continued to receive relief help from Millikan, who had swept floors in the Petty shop as a teenager, but the wreck had eliminated him as a serious contender for the championship.

"I just can't drive the car the way I want because my neck is still hurting," Petty said. "Dale was going to be hard to beat even if I had not had that injury."

Many in the racing fraternity thought the Pocono wreck might finally be enough to convince the Petty, who was 43, to retire at the end of the season. Some, like Yarborough, seemed to hope it would.

"Richard thinks he needs racing, but I can't believe a man needs anything that is killing him," Yarborough said. "I am sure he has burned himself down thin. How can a man love something like that so much?"

Petty tried to explain: "Any time someone does something he wants to do, he has got to sacrifice. Sometimes it hurts me to get into that race car and drive it, but I am doing what I want to do. I don't look at it as being stubborn. It is just that if I want to do something, I am going to do it – come hell or high water."

With Petty out, Waltrip was still talking confidently when he pulled into Clay Earles' picturesque Martinsville Speedway on September 28 for the Old Dominion 500. Although fifth in the standings, 185 points behind Earnhardt, he had finished first at Dover and second at North Wilkesboro on the previous two weekends.

"I want to win this championship more than anything else, and I think it can still be done," he said. "I lost the title last year during this stretch, and I believe we are going to win it in this stretch this year."

Winning the championship was not the only goal on Waltrip's agenda, and perhaps not the most important one.

Waltrip was at odds with his team owner, Bill Gardner, through most of the season – in fact, during most of the five years he had driven for the DiGard team. In 1978, he threatened to break his contract and leave. Instead, he renegotiated a contract that obligated him to DiGard through the 1983 season.

Now he wanted to leave again and frequently could be heard singing a line from a Johnny Paycheck song, "Take This Job and Shove It," as he walked through the garage area. He told Gardner he would not be back in 1981, but Gardner was determined that he would be.

"I asked Darrell what is bothering him and he says he just needs a change," Gardner said. "That is all well and good but it doesn't work well in a business situation. I can't think of any circumstances that would cause us to let him go. Darrell has a very big mouth and he says some things I don't like, but he is still a helluva race driver and an asset to our business."

When Waltrip left Martinsville, getting his release from DiGard was all he had to think about. He finished 21st after blowing an engine. But Earnhardt, despite taking a wild, spinning ride down the backstretch, had won his fourth race of the season.

On Lap 216, Dale was sent spinning off the second turn by a tap from Dave Marcis, the man he replaced in the Osterlund car the year before. Dale's car skidded down the backstretch without hitting the wall or collecting any of the cars whizzing by him on each side.

When the car spun back around, Dale shifted gears and continued on his way without losing a lap. "I said 'Thank you, Lord,' and kept going," he said later.

Dale also pulled alongside of Marcis to shake his fist at him.

Marcis replied in kind.

A couple of laps later, Dale said, he apologized to Marcis, a man who doesn't like to be shoved around on the tracks.

Asked how a driver could "apologize" in a race car, Dale smiled and answered, "The same way you can cuss a driver out. You do it with hand motions, and the other guy gets the message."

Marcis confessed to tapping Earnhardt's car into the spin. It was tit-for-tat, he added.

"There are things that have to be done, and you have got to do them. Earnhardt had been all over me all day long, and it was no good to let it go on. It was something that happened here at Martinsville and it had to be ended right here. Dale knew why I did what I did. Now it is over. History."

There were other dramatic moments in the race, too, before Dale sailed under the checkered flag. He was not assured the victory until Yarborough's Oldsmobile experienced a flat tire on the restart following the the final caution period. When he pitted to change tires, Dale took the lead for the remaining 13 laps.

"I don't know if I could have passed Cale if he hadn't had the flat. But remember, I was leading him and he couldn't pass me until we had a caution period and he got ahead of me coming out of the pits," Dale said.

With only four races remaining on the schedule, Earnhardt was holding a 105-point lead over Yarborough, second in the standings, and some were suggesting that Earnhardt, not Waltrip, was the one who should be seeking to renegotiate his contract.

Dale coolly advised everyone to forget rumors he was looking for a richer contract, even if he continued on to win the championship.

"Last January, Rod Osterlund and I came to an agreement

whereby I will drive for him five years. Unless something drastic happens, I will be driving for him five years, too. I have got all the money I want. If Rod paid me any more on a percentage basis, he would be crazy. He wouldn't be able to do justice for the rest of the team. I am satisfied."

But Yarborough was also laying new plans for the next season, which was a big reason Waltrip was determined to get out of his contract with DiGard. Yarborough had informed Junior Johnson that he no longer wanted to drive the full schedule and was leaving at season's end. Waltrip was Johnson's choice as his new driver if he could get his release from DiGard.

Yarborough's forthcoming departure from the Johnson team did not stir any ill feelings, however, that hindered the team's performance in the championship stretch run. Indeed, Yarborough was more determined to win the title since it was his last title run and something he wanted to give Johnson as a farewell gift. In eight seasons as Johnson's driver, Yarborough had won three championships, almost $3 million, and 55 races. He was only 40 years old, too. So why was he leaving?

The decision had been triggered by an incident earlier in the summer. Yarborough was on his way out of his house, running late for a business appointment, when he noticed his nine-year-old daughter, B.J., and some friends sitting around, doing nothing.

"Why aren't you riding your bicycles?" he asked.

"My bike is broke," his daughter replied.

"Why didn't you tell me about? I would have fixed it," Yarborough said.

"Daddy, I have told you, but you never have time to fix it," B.J. answered.

Yarborough immediately canceled the business appointment and repaired the bicycle. It was time, he decided, to spend more time with his family, even if it meant cutting back on his racing schedule.

"I had just been away from the family too much and too

long. My oldest daughter, Julie Ann, was 18 and she had grown up without me, and the same thing was happening with my two younger daughters," he later explained.

With four races remaining on the schedule – Charlotte, Rockingham, Atlanta, and Ontario – Yarborough knew he had to start cutting into Earnhardt's point lead. But he also knew that the Charlotte track, which Earnhardt considers home turf, was going to be a difficult place for him to do it.

Earnhardt is always pumped up for the Charlotte races, and not only because he knows that "half of Kannapolis is going to be in the stands pulling for me."

"This track is where I used to sit on the back of my daddy's pickup truck, parked in the infield, and dream about winning Winston Cup races and championships," he said.

The boyhood dream would finally come true in the 1980 National 500, but not before he and Yarborough thrilled the fans with a race-long battle that ended with Dale beating his remaining championship challenger to the finish line by less than two seconds.

Dale led 143 of the 334 laps around the one-and-a-half mile track, but he still needed – and got – quick service on pit road during his final stop to nail down his fifth victory of the season.

Led by Doug Richert, the Osterlund crew dumped in 20 gallons of fuel and changed both rightside tires in only 13 seconds – four seconds quicker than Yarborough's crew needed to complete his final stop.

In Victory Lane, Dale hugged his mom, who had tears in her eyes, and declared, "It is a great, great feeling to win this race, at this track, at such an important time in the season."

Dale might have been the least-experienced championship contender in Winston Cup history, and Richert the youngest crew chief, but they had a relatively comfortable 115-point lead over Yarborough to take into the final three races.

For eight months people had been telling Dale he would not win the championship. Back in March, after he won back-to-back races at Atlanta and Bristol, he later recalled being told, "Dale, you got a good future in this sport, but it is ahead of you. You ain't got the experience to be thinking championship. You would have to beat Richard and Darrell and Cale. Boy, you ain't got a chance."

Dale listened, got a little mad, smiled and said, "I am gonna win it."

In June, after Elder quit, people were saying, "Boy, you ain't going to win it now. Not without Jake. All you got now is a 20-year-old crew chief and Jake has gone with Darrell. Cale has got Junior, and Richard's got his brother, Maurice, and Dale Inman, and they know how to win championships. Boy, you ain't going to win it now."

Earnhardt listened, got redder in the face, and replied. "I'm gonna win it."

Not only was he confident, he even told skeptical critics how he would become the first second-year driver to win the championship.

"By winning races, driving flat-out," he said. "You people talk about pressure. But I don't feel any pressure. The pressure is on them. If I win enough races, they can't catch me."

Waltrip, of course, had tried a similar strategy the year before and it blew up in his face. Now people were telling Earnhardt he was making the same mistake.

"Boy, you got a good lead and all you got to do is protect it. You take too many chances and you try to lead too many laps when it doesn't count. You just be a little bit more patient, and you might win this thing."

Dale shook his head and said, "I went to Martinsville and Charlotte to win the races, not to stroke for points, and I want to win a couple more races before the season ends, too."

Dale had won the last two races with a heavy foot, but he also had been extremely fortunate. There was the skirmish with Marcis at Martinsville, and at Charlotte he had engaged Petty in another potentially-dangerous bumping duel.

It was on Lap 108 when Petty was trying to pass Earnhardt to make up a lost lap. Dale pulled up on Petty too hard in the third turn and almost spun him sideways. Off the next turn, Petty suddenly steered his car into the side of Earnhardt's and they popped together once again.

"I deserved it. I had driven all over Richard and it was my fault. I apologized to Richard after the race," Dale said. "But I don't feel I am being any more aggressive than the other drivers. I know Yarborough isn't going to back off. I am not either. The only way I know to drive a race car is flat-out."

The day before the Rockingham race, for which Yarborough qualified second and Earnhardt third, Petty made an interesting observation about the championship battle.

"Dale has had good luck for so long, it is bound to fall out from under him eventually. It is just a matter of time. But it is going to have to happen pretty soon if anyone is going to beat him for the title."

Events in the next day's American 500 made Petty look like a prophet.

Dale's streak of good luck crashed into the wall, not once but twice, and Yarborough drove to a victory that he vowed had opened the door to winning the championship. With Earnhardt finishing 18th, Yarborough chopped 75 points off his lead and trailed by only 44 points with the races at Atlanta and Ontario remaining.

"I can catch him now. He has to know that I am coming," said Yarborough, his blue eyes twinkling in the sunshine that had broken through a thick layer of clouds midway through the race.

It was the sunshine, Yarborough claimed, that ushered him to his fifth victory of the season. "At the start of the race my car was running rich. There was too much air getting into the carburetor because it was so humid. When the sun came out, it thinned down the air and that made my car as fast as any on the track."

Dale, who had taken his car to the lead on Lap 97, said he drove through some oil to cause his first collision with the wall. "The second time that it happened, a tie rod broke on the left front. The old race car took a pretty good beating today."

Dale's race car wasn't the only thing to take a beating. So had his solid lead in the championship standings. "But I am still in the lead and I plan to stay there," he said. "Cale can talk all he wants about beating me. But it is going to take more than talk."

During the 10 days before drivers and crews arrived at Atlanta International Raceway to begin practice and qualifying for the Atlanta Journal 500, a Charlotte television station reported that Yarborough had injured a leg and would not be able to compete in the race.

Yarborough was still upset with the erroneous report when he got to the speedway. "I just sprained my ankle a little bit," he said. "I was chasing a cow on my farm and fell. But there was no injury. I am fine and my leg is fine. I just can't understand how some stuff gets so overblown."

Overall, though, Yarborough was in a good mood and still riding an emotional high from his Rockingham victory.

In the Earnhardt camp, it was a different story. Dale was on edge and clearly irritated by reporters asking the same questions: Was he finally feeling the pressure? Was he worried Yarborough could make good on his boast to take the title from him? Was he going to change his "flat-out" style of driving?

"What can I change?" he asked. "You know how I have run all season long. Why should I change? Cale is not going to change no strategy. Why should I? I have said all year that I was going to try to win the races and let the points take care of themselves. That is the way it is going to be. Whatever happens will happen. I remember when Richard Petty closed to within 13 points of me and people started talking about pressure. I didn't worry then. Why worry now?

"If I don't win the championship, what am I going to do? It

won't be because I didn't try. Besides, people have been saying all year I couldn't win it. I am just a sophomore on this circuit, and I am not supposed to be doing as much as I have done.

"That is what people say. But I don't believe it. I feel natural to be where I am. All I have been doing is racing, driving the car as hard as I can. I won't be happy if I don't win the championship. I don't like finishing second in anything."

Yarborough was doing all he could, too, to make Earnhardt more irritable, it seemed. He reminded reporters that Dale's hard-driving style had not made him popular with many drivers.

"Not many have said it publicly, but there have been races when Earnhardt was not so gentlemanly, and I think a few drivers have told him that," Yarborough said.

Digging the needle deeper, Yarborough continued, "I have been through these championship battles a few times and Dale hasn't. So you can figure out where the pressure is. I am not denying that I want to win this championship. But if I don't win it, well, I have won it three times before. Dale has not ever won it."

Dale certainly had the right to feel pressure when he drove through the infield tunnel at the one-and-a-half mile track early Sunday morning with only 44 points separating him and Yarborough, but Yarborough had to feel some pressure, too.

Sure, he had won three previous championships. But this would be his final chance to win another. Dale's career was just beginning. There would be other opportunities for him.

Yarborough was making a mistake, if he thought his stinging comments the previous day were going to intimidate his young opponent. If anything, the comments served to fire up Earnhardt, who became even more determined that Yarborough was not going to have an easy day, no matter what.

Neither Yarborough nor Earnhardt qualified well. Yarborough started 12th and Earnhardt 13th. When the race began, Bobby Allison and Darrell Waltrip were dueling for the lead when John Callis blew an engine in his Ford and both were caught up in the accident. Earnhardt and Yarborough were still trying to get to the front and thus avoided the string of wrecks that caught Allison and Waltrip.

Following the caution period, Yarborough drove into the lead on Lap 42 and led all but 18 of the remaining 287 laps, with Neil Bonnett the only other driver finishing with him in the lead lap.

Dale led only once and finished third after losing a lap during a green-flag pit stop. But, as he had promised, what should have been an easy day for Yarborough ended in a nerve-rattling, temper-igniting experience.

Three laps from the finish, Earnhardt, a lap down and in third place, pulled alongside Yarborough and raced him door-to-door the remaining miles.

Yarborough was brimming with anger when he reached the press box several minutes after taking the checkered flag.

"Earnhardt didn't have any business doing what he was doing those last three laps," he said. "I think that showed the pressure is getting to him. That was the worst piece of driving I have seen anyone do since I have been in this sport. It seemed he would rather take both of us out of the race than to let me win it. It was a stupid move on his part."

Yarborough conceded he may have been equally as dumb for not slowing down and letting Earnhardt pass him, since Bonnett, in second-place, wasn't close enough to him to make a challenge for the victory.

"I was just so mad at what he was doing, I was determined that hell could freeze over before I would let him get on by me," Yarborough explained. "But NASCAR should have done something. What he did was foolish, and he did it out of spite, trying to keep me from winning."

Dale took Yarborough's complaints with a mischievous grin and a shrug.

"I wasn't going to wallow on him or anything like that," he

37

said, "but those last three laps were thrilling as hell. If Cale was worried, he could have let me go. He didn't back off any, and I didn't either. He is a racer and so am I."

Dale was aware of scoring errors in previous NASCAR races and claimed he was not positive that he was a lap down.

"You know, if the scoring had been wrong, and I had been in the same lap with Cale, I could have gone on and won the race. I was just trying to win the race, that is all. My daddy taught me long ago to never think anything is right, or to take anything for granted."

Yarborough wasn't buying that.

"Dale had been a lap down all day, and I even had him almost two laps down at one point. If I had thought he would do something crazy like that, I would not have let him stay that close to me. I could have gone off and left him with about 20 laps to go."

As angry as Yarborough was, he had the consolation of having trimmed another 15 points off Earnhardt's championship lead and would go into the final race in two weeks at Ontario trailing by only 29 points.

"I am going to whip his butt," Yarborough declared.

But he didn't have the last word.

"I'm still leading, ain't I?" Dale said.

Dale's display of defiance in the final three laps was an appropriate prelude to an announcement the following day that the Osterlund team had signed a multi-year sponsorship agreement with Wrangler, which sold its sportswear products under the slogan, "One tough customer."

"We see our association with Winston Cup racing and most specifically Osterlund Racing and Dale Earnhardt as a natural extension of our advertising posture," Wrangler Group executive Bob Odeare said.

Jack Watson, the director of advertising for the Wrangler group, agreed. "We came up with what we think is a perfect fit for our bluejeans and sportswear. We have a driver who fits our program like a hand in a glove. Dale Earnhardt is certainly one tough customer."

Earnhardt was delighted with the new sponsorship because it made the team more stable financially, and it proved he was the type of driver who could attract the attention of the corporate world.

Even more, he liked the idea of people thinking of him in exactly the words of Wrangler's slogan: "One Tough Customer."

After the fireworks at Atlanta, speculation ran full-bore in the two weeks leading to the final race of the season. What would happen when Earnhardt and Yarborough met at Ontario to decide the national championship?

Yarborough kept insisting that Earnhardt proved he was feeling the pressure by his driving in the final three laps at Atlanta.

Dale, who seemed less tense than he had been before the Atlanta race, kept reminding reporters that the pressure had to be on Yarborough, because he was the one who was 29 points behind.

If Earnhardt finished as high as fifth and led a single lap to collect the five bonus points, he would win the championship, no matter what Yarborough did. "But I am not thinking about finishing fifth," he said. "I want to win the race. That is how I want to win the championship."

Once the talking stopped and the green-flag dropped, both drivers were strictly business, each trying to do what he had to do to win the title.

Dale bolted to the front on the eighth lap to collect the five bonus points, then began falling back through the field. During a green-flag pit stop on Lap 71, he dropped a lap down to Yarborough, who was leading the race.

Dale made up his lap with the help of a caution flag on Lap 152 of the 200-lap race and moved back up to fifth place, where he needed to finish to win the title. Then misfortune hit.

With 17 laps remaining, Dale wheeled his blue and yellow car, which was carrying the Wrangler logos for the first time, down pit road. The plan was to stop just long enough for a splash of fuel. But a crewman, who had not gotten the word, thought the stop also was for outside tires and began to change the right rear.

He had removed three lug nuts when Earnhardt, unaware that the tire change was in process, mashed the accelerator and ran over the jack in his haste to get back onto the track.

NASCAR officials waved the black-flag ordering him to return to the pits for a stop-and-go penalty for running over the jack. Dale ignored the black flag for three laps before finally returning to pit road, where the three lug nuts were replaced.

Despite this setback, he remained in the same lap with the leader and finished fifth to clinch the title. Yarborough finished third and ended the season 19 points behind Earnhardt.

"It must have looked like we were trying to give the championship away," Dale said after the race, "but we did what we had to do to come back from the bad luck and win it anyhow."

The big mystery was how Dale was able to stay on the track at speed without wrecking during the laps he drove with three lug nuts missing from the right rear wheel.

"The Man Upstairs was certainly with me," Dale said. "If that wheel had come off, or caused me to wreck, the whole season would have gone down the drain."

The heavy lines of concern that dug deeply across Dale's face in the final weeks of the championship race seemed to have disappeared, and he returned home to go a three-day deer-hunting trip to South Carolina.

"I had made up my mind that I was going to do that – win, lose, or draw," he said later. "I never even fired my gun, but it was a wonderful three days, just unwinding by myself. There are not any telephones out there in all those trees."

Dale finally confessed that he had felt strain from his first Winston Cup battle.

"The pressure was there, but it didn't come from Cale. That was just racing, the easy part. The pressure was from the fans, the press, and my family. What was I going to say to them if I didn't win the title after leading all year?"

Dale had accomplished something no other stock-car racer had done by winning the rookie title one season and the championship the next. But he seemed less impressed by it than anyone else.

"I don't think I am the best driver on the circuit," he said. "I may be only the 15th or so. Winning the championship just means that I did the best in the points race this year. I do feel I am one of the best drivers. I have always had confidence in myself. If you don't have that, you won't be successful.

"But I have a bunch to learn. When I stop learning will be the day I die. Being the best means you know everything there is to know about all of the tracks and all of the crew chiefs and other drivers. I don't think anybody is close to that. When anyone thinks he doesn't need to learn any more, that is the day when he will get his."

What Dale wanted now, he said, was more titles.

"I have won one, but my goals don't end there. Cale won three straight and I'd like to win four straight. Then I will think about being the first driver to win eight championships."

That was looking a long way down the road, and Dale told interviewer Steve Waid, that he really didn't know how many years he would have in the sport.

"I know what I am doing now will not go on forever," he said. "This is the last step for me as far as my racing career goes. I have gone from Late Model Sportsman racing to part-time Winston Cup racing to full-time Winston Cup racing. I feel like I have 10 years in this sport. At least five.

"What happens after that? It will be determined by what I do with myself, how well I invest my winnings, or how well I educate myself in preparation for another career. Maybe I will go back to school and be a lawyer. I know you have to have a dollar to make a dollar. I used to borrow a dollar to make a dollar and then I would owe a dollar."

Dale also told Waid that he felt an emptiness caused by the two unsuccessful marriages.

"Honestly, if things hadn't happened the way they did with my family, it would do me much prouder to have them right here with me right now," he said. "This is something I wanted all my married life. My daddy did right by his family. He raised the kids, sent them to school and did right by them. They came first. Forgetting all the bad times I had, I wish that I had finished school for my father.

"Circumstances being what they are, I don't have my family with me right now. But I have a good relationship with my kids. They love me and they know they have a home right here, just like they do with their mother.

"I miss the security of having a wife and kids with me. I am so involved with what I am doing and I am gone so often and so long it would make it very tough to have the kids here. I don't think it would be the ideal situation. But there is no substitute for them."

If Dale's personal life was not what he wanted it to be, there were no complaints about his career, which seemed to be rock-solid in a period of numerous driver changes within the Winston Cup teams between the 1980 and 1981 seasons.

Yarborough left Junior Johnson to drive a limited schedule for M.C. Anderson's team. Waltrip bought his way of his DiGard contract and was hired to replace Yarborough as Johnson's new driver. Bobby Allison left Bud Moore and took Buddy Baker's seat in the Ranier car, and was replaced by Benny Parsons. Baker moved over to Hoss Ellington's car, and Ricky Rudd, a young driver from Chesapeake, Virginia, got his first top ride by taking Waltrip's vacated seat in the DiGard car.

In addition to Rudd, there were other new and talented drivers who made appearances on the circuit during the 1980 season. Rusty Wallace drove a couple of races for Roger

Penske, and finished second in his Winston Cup debut in the first Atlanta race. Tim Richmond, the 1980 Indianapolis 500 top rookie, joined the stock-car circuit for five races, and people began noticing a young, red-haired Georgian, Bill Elliott, who had been running in selected events the past few years. Another newcomer seeking a competitive ride was Geoff Bodine, a big winner on the Northern Modified circuit.

They, along with Waltrip and Mark Martin, who was set to run five races in 1981, were to become Earnhardt's major challengers during the next decade.

4

'Get over here, Rod has sold the team'

If stock-car racing fans were overwhelmed by the rash of changes and new faces arriving on the circuit, they were to be thoroughly shocked by more circuit-shaking developments once the 1981 season was under way.

The first bombshell exploded only a couple of days after Richard Petty outsmarted the competition to win his seventh Daytona 500.

Petty, relying on strategy plotted by his cousin and long-time crew chief Dale Inman, grabbed control of the race during his final pit stop when he paused only long enough for his red and blue No. 43 Buick to gulp down 10 gallons of fuel.

Two laps earlier, the pre-race favorite, Bobby Allison, who won the season-opener at Riverside, ran out of fuel and pitted to get a full tank and two rightside tires. It seemed like the thing to do for three other contenders – Earnhardt, Rudd, and Baker, who also took on tires and a full tanks of fuel and were in the pits more than 17 seconds.

Petty came in two laps later and needed only eight seconds to get one can of fuel, just enough to get him to the finish line.

When Petty pulled back onto the track, he held a 10.7-second lead over Allison and a 7.78-second lead over Earnhardt, Rudd, and Baker. Allison chased down the trio in front of him to finish second but he could not make a serious challenge to Petty, who crossed the finish line eight seconds ahead of him.

"Dale Inman told me about halfway through the race the tires were not wearing out and would not be a problem for us," Petty recalled later. "Dale has full authority in the pits. If he had changed all four tires or had sent me back out on just three wheels, that was his decision.

"When Bobby slowed down on the backstretch, the other three slowed down with him. They wanted to make their pit stops when he did so they could watch what he did and stay in the draft with him since he was supposed to have the best car. But we had our own strategy. We didn't go along with the crowd. Dale told me all I needed was one can of gas and that is all I got.

"Give Dale Inman the credit for this victory," Petty said. "All I did was stick my foot on the accelerator and hope the car would go fast. Dale did the rest. I didn't outsmart anyone. But Dale sure did."

Inman, who had walked away from an interview in Victory Lane because of the tears that began choking his voice, released a statement two days later that he was leaving Petty's team.

"I am going to become vice president in charge of racing operations for Dale Earnhardt's Osterlund team," Inman said. "I have had a long and happy relationship with Richard and Petty Enterprises. The decision to make the move didn't come until after hours of discussions with close friends with whom I have worked for so long. I have accepted this new position as the biggest challenge of my career, and all I want is to contribute to the Osterlund team."

Petty and Inman had been inseparable for most of their lives. They played together as kids and worked on the race cars of Richard's father, Lee, who began the family racing business.

Inman, whose grandmother was a sister of Richard's grand-mother, joined with Richard's brother, Maurice, in building and maintaining the cars that Petty had driven to 193 career victories and seven championships.

"Dale was my best friend as a kid, and he still is," Richard Petty said. "As kids we did everything together. Racing bikes, playing football, and just messing around. I did more with him than anyone else."

Inman expressed sincere regrets about breaking up the successful relationship with Petty. He said the friendship would continue but he looked forward to working with Earnhardt, the new superstar on the circuit. "Dale has had a lot of success the first two years on the Winston Cup circuit and I have got a hard act to follow," Inman said.

He couldn't imagine just how hard it would be, however.

Unknowingly, he had set himself up to become involved in in another bombshell, one that would explode in the lap of an unsuspecting Dale Earnhardt.

After two spectacular seasons, Dale was off to another decent start in 1981 with the fifth-place finish in the Daytona 500. But, despite Inman coming aboard, he failed to win a race through the first half of the season, and not until the 14th race did he collect a second-place finish.

Once the darling of the Southern racing media, Dale was quickly gaining a new reputation for being moody and temperamental. He was no longer as approachable as he had been earlier in his career. He didn't talk much and he smiled less.

Worst of all, the luck that had been so good in his championship season was now coming up all bad.

He wasn't winning races. The car wouldn't run at the front of the field, or when it did there was an eventual mechanical problem. And Dale was spoiling a few of his own chances by becoming involved in wrecks, some of his own doing, such as when he drove the car too hard into the fourth turn at Darlington and smashed into the wall.

After the accident, Dale told his crewmen over the radio that he was "sick." Thinking Earnhardt was ill, Richert asked if he wanted a relief driver.

Cursing, Dale replied, "I mean that I am sick because I hit the wall. Don't ever ask me if I want someone else to drive my race car!"

Dale spent the day after the Darlington race in his boat on Lake Norman. "That made me feel better, and the next day I called Rod and told him what had happened at Darlington. Then, I went by the shop and talked to the mechanics and told them that I was sorry it had happened," he recalled later.

Just before the Winston 500 at Talladega in early May, Dale tried to explain the frustrations he was feeling.

"It is hard as hell to keep falling out of races, hard as hell to smile some of the time. But I got to do it. I got to stay positive and go on. It is just tough to come off a winning season, to be the champion, and not be winning races. I am as hungry now as I have ever been. I never feel pressure when I am in a race. I love tight racing. That is what I enjoy the most. The pressure comes from other places. We have got a big sponsor to please this year. Last year I won a lot of money and this year I'm not winning as much. I worry about my family. My crew members work so hard. I hurt more for them than I do for myself.

"I get ill and upset, but I am not the only one ever to do that. Hopefully, I can overcome my mistakes. Some writer said I was acting like a prima donna. That is just not true. I have my moods and my ways. Maybe I have cut a writer off a time or two. But this hasn't been a good year for me. It hasn't been all roses. Never has been. But when you are winning, everyone is patting you on the back. It is easy to smile and be happy then.

"When you are losing, everyone wants to know why. You get all the negative attitudes. It is a hard situation to handle."

Meanwhile, Waltrip was making the most of his new association with Johnson. He won five races during the first half of the season, and Bobby Allison, even more successful with his new Ranier team, had won four races to build a whopping 256-point lead over Waltrip in the championship standings.

Dale was fourth in the points, 329 behind Allison, but hopeful he could turn things around in the second half of the season. What he didn't know, however, was that things would get worse, not better.

His team owner was experiencing a serious cash-flow problem and had decided to sell the team to Jim Stacy, a man who had little respect among the stock-car racing fraternity.

The deal was completed the last week in June, as Inman and Richert were finishing preparations on the car they would take to Daytona for the Firecracker 400, the race in which Dale had revived his title charge after Elder's departure in '80.

Dale, who trusted Osterlund like a father, had no idea Osterlund was even thinking about selling the team until he received an early-morning phone call from Wlodyka.

"It really threw me," he recalled later. "I got the phone call at 6:30 in the morning from Roland and he said, 'You had better get over here to the shop. Rod just sold the team.' I asked Roland if he was kidding and he said, 'No, you better come on over. Rod has sold the team.' "

Earnhardt quickly dressed and made the short trip from his house to the shop.

"I get there and all of Stacy's people are milling around. Boobie Harrington and these other guys are writing down all this stuff that was there and I am looking at this and saying 'What is going on?' Then big Stacy rolls in and he is prancing around the whole place, smoking his cigars, and then Joe Ruttman and his wife come in and I am going, 'Oh, boy. I have lost my deal now. This is the end of me,' you know.

"I just couldn't believe this was happening. I had the five-year contract with Osterlund. We had won the championship and had a rich sponsor. It had not been a good first-half of the season for us, but there was no reason to think something like this was going to happen.

"I was in the office with Stacy and his people and Rod walks in. He didn't expect me to be there. He came in to sign the final deal, and when he saw me, Rod asked everyone else to leave.

"He told me, 'Look, I am going to sell the team and you need to stay with Stacy.' I asked Rod why he was doing something like that. I told him it was like he was selling me to these people. Rod told me again that it was best if I stayed with Stacy, and that Stacy would take care of me. I told him that I would."

Earnhardt remembers that after Osterlund signed the papers he left and Stacy returned to the office.

"Stacy told me, and these are his words, he said, 'Let me tell you, Dale, I don't know how you feel about it, but this is how I feel. If you want to drive that race car out there, you can stay here and you can drive that race car. But if you don't want to drive that race car, you can go home and it really doesn't matter to me.'

"I said, 'Well, I reckon I will just stay and drive that race car for you,' and I eased on out of there and went over to my house. I didn't know what to do.

"Dale Inman was telling me not to worry, everything will be all right, that Stacy was going to run two cars and all of this stuff. So, they got to running two cars and I'm driving and I'm going, 'I hate this, I hate this,' because they were shoving stuff down my throat and they were doing this and you were wondering what they were doing here and there. Stacy was bragging about this and he was going to do that, and I didn't know what was going on, except that I didn't like any of it."

It had been four years, almost to the week, that Stacy had first appeared on the NASCAR circuit.

Harry Hyde brought Stacy, a big man who liked to wear open-necked shirts and smoke big cigars, into the infield press room at Daytona just before the Firecracker race and introduced him as an angel – his personal angel.

For several years Hyde had built fast cars and won numerous races and one championship for Nord Krauskopf under the sponsorship of Krauskopf's K&K Insurance Company. When Krauskopf retired as president of the company, he told Hyde to sell all of the racing equipment and lock up the shop. Hyde thought he was out of work until Stacy came to the rescue.

Stacy, who reportedly had made millions of dollars from a coal mining business, gave Hyde a check to give to Krauskopf as a down payment and told Hyde to spend whatever it took to win races.

A couple of years later, Harry Hyde and Jim Stacy were not speaking to each other, except through lawyers. When Hyde spoke to others about Stacy, he turned red in the face.

The two men exchanged numerous law suits and Hyde almost went bankrupt fighting the legal battles, all of which were settled in his favor. It was a major surprise when Stacy showed back up on the circuit with enough money to buy a championship team.

"Rumors are flying," said Inman when the Stacy team pulled into Daytona for the Fourth of July race. "For awhile, I heard Stacy didn't have enough money to meet the payroll. Now, I hear NASCAR is worried that he might buy every race team out here."

Stacy had his name on three cars entered in the Firecracker. He owned Earnhardt's car and Joe Ruttman's car, which was prepared by Harrington, and he was sponsoring another car, driven by Lennie Pond. The word was Stacy had come into considerable money in recent weeks by closing an international coal deal.

Harrington, who had left Hyde to remain with Stacy, was named general manager of Earnhardt's team. He had only good things to say about his boss.

"Jim Stacy is the nicest man I have ever met," Harrington said. "When I left Harry and went with Stacy, people told me that I was crazy and that Jim couldn't stay in racing. Well, Jim told me a year ago he was going to buy the Osterlund team. It took him a little longer than he expected, but he's done it.

"If Jim had $6 million, I believe he would spend every dollar except one on race cars. Then he would spend that one dollar to get into the race track to watch it."

Meanwhile, Dale was trying to take Inman's advice and stay cool. When reporters asked about Stacy, he replied, "I don't know the man. I can't say much about him until I get to know him."

Inman and other members of the crew tried to look on the bright side. At least, Stacy had replaced Wlodyka, who had problems with almost every driver and crewman who worked for Osterlund.

"Roland kept everyone on edge, and we will be a better team because he is gone," one crewman predicted.

Harrington vowed to stay out of Inman's way. "I will just try to make his job easier. I have always been a team man. We will celebrate together when we win and we will cry together when we lose," Harrington promised.

If things were going to get better, Dale couldn't see it. He finished 35th in the Firecracker, seventh in the next race at Bristol, and 11th in the summer race at Pocono. Not only was he still failing to win, Dale didn't see a future for himself in Stacy's plans to build a racing empire.

When the circuit moved to Alabama in late July for the Talladega 500, both Earnhardt and his sponsor, Wrangler, had learned enough about Stacy to know they had to find another home.

"Stacy told Wrangler the same thing he told me, that if they didn't want to stay with him they could go someplace else," Dale later recalled. "So the Wrangler people were talking to me, saying that we needed to do something, and I had told Dale Inman before going to Talladega that I was going to quit. I just didn't have any place that I could go."

Dale talked to Junior Johnson, who had inquired about his

availability after his rookie season, but Johnson's new driver, Waltrip, was in the midst of a championship battle with Allison.

"I liked Dale as a driver, but Darrell was in the title fight and I just didn't have the time to take on someone else right then," Johnson said.

Dale made no secret that he was dissatisfied with Stacy and was hunting a new ride.

With rumors swirling through the Talladega garage, Dale advised reporters, "Stay tuned. Something may happen in the next couple of days. I am talking to some people, but you don't leave a good car to jump into a bad one. You wait to make your move at the right time."

On Saturday, Dale met with Stacy at the track and was told again if he could find a better ride that he was free to accept it. Stacy then met with reporters and outlined his position.

"I am going to own or sponsor five cars in 1982 and I hope Earnhardt will be driving one of them. But if Dale can get something better and wants to go elsewhere, I have no problem with that."

Stacy contended the only time Earnhardt had expressed dissatisfaction with him was on the morning he bought the team.

"I think Dale was in total shock. He didn't know if we were going to give him a total effort. He worried because we were going to have more than one car. Those are normal concerns. I will do my best to make sure all of my drivers have equal equipment. The cars and engines will be built equal. I don't really care which one wins the races."

Following the Saturday meeting, Dale seemed resigned to remaining with Stacy, simply because there seemed to be no other place for him to go. Stacy claimed Earnhardt told him that he was going to stay and "win races for you."

All of that changed Saturday night when Richard Childress, who had struggled as an independent car owner-driver on the circuit since 1970, met Dale at the Downtowner Motel in Anniston and offered Dale and his sponsor an option.

Giving up his car for someone else to drive was the hardest decision he'd ever made, Childress said later. But he had hunted and fished with Dale, and he thought they could make it work. With all the changes in racing, Childress knew he couldn't keep going on his own anyway.

"A few years earlier, Harry Ranier had come along, and it was not long before a few other money people started coming into the sport and building strong teams," Childress said. "It was getting to be lot different than when I started out, and I only had to race the four teams owned by Junior Johnson, the Wood Brothers, Bud Moore, and the Pettys. There were other good teams out there, but those were the Big Four, and you could make a good living racing as an independent in those days if you finished close behind them.

"When the money men started coming into the sport, I could see that things were changing. I could see where an independent just wasn't going to make it. The rich teams were hiring away the good mechanics. Tim Brewer, my crew chief, left in 1976, and I kept losing other people. With circumstances being like they were, I felt I had to do one of two things: own a racing team and get a driver, or sell the racing team and drive for someone else.

"Since my record was not good enough to get a ride with one of the top four or five teams, I felt my future would be better as a team owner. So when Dale talked to me at Talladega about driving my car, I went to Junior Johnson and told Junior I needed to talk to him. I knew he would give me good advice.

"We went to the motel, sat there in Junior's room, and he told me there was more need for car owners than for drivers."

Saturday night, Childress met with Earnhardt, Bob Odeare of Wrangler, and Phil Holmer, a representative for Goodyear, and laid the plans for beginning his new career as a Winston Cup car owner.

In the next day's race, Dale charged from his third-place starting position to lead a few laps before dropping back into the field. On Lap 83, he coasted into the garage with a broken transmission. He climbed out of the car and told Stacy, "I don't have anything against you, but I can't drive for you anymore."

Stacy took a long draw off his cigar and said goodbye.

No one on the Stacy team was surprised that Earnhardt was leaving and there were few regrets.

"I certainly wasn't surprised," said Harrington. "I just could never understand why he was so unhappy when he was with us. We bought the place out, and he couldn't get over it. Osterlund sold it, but Dale kept blaming us for buying it."

Harrington predicted the Stacy team would be better off without Earnhardt. "I would not be surprised if Joe Ruttman won a race for us real soon," he said. "Joe is a team builder, an easy-going guy, not the type who is moody, or flies off the handle so easily."

Dale could not be sure he was going to win races quickly with Childress's team. He just knew life had to better because Childress was a racer.

"I had won races my first two seasons and had just won the national championship, and Stacy made me feel like I was a peon in the world and without any credentials," Dale said later. "Richard said he would make every effort to give me a good car, and I knew that I could trust him."

Fielding a car for the defending Winston Cup champion was a tall challenge for Childress, who never had enough sponsorship money as a driver to compete at the front.

"The money that Wrangler was paying to sponsor my car for the final 10 races of the 1981 season was the most money I had ever seen," Childress said. "They were going to pay me so much a race, and Goodyear was going to help us with tires. I went out and hired a bunch of new people, some of them from Stacy's shop, and bought all new engines and the other stuff that I needed to build good race cars.

"When it was over, I was in debt $150,000. I was in worse shape than I was to start with. I was just devastated by the amount of money I had spent. I knew I had to do it, though, and we impressed a lot of people. We almost won a couple of races and Dale led a lot of laps.

"Wrangler came back and put $75,000 more into the team to help me out. I had to carry the other $75,000 over, had to finance it and hock about everything I had to make it work."

Earnhardt's best finishes were a couple of fourth places, at North Wilkesboro and Riverside. He placed sixth in the Southern 500 at Darlington. He was leading late in the race at Charlotte before the car developed an ignition problem, and he was running strong at Atlanta before engine failure put him out.

Childress recognized that his team simply was not ready to take on the giants of the Winston Cup circuit. He remained convinced, however, that Johnson had given him good advice and he never thought about returning to driving.

He knew that Dale had the ability to win races, even another championship, if he could produce a competitive team. It would be a couple of years, at least, however, before he could build his own team to that level.

In what must be regarded as one of the grandest and most unselfish moves in stock car racing's not always honorable history, Childress decided to sacrifice the richest sponsor he ever had for the good of his new driver and hunting buddy.

During Southern 500 week in September, Childress told Earnhardt that they needed to have a little talk about next year.

"I can remember that day as well as if it were yesterday," Childress said later. "Dale had an old Pontiac, and we left the race track early because we already had qualified. We rode down the road, just riding around, talking, and Dale asked me what I thought he ought to do.

"He says, 'I can drive for you. I can drive for Harry Ranier. Or I can drive for Bud Moore. You are a race-car driver, what would you do?'

"I told him that knowing my operation, my finances, and where I was at, and knowing Ranier's situation, that Jim Stacy was rumored to be going to buy it, and Bud Moore, with the time, the experience, the money, and the situation that he's got, I'd have to go drive for Bud Moore.

"I didn't try to keep Dale with me. I was honest about it because I knew I was just not in a situation to run an ex-champion. I just didn't feel it would be a good move. I didn't really feel comfortable either being a car owner and former independent race driver and telling the reigning Winston Cup champion how to drive the car, or what to do. We just kind of let it work itself for those 10 races and then at the end of the season he and Wrangler left for Bud Moore's team."

When Dale left, Childress told him that someday he hoped to have a team good enough for his talents and maybe they could get back together again.

"That's how we left it," Childress said.

Dale completed the season winless, while Waltrip made a rousing comeback in the final 10 races to defeat Bobby Allison and win his first Winston Cup championship. Allison, who led by 70 points with 10 races remaining, lost the title by 53 points despite winning the final race of the season at Riverside.

An interesting footnote to the 1981 season, and Waltrip's championship, is that it was at Riverside – and not at Talladega, as most fans believe – that Childress drove his final Winston Cup race.

"Junior Johnson had taken two cars out for the final race, and he wanted someone to qualify the second car in case something happened to Darrell's," Childress explained. "He asked me if I would qualify the second car and start it in the race. I had to talk to Dale about it. I told him that I would start the car, drive it a few laps, park it, and then get in the pits to help him and our team. I did it, and I've been able to tell people that I ended my career driving for Junior Johnson."

Childress, who drove only five laps, finished 39th and went to his team's pit to help Earnhardt end his season with a strong fourth-place finish.

5

'You never forget the hard times'

After such a bright and promising beginning of his career, Dale's failure to win even a single race in the 1981 season pressed him to defend himself against allegations that success had come too quickly and he wasn't fulfilling his promise, that he spent too many nights partying at his home on Lake Norman and too little time concentrating on racing.

"Some people were talking like I was drinking and partying all night, every night," he remembered later. "Well, I did have the home on the lake and I did have friends coming by. I was a bachelor. But I didn't go to extremes. I didn't have wild parties. I didn't spend my nights with wild women. That stuff just wasn't true.

"The people who came by were racing people. They would come down for a cookout, to go water skiing, and they would bring their wives. We didn't raise any more hell than anyone else having a cookout.

"I would take a drink of Jack Daniels sometimes, but I didn't drink every day – sometimes just one beer in a week. I said my prayers and read my Bible, too."

Dale had high hopes that the new season would turn his career back around, and leaving his friend Richard Childress to drive for the established Bud Moore Ford team seemed to give him the chance to do that.

"Winning again is not going to make up for going through that run of disappointments in 1981," he said. "You don't ever forget the hard times. Nothing can wipe them out. But good drivers survive them."

Moore had fielded cars for some of stock car racing's greatest drivers. The late Joe Weatherly won back-to-back championships for him in 1962 and 1963. More recently, Bobby Allison won 14 races in Moore's cars from 1978 to 1980, and Benny Parsons won three in 1981.

Moore, whose garage is in Spartanburg, S.C., was one of the best-liked and most respected car owners on the Winston Cup circuit. He had been involved in stock car racing since returning home from the European battlefields a hero – the recipient of two Bronze Stars and five Purple Hearts – following World War II.

Moore says the first Bronze Star was presented for being on the front lines for nine months and 14 days without getting wounded or evacuated.

The second Bronze Star was presented for Moore leading an operation that resulted in the capture of five German officers and 24 enlisted men.

The only complaint against Moore was his stubborn loyalty to Ford Motor Co., whose cars he had raced during most of his career. Allison, who won more races than anyone else for Moore, tried for two years to persuade Moore to switch to General Motors before Allison switched himself to another team.

Allison contended that a Ford team could not compete successfully for the national championship because General Motors had continued to develop and widely distribute high performance parts following the withdrawals of factory sponsorship in the early 1970s.

General Motors teams won 26 of 31 races in 1980 and 22 of 28 in 1981. But Michael Kranefuss, the director of Ford's racing program, promised more help would be provided for teams racing Fords in the future.

"Things are changing," Kranefuss said. "It will be noticeable in 1982 and more so in 1983. We are tired of having our nose rubbed in it by the other factory."

That was good news for Earnhardt, one of the few drivers making team switches for the new season. Allison, after only one season with the Ranier team, moved over to replace Ricky Rudd in the DiGard car. Parsons, who had left Moore, went to the Ranier team, and Rudd replaced Earnhardt on the Childress team, which had signed Piedmont Airlines as its new sponsor.

There also was a change in the Winston Cup schedule format. Instead of sending the teams to Riverside to open the season in January, the season began at Daytona in February, a move that pleased all of the teams.

The driver drawing most attention in the events leading up to the Daytona 500 was Waltrip, who had won his first Winston Cup title the previous year, his first driving for Junior Johnson.

Waltrip also stirred considerable controversy during one of the 125-mile qualifying races, which are run on the Thursday preceding the Daytona 500 to help decide starting positions for the big race.

Buddy Baker was at the lead of a six-car pack when Waltrip, sensing rain was about to put the race under caution, wheeled out in an effort to get close enough to take the lead from Baker. Suddenly, Waltrip decided he didn't have the power to get around Baker by the time they reached the start-finish line, so he tried to salvage second place as a line of other cars prepared to draft by him.

Waltrip cut into the line ahead of Earnhardt, who had to hit his brakes hard to avoid wrecking. Neil Bonnett, closely following Earnhardt, tapped the rear of Earnhardt's car and slid down in front of Ron Bouchard.

Waltrip succeeded in finishing second, just ahead of Earn-hardt, but Bonnett dropped back to seventh and Bouchard all the way to 11th. Waltrip was severely criticized by most of the drivers caught in the high-speed jam session.

"I think Darrell saw he was going to drop from second to sixth in a hurry and he turned right into Earnhardt's front bumper," Bonnett said. "I had to get on the brakes real hard and when I did Ron and I got together. I was just trying to save a lot of beautiful race cars from being a pile of junk. I really think some people are going to have to put a little more thought into what they are doing on the race track."

Dale, who was driving the Moore Ford for the first time, was more philosophical. "I guess you could say that was just racing. But it was a little too close. I don't blame Bonnett and Bouchard for not thinking it was a wise move on Waltrip's part. He just tried to take a little space that I happened to be in. The move worked for him, because he finished ahead of me."

The most stinging criticism came from Richard Petty, who was watching from the sidelines after already competing in the first qualifying race.

"One of these days, Darrell is going to kill someone if he keeps driving like that," Petty said.

That brought a strong reply from Junior Johnson, Waltrip's team owner.

"That kind of talk isn't going to stop us from racing," Johnson said. "It seems Darrell is damned if he does, or damned if he don't. Well, they can go ahead and damn him for doing, because he is going to keep on doing. I don't think Richard Petty has any business commenting on a man's driving style. Why someone would make a comment like that, I don't understand."

Johnson suggested other drivers were just jealous of Waltrip, who had won 12 races the previous year. "People used to criticize Cale Yarborough the same way when he drove for me," Johnson said.

"I think people are just mad because they can't beat our car. The only thing Darrell did was beat a bunch of them to the flag. If he had finished 10th instead of second, everyone would have been tickled to death with the way he drove. But Darrell didn't do anything wrong. He wants to win races, and I don't see him doing anything no one else out there isn't doing.

"When it comes down to racing for the flag, if someone loses, he should be man enough to say that he just got beat. It seems Darrell catches more criticism than anyone else. Everyone who races sometimes sticks his nose in places he shouldn't. I have seen Petty do it plenty of times. But they get beat and it seems to hurt their feelings and they want to cry about it."

Dale, often criticized during his first three years on the circuit for being too aggressive, wouldn't disagree with anything Johnson had said. In fact, he would say the same things to Johnson, Waltrip, and others in years to come when he had the car to beat on the circuit once again.

It did not take long for Dale to suspect that he would not reestablish himself as a consistent winner during the 1982 season. The only trophy he got at Daytona was for winning the Goody's 300, a Late Model Sportsman race, on the Saturday before the Daytona 500, and that was not in Moore's Ford.

He had wisely used race traffic to hold back a challenge from Jody Ridley on the last lap to win that race. "I had planned to draft Dale until the last lap and try to draft around him," Ridley said later. "But the slower cars spoiled that strategy for me. I was hoping they would move out of the way and let Dale and me race to the flag. They didn't and I ran out of room. I never got the chance to make my move."

"I was fortunate the traffic was there," Dale said, "but, man, it feels good to be back in Victory Lane. I just hope we can do it again on Sunday. That is the race I want to win."

In the Daytona 500 the next day, Dale made an early charge from his 10th-place starting position to pass Harry Gant for the lead on Lap 14. But after swapping the lead a couple of times with Bobby Allison, Dale was forced out of the race on only the 44th lap because of engine failure. He finished 36th, one position behind Rudd, who also had engine failure in his first race with the Childress team.

General Motors cars swept eight of the top 10 finishing positions and Buick drivers Bobby Allison, Cale Yarborough, Joe Ruttman, and Terry Labonte finished one through four. The top Ford was driven by Bill Elliott, who was fifth but two laps down.

Meanwhile, it was a good day for Jim Stacy, who had his name on seven of the 42 cars in the starting field. Ruttman, driving the car that Earnhardt left, was third and Labonte finished fourth in a Buick that Stacy sponsored. Stacy also sponsored cars for Jody Ridley, Ron Bouchard, Jim Sauter, Dave Marcis, and Benny Parsons, all of whom finished ahead of Earnhardt.

The next two races, on the short tracks at Richmond and Bristol, made Dale more optimistic about his future with his new team. At Richmond, he finished fourth in the rain-shortened Richmond 400. The race was won by Marcis in a Stacy-sponsored Chevrolet. Richard Petty was second and Parsons, in a Pontiac bearing Stacy's name, was third.

Dale made another strong run for victory in the Valleydale 500 at Bristol, leading 255 laps before Waltrip passed him and led the final 103 laps to victory. Dale finished second.

Returning to the superspeedways at Atlanta and Rockingham, Dale encountered more disappointments that were typical of his first season with Moore. He won the pole at Atlanta with a speed of 163.774 miles per hour and led 155 laps until engine failure forced him out after 211 laps.

It was a similar story at the one-mile North Carolina Motor Speedway in the Hodgdon 500 a week later. Dale led early but was eliminated less than halfway through the race because his engine overheated.

Finally, the long, nerve-shattering slump ended a week later at Darlington. It was Dale's first tour victory since Charlotte in early October of his 1980 championship season, and it was almost denied him by Yarborough, the driver he had beaten for the title.

Only 13 laps from the finish, Yarborough charged hard into the third turn to slip under Earnhardt for the lead. On the following lap, Dale beat Yarborough through the first turn to regain the point.

Yarborough, who had won the week before at Rockingham, made a strong attempt to snatch the victory from Earnhardt at the finish line. He drove hard off the fourth turn and swooped to the inside of Earnhardt, who held on to win by only half a car length.

"We finally showed what we could do when the car stays together," Dale said, his face showing relief. "I had kept promising my sponsor, Wrangler, that I was going to win again, and they kept saying, 'We know you are.' They never put any pressure on me, and I appreciate that.

"There were times last year, and this year, too, that we should have won races. But we didn't get the breaks that we needed. Today we did."

Dale did get some timely breaks. Three times he barely missed cars that wrecked in front of him. "Once, when Neil Bonnett bounced off the wall, I don't have any idea how I missed him," he said. "I thought I was going to rip into him. He just came off the wall in front of me and somehow I managed to miss him."

In addition to getting the breaks, Dale had a strong car that led 182 of the 367 laps, and he did a splendid job steering it through the knots of traffic and narrow turns of the old speedway.

Asked if he thought his next victory would come quicker and easier now that the slump was broken, Dale replied with the wisdom gained during the long run of frustration and disappointments.

"We are capable of winning a lot of races, but it is never easy to win on this circuit. There are too many good cars and lots of money being put behind them. You just have to avoid trouble and be around at the end to have a good chance of winning."

Unfortunately, for the remainder of the 1982 season, Dale had more trouble than opportunities for victory. The Darlington win would be his only one of the year on the circuit as he failed to finish 18 of the 30 events, mostly from engine problems.

But if Dale had reason to wonder if he had made the right move by going to a Ford team, he had other reasons to be convinced he made the right decision in leaving Stacy during the middle of the 1981 season.

As predicted by many, Stacy's racing empire crumbled amid controversy following the impressive showing by his cars in the opening races of the season. Ruttman, who had taken over Earnhardt's car, quit Stacy without explanation after only five races to drive for the Rahmoc team.

Dave Marcis, who won the first Richmond race in a Stacy-sponsored car, had financial support from Stacy withdrawn in June because of a good deed he had done by giving Bobby Allison a push toward Victory Lane in the race at Pocono. Allison was leading Tim Richmond, who had replaced Ruttman in the Stacy-owned car, late in the race when his car ran out of gas during a caution period. Marcis, who was a lap down and out of contention heeded a request for assistance from Allison. He pushed Allison's car around the track and down pit road.

After refueling, Allison returned to the track without losing a lap. He charged past Richmond to regain the lead and went on to win.

Stacy pulled his sponsorship, worth about $75,000, because of Marcis's action. "I have helped other guys out like that, and others have given me a push before," Allison said afterward. "I can't believe Stacy would drop his sponsorship because of that."

It surprised Marcis, too.

"On this circuit we have always helped out each other," he explained. "If I hadn't helped Bobby, someone else would have. A NASCAR official told me that they would have sent out a truck to push him around the track if none of the drivers had been willing to do it."

A few weeks later, without explanation, Stacy also withdrew his sponsorship from Terry Labonte's team, while Labonte was leading the Winston Cup championship standings. Labonte failed to hold the points lead and the championship race turned into a rerun of the 1982 season.

Waltrip, again rolling to 12 victories, made another late-season comeback to defeat Allison for the his second consecutive championship. Waltrip took the lead by finishing second at Dover in September and reeled off a four-race string of victories at Martinsville, North Wilkesboro, Charlotte, and Rockingham.

At the end of the season, Stacy was sponsoring cars for only Ron Bouchard and Jody Ridley. But he had come up with a winner for his own car in Tim Richmond, who won the Budweiser 400 on the Riverside road course in June and repeated in the season-ending Winston Western 500 in November, beating Ricky Rudd by seven seconds.

Dale closed out his dismal season with a last-place finish, completing only eight laps before an oil leak put his Ford out.

After beginning the 1982 season with his name on seven cars, Stacy would not have his name on any a year later.

Richmond, who bought a home on Lake Norman and become one of Earnhardt's closest friends, was named to drive for a new team fielded by drag-racer Raymond Beadle in 1983.

6

'Earnhardt would give an aspirin a headache'

While the 1982 season was a bundle of mechanical failures and disappointments for Dale Earnhardt, he did score one major triumph in his personal life by marrying Teresa Houston, a slender and beautiful woman who frequently was mistaken as one of the beauty queens when she was around the race tracks.

Teresa grew up in racing, so she understood the demands that the sport placed on her new husband. Her father was Hal Houston and her uncle was Tommy Houston, a longtime star on the Busch Grand National circuit. "My dad and uncles raced, and if they weren't at a race track they were working on race cars," Teresa said once during an interview with Deb Williams.

Teresa first noticed Earnhardt when he was competing in a race at Hickory Speedway, but it was several years later before they began dating. "My first impression of Dale was that he was very energetic and a go-getter. He seemed to be a lot of fun, too."

Shortly before the marriage, Dale had gained custody of

Kelly King and Ralph Dale Jr., his children from his second marriage.

"From the first time we met, Teresa and I have been friends," Dale said later. "But it was several years after I met her that we began dating and then got married. That was the best business decision I have ever made, too. She has been good for me in business, and was good for me as a friend.

"She was there when I didn't have anything, and she has stuck in there with me. She was there through the bad times until we finally got something. She came right in and was mother to my kids from the previous marriage, and she has got a good business head on her shoulders and makes smart business decisions."

With his personal life on solid ground for the first time since he began his Winston Cup career, Earnhardt was hopeful he could renew his winning ways on the tracks, too.

The Ford teams had their noses "rubbed in it" again during the 1982 season as General Motors cars won 28 of the 30 races.

The only Ford victories were by Earnhardt at Darlington in April and Neil Bonnett at Charlotte in May. But, as Kranefuss had promised, help was on the way and the first visible signs were the new, stream-lined Ford Thunderbirds in the garage at Daytona International Speedway when preparations began in early February for the season-opening Daytona 500.

Major driver changes during the offseason included Cale Yarborough hopping from the M.C. Anderson team to drive the Ranier Team Pontiac for the major races only Neil Bonnett leaving the Woods team to drive for Rahmoc, and Buddy Baker taking Bonnett's place in the Woods' Ford. Anderson, unable to persuade Yarborough to accept a $1 million offer to run the full schedule, folded his team, and his top mechanics, crew chief Tim Brewer and engine-builder Harold Elliott, signed on to prepare cars for Tim Richmond, driving for the new team fielded by Beadle.

Dale, who had signed a two-year contract with Moore, was

anxious to test the new Thunderbird in a race and the first opportunity came in the Busch Clash, which he had sat out the previous season after failing to win a pole position in 1981.

Dale barely had settled into the driver's seat of the blue and yellow Ford when it began belching smoke. The problem had no affect on the performance of the car, however, and he was determined to ride it out until NASCAR flagman Harold Kinder waved the black flag, ordering him to pit road on the ninth lap of the 20-lap race.

Realizing that he would be out of contention if he made a pit stop during such a short race, Dale ignored the black flag and continued to race until a last-lap collision took him out. Neil Bonnett passed Darrell Waltrip on the final lap to snatch the victory.

NASCAR officials and other drivers were furious that Dale had ignored the black flag. Buddy Baker blamed an oil-covered windshield for his involvement in the final-lap wreck that included Earnhardt and Terry Labonte.

"Dale Earnhardt would give an aspirin a headache," Baker fumed.

The next day NASCAR fined Earnhardt $10,000, the heaviest penalty ever given a driver for violating race procedure.

Dale immediately announced that he would appeal the fine.

"I know some of the drivers probably have hard feelings against me because of what happened," he said. "I don't blame them. But I wanted to win that $50,000 first-place money as much as they did. NASCAR put us out there to race for $50,000, threw the green flag, and then expected me to quit. There was a lot of smoke, but I don't think much of the oil was getting onto the track. I don't think Darrell Waltrip, Buddy Baker, or anyone else would have quit that race if they had been in my place.

"In a 20-lap race, if you pit you lose. It is as simple as that. I decided to ignore the black flag and argue my case afterwards."

Bud Moore supported his driver's decision. The smoke was caused by a minor engine problem that didn't affect the car's performance, he claimed.

"I am upset with the fine, but I am not mad at NASCAR," Dale said. "I know they had to do something. I broke their rules, and I have to pay the price. But I think the price is too much for what I did. If I had slapped Bill Gazaway (NASCAR's director of racing competition), the fine might not have been that much. They are taking all the money I won in the race away from me. I did something wrong, but there was something wrong when they threw the flag for that race.

"In the drivers' meeting, they told us to be careful and to respect the other drivers. Hell, that went off the board on the first lap."

A day later, a NASCAR appeals board agreed with Earnhardt that the fine was excessive. The board reduced the fine to $5,000, $2,000 of it refundable if in the next 10 races Dale conducted himself "to the extent and spirit of the NASCAR rules."

Despite the oil leak, Dale was pleased with the way his new Thunderbird ran and handled during the Busch Clash, and he was even more enthusiastic after the 125-mile qualifying races on Thursday when he won a high-speed chess game against A.J. Foyt.

Foyt, driving a Chevrolet Monte Carlo, led 22 consecutive laps before Earnhardt spearheaded a three-car parade around him on the final lap. Baker, in another Thunderbird, finished second and young Kyle Petty, in a Pontiac, was third.

"I think my car was strong enough that I could have taken the lead much earlier, but the place you want to be on the last lap is second-place, so you can use the slingshot," Dale said, referring to the way a trailing car can shoot from the draft of the lead car to get a sudden surge of power.

Foyt was not surprised that Earnhardt and the other two drivers had passed him so easily. "There was nothing I could do to stop them," he said. "My car was a little loose and they just came under me. The only chance I had was to use a slower car to block them, but there wasn't any when I needed it."

Winning the 125-mile qualifier was a solid confidence-booster for Dale and the Moore team. But the race that counted was the Daytona 500, and in it there was only more frustration of the kind the team had experienced during the 1982 season.

Earnhardt drove by Joe Ruttman to take the lead on Lap 61, but two laps later the engine blew and he coasted back to the garage to finish 35th. His only consolation was that a pair of Fords, driven by Bill Elliott and Buddy Baker, finished right behind Cale Yarborough's winning Pontiac, and Dick Brooks took fifth place in his Junie Donlavey Ford.

"The new design certainly makes the Fords more competitive on the big tracks than they were a year ago," Dale saidd. "But you've still got to be there at the finish to win the race."

Moore took an old-style Ford, which had performed well on the short tracks the year before, to Richmond for the next race. It ran strong all day but excessive tire wear prevented Dale from getting his first victory of the season.

Bobby Allison gained the advantage he needed to beat Earnhardt by only a half-second when he ducked into the pits on his final stop to take on a couple of gallons of fuel to get him to the finish line. Dale was in his pit for 15 seconds during his final stop to get a change of left side tires and fuel.

Allison had a 3.4-second lead following the final round of stops. He built the margin between him and Earnhardt to 4.5 seconds when Earnhardt got ensnarled in a traffic jam.

After clearing the slower traffic, Earnhardt steered his Ford around the track at dare-devil speeds while attempting to overtake Allison. He came up only a few yards short.

"If the race had been a few laps longer, I would have caught him," Dale said. "Time ran out on me. It was hell catching him and then not having enough time left to get the victory."

At least Dale had come within a whisker of victory, and he had not experienced any mechanical problems with the Ford.

That was more than he could say about the next few races in which he finished 33rd, 34th, 13th, 29th, 26th, 24th, and 24th again. He failed to finish five of the events because of engine failures and he wrecked in two others.

Once again he had gone more than a year without a victory on the Winston Cup circuit, and the streak of bad finishes already had eliminated him from any chance of winning the national championship. In the first nine races, his Ford had been running at the finish in only one, at Richmond, where he finished a close second to Allison.

Some critics in the grandstands were blaming the mechanical failures on Dale's rugged style of driving. But those closer to the sport knew differently.

"Most of the stuff breaking on the car doesn't have anything to do with how hard he drives," said Tim Brewer, crew chief for Tim Richmond. "You can believe this, too, buddy. Earnhardt is still as good or better than any driver out here."

Dale never doubted his own ability either. When Moore's Ford was running good, he took it to the front of the field, and he insisted he would not change his hard-driving style.

"My foot is made to go all the way down on the accelerator, not just halfway," he said. "I can't stroke. I ain't built that way."

The run of mechanical problems bore down heavily on Dale. "If the car doesn't blow up, it seems that I am a victim," he complained after being trapped in an accident involving Dave Marcis and Geoff Bodine at Martinsville. "Sure, it is frustrating. I drove 40 laps at Wilkesboro and then had to sit there and watch the rest of the race because the engine blowed up."

He wished that Moore would switch to a General Motors car. "If it was my decision, I would have bought one at Daytona when I rolled in there in February," he said. "But that is Bud's decision. He is the car owner. A man who once drove for Bud gave me a good suggestion when I went there to drive for Bud. He said, 'You just drive the car, don't offer advice,' and I have tried to do that."

But Dale knew that he could change matters if he so chose and that that likely would be the case.

"I will stay here with Bud for the remainder of the season," he said in May. "Then we will talk. But it is safe to say that I might be somewhere else next year. I just want to win some more races. I appreciate the hard work Bud and his team have put into the car, and I don't mean to fault him. He is just as disappointed as I am that we are not winning. But he is a dedicated Ford man, and I am not sure that is the way for me to go. I can't seem to get along with the Ford people."

Dale wasn't the only Ford driver having problems during the first half of the season. General Motors drivers swept the first 15 events before Buddy Baker won the Firecracker 400 at Daytona in July.

Dale broke his 15-month non-winning streak in the next race, two weeks later, by leading 212 of 420 laps to beat Darrell Waltrip by 11 seconds to win the Busch 420 at Nashville.

After another engine failure sidelined him at Pocono, Dale won his second race in the Talladega 500 on July 31.

He led a total of 44 laps on the 2.66-mile track but he had to slingshot by Darrell Waltrip on the final lap to get the victory by a half-car length.

Three victories in four races certainly indicated that the Ford teams were finally making strong headway, but it wasn't enough to convince Dale that he should stay with a Ford.

"I talked to Bud and told him I had to go somewhere else, that I just couldn't stand it," Dale recalled later. "Bud said, 'Well, how much money will it take to get you to stay with me?' I had to give Bud a figure, which I did. Bud talked to Wrangler, our sponsor, and they said they couldn't do that. Some of the Wrangler people told Bud that they were going to stay as his sponsor and that I could do what I wanted to do."

When Dale studied the possibilities for the coming season, however, he didn't see many. Junior Johnson had sold half of his team to Warner Hodgdon, a West Coast businessman, and was committed to fielding cars for both Waltrip and Bonnett. Yarborough was having a good year with the Ranier team, driving a limited schedule, and Bobby Allison was en route to his first Winston Cup championship in the DiGard Buick. That left the Rahmoc team, which Bonnett was going to leave to drive for Johnson, and a new team being formed by Harry Hyde. Neither interested Earnhardt.

Even when Dale gave Moore notice that he was looking for another ride for 1984, he had a good idea where he would like to go. Richard Childress, who had told Dale two years earlier that his team wasn't good enough for him, had emerged as a competitive force on the circuit with driver Ricky Rudd.

Rudd won pole position for the Daytona 500 in Childress's Pontiac with a speed of 198.864 miles per hour, then scored the team's first victory at Riverside in June. He also won at Martinsville in September. It was at that race that Rudd first heard rumors that Earnhardt was interested in returning to the Childress team.

"Richard and I both still have a lot to learn, but we have been able to grow together," Rudd said. "I don't know, and Richard says he don't know, what is going to happen for next year. I think we are both smart enough to know it has taken a couple of years for us to reach this point, and neither of us wants to throw it away. But there are other people who can see this has become a successful team, and they might want that success. A car owner might want to hire the driver away, or a driver with good sponsorship money might want to buy his way into the car. I know there are other drivers who would like to have what I've got right now."

Actually, several drivers had expressed interest in the Childress team after Earnhardt left in 1981.

"After Dale and I agreed that he should go to a more established team after the 1981 season, I had a lot of drivers who were interested in driving my car, because it had run so good in those 10 races with Dale in it," Childress recalled later.

"Benny Parsons was one driver that talked about driving for me. But Piedmont Airlines had approached me about sponsoring my car, since Wrangler was going to go to Bud Moore's with Dale, and they wanted me to get a young driver. Ricky had run good with DiGard in 1981, but he had never won a race. I told him that if he would come with me that I thought we could win some races. We got together, and about halfway through the first season with Ricky things started clicking good for us.

"It was a good situation for both of us. Ricky had an ex-driver who could help him out. I rode him around Riverside and showed him some things. I felt comfortable talking to him because he was a young driver, and I had the confidence that I could help him with some things. So, that relationship was great for both of us. He couldn't win with DiGard, which had good equipment, and in our two years Ricky won six poles and two races.

"So at the end of the '83 season, I felt more confident in our team, our finances, and everything. If Earnhardt wanted to come back, which he had said he did, I felt we were in position to give him a good car that would run up front and win races."

There was another major decision confronting Childress. His team had developed to such a highly competitive level that it had caught the attention of Mike Curb, a West Coast businessman and music producer. Curb wanted to buy Childress's team and let Earnhardt drive the car.

"Mike was talking to both me and Dale, saying he wanted me to run the team and Dale to be the driver. We talked and talked about it, and I lost a lot of sleep over it," Childress said.

"I had someone wanting to buy my team and was offering me more money than I had ever seen at one time. I had a man bring me a check and lay it in front of me. I was thinking that I could take it and leave the country, you know." He laughed.

"But I wanted to keep the team. You know, I had got it that far and we had won races with it, and I knew out there in the future there was a lot more to be gained."

After Childress turned down Curb, Wrangler re-entered the picture and told Childress the company would like to sponsor him and Earnhardt as a team again. "They told me that they wanted Dale and me back together and said they could put Ricky in another car, which was Bud Moore's, because they had another year left on their contract with him. That is what we ended up doing."

During his own career as a driver-owner, Childress's best season was in 1980, when he had 10 top-10 finishes and won $157,400. But in 285 races he had scored no victories and had finished only six times among the top five.

In only his second year as a team owner, his driver, Rudd, won $257,585, two races, and had five other top-five finishes. Still it had been difficult for Childress to give up racing himself.

"I had run like 250-something races without ever missing one," he recalled."I think only myself, Benny Parsons, and Richard Petty had a string of consecutive races that long. But opportunity knocked. Wrangler was offering the money and I could put Dale in the car to show what it could do. I could run a hundred laps at a time, or lead through one pit stop, but I just didn't have the money, or the drive, whatever, to keep it going for the whole deal.

"I had bills I had to pay. I had people working for me I had to pay. I lived in a five-room house that my family lived in until 1980 because I put every penny I had back into my race team. My wife, Judy, and my daughter, Tina, were both understanding. They knew I was doing what I loved, and that was driving race cars. I kept telling them that someday we were going to get a break, and we were going to make it. I think, if anything, we were closer back then. We are still close, but then we were struggling for everything."

While as a driver Childress never had the sponsorship money to win races on his own, he always showed up at the tracks with a car that looked stronger than it was. "Even back in

1976, the Saturday night before the Daytona 500, I went down to a T-shirt shop and had shirts made up for all of my crew guys. They had my car number, 3, on the back, just to make them look professional. We didn't have money for uniforms."

Childress, who grew up in Winston-Salem with Junior Johnson his racing hero, had gotten the No. 3 for his own Winston Cup car when it became available. It was the number that Johnson used during most of his driving career.

"To have the number Junior Johnson raced and made famous was a big honor to me," Childress said. "When Dale left Stacy, Wrangler tried to take the No. 2 with them, because they had used that number in all of their advertising. But Stacy wouldn't let them have the number, so we kept my number, 3, and I'm glad we did, the way things turned out."

Eventually, only a few old-timers and racing historians would remember that Johnson was the first to make the No. 3 famous. With Earnhardt and Childress back together again, it would become the symbol for what was to become one of stock car racing's greatest teams.

7

'The greatest stock car race ever'

Nobody has discovered a magic formula for building a winning team on the Winston Cup circuit.

Many rich team owners have hired talented engine builders, crew chiefs, and drivers from other successful teams only to discover that while cubic dollars can overcome many obstacles in racing, that alone can't guarantee success. During the '60s, '70s and '80s, several teams enjoyed the "right combination" for a couple of seasons but only a handful dominated for several years with the same driver.

By far, the most durable and successful combination was Richard Petty driving for his family-owned Petty Enterprises. Bill Elliott also became a consistent winner with a family-dominated team that was owned by Harry Melling. The best non-family operations to enjoy long-lasting success with the same drivers were: the Wood Brothers' team with David Pearson, from 1972 to 1978; Junior Johnson's team with Cale Yarborough, from 1973 to 1980, and with Darrell Waltrip, from 1981 to 1986; and Fred Lorenzen, who dominated the superspeedways while driving for Holman-Moody from 1961 to 1967.

Lorenzen, who retired because of health problems when he was only 31, made a rare visit back to the circuit to attend the 1991 Motorcraft 500 at Atlanta International Raceway and was impressed most by the Dale Earnhardt-Richard Childress combination, which reminded him of his old race team.

"Dale Earnhardt is the best driver I have ever seen," said Lorenzen, who once raced against Curtis Turner, Fireball Roberts, Joe Weatherly, Richard Petty and David Pearson. "But what makes him so successful are the car owner and crewmen around him. They just expect to win every time out, as I did when I was driving for Holman-Moody. None of them wants to accept losing.

"That is what makes a great team, getting the right people and having them all work together. It is the car owner, the crew, the mechanics, everybody doing their jobs and making it work. Dale is a great driver, and Childress is the mechanical genius behind the whole operation, just as Ralph Moody was for my team."

Dale had won nine races, six for the Osterlund team during his first two years on the circuit and three while driving for Moore in 1982 and 1983, and Childress had won two races with Rudd in his second full season as a team owner before he and Earnhardt reunited for the 1984 season. It is safe to assume both would have continued to win races had they not gotten back together. It is just as probable that neither would have enjoyed the same success that they would achieve as a team.

"It is very difficult to explain why one combination of a car owner and driver works so well and another combination involving the same people doesn't," says Childress. "In the case of Dale and me, I think a lot of it has to do with us having similar backgrounds.

"We both came up the hard way. We have got a lot of things in common. We both lost our dads by heart attacks, and we both know what that is like, although I was only five years old when my father died and Dale was older than that.

"We both had to work for everything we got. Nothing was just given to us. He had to go out and work on his race cars to make things happen and I did, too. I have the greatest respect in the world for him as a race driver and a human being. We have equal respect for each other, not only as professionals, but as human beings, and I think that helps us both out.

"We all have problems, and when I do, I feel that I can talk to Dale about it. If he has a problem, he feels he can talk to me about it. That's just the way it is. It is hard to give a clear reason for our success together, but a lot of it is that we both can relate back to what it was when we got into this sport, and how we had to struggle to get to where we wanted to go."

Dale agrees that mutual respect and a relationship that extends beyond the race team was a foundation for success for the two from the beginning.

"Richard is my boss, because this is his race team and he calls the shots," he says. "He is also one of my best friends. We race together and we fish and hunt together. Richard is the kind of guy you like to be around because he is a lot of fun. He is a man you want to race for because he is a winner. He will work all night and day to build a perfect race car, and he will stick with you every lap of the race to make sure everything is all right."

Richard Childress was only 10 years old when he got his first job in racing. He sold peanuts in the grandstands at Bowman Gray Stadium in Winston-Salem during the weekly Modified races.

"I had to beg to get the job, and it wasn't just to make some money," he recalls. "I really wasn't interested in selling peanuts, you know. I didn't have the money to buy a ticket to get into the stadium to see the races and the job got me in free. Racing was all I could think about, even back then, just as it was for Dale when he was that age. I had to walk about eight miles round-trip from our home, just outside Winston-Salem, to get to the race track and back."

Childress bought his first race car for $20 and began racing when he was 16 "I guess that is about as close as you can come to starting on the bottom," he says.

"I was racing in what was called the hobby division, and I kept trying to work my way up, trying to see how far I could go, and knowing I wouldn't be satisfied until I got to the Winston Cup circuit. I didn't have much money, just a lot of dreams in those days."

In 1969, Childress was driving in NASCAR's Grand American Series. He was among the drivers from that circuit who agreed to fill out the field when most of the top Winston Cup drivers boycotted the first Talladega 500 at Alabama International Motor Speedway.

"I won about $6,000 in that race. Man, I didn't know there was that much money in the world. I took it and started my first race shop," he recalled.

He moved up to the Winston Cup circuit in 1972 as an independent driver and his best season was in 1975, when he finished fifth in the Winston Cup championship standings. "I used the money I won that season to buy the land where I built my present shop," he said.

Even when Childress was struggling through the early years of his career and could afford to pay his crew chief only a few dollars and expenses, he had a good eye for talent. Barry Dodson and Tim Brewer, who became two of the most respected crew chiefs on the circuit, began their careers as teenagers working for Childress.

Childress came up with another "find" in 1980 when he hired Kirk Shelmerdine, a jobless 22-year-old, to work for him in the engine room at his race shop. Midway through the season, when Dennis Connor resigned as crew chief, Childress asked Shelmerdine to fill in at that position for a few races.

"When Dennis left, Richard said he would like for me to look after things until he found someone else," Shelmerdine says with a laugh when telling how he got the job. "I guess good help is hard to find, because it has been a long time since then and he still hasn't found someone else."

Actually, Childress realized he couldn't find anyone better to fit his needs, and Shelmerdine never found adequate reason to go anywhere else.

Shelmerdine, a native of Philadelphia, originally drifted south in hopes of becoming a Winston Cup driver, and he still competes in minor events when he finds the time. In the late 1970s, he went to work for James Hylton's independent Winston Cup team and later was with the DiGard team during Darrell Waltrip's controversial tour.

"That was an experience," says Shelmerdine. "Darrell was in the middle of his contract dispute with Bill Gardner and everyone on the team was mad at each other and threatening to quit. Buddy Parrott was the crew chief and he was fired. Jake Elder came in for a little while after that. I was there for nine months and it was total chaos the whole time.

"That was my first taste of big-time racing. I thought if it was going to be like that, I didn't know if I wanted to stay in racing or not."

He learned how enjoyable racing could be when he went to work for Childress. "Richard has a real knack for keeping people interested and focused on their jobs. The people who work for Richard are all dedicated to doing whatever they can to make the team a winner," Shelmerdine says.

Despite the progress Childress's new team made during the two years Earnhardt spent driving for Bud Moore, Childress did not think it was quite ready to make a serious run at dominating the circuit. With the solid sponsorship of Wrangler, he wasn't being pressured to take quick-fix short cuts to rush the team into something it wasn't ready to handle either.

"I talked with Dale and Kirk during the winter before the 1984 season and we spent a lot of time planning how we wanted to run the season, and what goals we wanted to accomplish," Childress recalled. "We knew if we were going to be successful we were going to have to develop durability. We decided to concentrate on reliability during the first half of the season.

"We knew we had to build equipment that would last before we could start winning races during the second half of the season, and we knew it was going to take some time for all of us to start adjusting to each other. Our purpose wasn't to go out and set the world on fire that first year. We felt we were going to be competitive and that we were going to win some races, but the main thing we wanted to do was to work on durability and get the team going in the right direction."

The team got off to an excellent start in the Daytona 500, where Earnhardt finished second to Cale Yarborough, who became the first driver since Fireball Roberts in 1962 to win pole position, a 125-mile qualifying race, and the 500.

Yarborough, who was driving a Chevrolet for the Ranier team, drafted behind Darrell Waltrip through most of the final laps with Earnhardt riding tightly on his rear bumper. Everyone, including Waltrip, knew Yarborough was just waiting to sling-shot around Waltrip on the final lap.

"I knew the whole time what Cale was going to do, and worst of all, I knew there wasn't anything I could do to stop him," said Waltrip. "I was wanting to hook up with Cale and for me and him to get away from Earnhardt and everyone else. But when Cale came out of the pits and pulled up behind me after his last stop, I knew the scenario. I had seen it a few times before."

The year before, Yarborough was carrying an in-car microphone and told the national television audience that he would slingshot by Buddy Baker for the victory. "I was just hoping Cale hadn't told the whole world that he was going to roar by me, like he did to Buddy last year," Waltrip said. "I had asked him if that ever happened with me sitting there in front of him not to do me that way. When Cale went by me, he was going so fast that he just sucked Earnhardt on by me, too."

Dale figured he had done all he could by finishing second.

He had hoped Yarborough would make a mistake by passing Waltrip too soon and he would have enough time to use the sling-shot to get by Yarborough. But Yarborough was too smart, and his car too strong, to allow that to happen.

"I just took what I could get," Dale said. "The car was a little down on horsepower all day. I could draft with them, but nothing else. I wanted to be behind Cale because if I had been in front, he would have done to me what he did to ol' Darrell. When Cale went by Darrell, I used the wind to get by, too. It got a little close between Darrell and me at the end. I laid my car real close to his to get all the wind off him that I could."

Dale finished one second behind winner Benny Parsons in the Coca-Cola 500 at Atlanta, and was also runnerup in the World 600 at Charlotte, and the Miller 400 at Michigan International Speedway during the first-half of the season.

While failing to win, he still held a 47-point lead in the Winston Cup standings at the halfway mark, following an eighth place finish in the Firecracker 400 at Daytona. He started the Firecracker on the outside pole and was a strong runner during the first half until a broken rear shock spoiled his hopes.

The biggest news of the day was at the front of the field, where Richard Petty barely beat Cale Yarborough to the start-finish line to begin a race-ending caution period for the 200th victory of his career. Among those cheering his accomplishment was President Ronald Reagan, who for a few minutes joined announcer Ned Jarrett in the radio booth to describe the race for Motor Racing Network listeners.

"Here they come...there they go," the President said. "The blue car is just about to pass the white car."

President Reagan didn't have any trouble recognizing the significance of the victory or the driver of the winning red and blue No. 43 Pontiac. The president had met Petty, himself a Republican politician and Reagan supporter, previously at White House dinners. This time the president met The King on his own turf to offer congratulations.

Yarborough and Petty bumped several times as they battled back to the caution flag, each knowing the race would not restart under green. Petty won by only a few inches. "I can't believe you were bumping each other like that at 200 miles per hour," Reagan told Petty.

For Petty, the victory was special. "The 200th is a big win because it is Daytona. It is a big deal because it is July Fourth and the first time a president has attended one of our races. All of that combined, makes it just a big, big deal. That is the best way to describe it," he said, flashing a wide grin.

Earnhardt was happy to see Petty get the 200th victory he had been chasing since winning at Dover, Delaware, in May. More pleasing, however, for Earnhardt was being the new points leader and the feeling that his first victory with the Childress team was not very far away.

"We spent the first half of the season concentrating on endurance, and it paid off. Now we are in perfect shape to get our first victory," he said as the team prepared for the Talladega 500 at Alabama International Motor Speedway in late July.

While Earnhardt has special feelings about each of the race tracks on the Winston Cup circuit, he loves to race on none more than the high-banked track at Talladega. That was especially true before 1988 when NASCAR began requiring teams to use carburetor restricter plates in an effort to keep racing speeds below 200 miles per hour.

The big track between Birmingham and Atlanta has been trademarked by controversies, strange happenings, and spectacular finishes since Bill France, the founder of NASCAR, built it as a sister track to Daytona in 1969. France, who occasionally had problems with Florida politicians, had a strong friendship with former Alabama Gov. George Wallace, and France thought it would be nice to have another major track, in case he ever felt the need to move NASCAR out of Florida.

However, according to local legend, France made a mistake by building what would be called "The World's Fastest Speedway," on top of sacred Indian burial grounds. The Indian tribe, forced from the land many, many years before, supposedly left behind a curse for any who dared to disturb the burial grounds.

When a field of more than 40 race cars crank up and thunder around an enclosed bowl of asphalt at more than 200 miles per hour, you have to figure if any spirits were left behind, they are apt to be disturbed.

France ran into an immediate problem when the track opened for its first race in 1969. Most of the top drivers said the pavement, which had some big holes, was not safe and they organized a boycott. France responded by recruiting whatever cars and drivers he could find, including Childress and his Grand American car, so he could hold the race as scheduled.

It was at Talladega in 1973 that Bobby Isaac drove his Bud Moore Ford into the garage without advance notice.

"What is wrong with the car?" a stunned Moore asked.

"Nothing," replied Isaac.

"Why did you drop out of the race?" Moore demanded.

"I heard a voice that told to me to quit," answered Isaac, who also quit Moore's team and retired from the sport, although he attempted an unsuccessful comeback a few years later.

There also have been weird electrical outages at the track during races, and a couple of times tornadoes could be seen whirling within miles of the track during race weeks.

There are several strange faces in the crowd of Talladega 500 winners, too. Bobby Hillin, Lennie Pond, Dick Brooks, and Richard Brickhouse got their only Winston Cup victories in the event. James Hylton won the 1972 race for the only superspeedway triumph of his career.

At wide-open speeds, the Talladega track is the most competitive in motorsports and it is not unusual to see cars switching the lead three or four times during a single lap as they break in and out of the draft, which was considerably more effective before the carburetor plates and the smaller, sleeker cars.

Racing at Talladega was at its best in the mid-1980s, when drivers pushed single-car qualifying speeds beyond the 200-miles-per-hour mark, and raced bumper-to-bumper, fender-to-fender at about the same pace.

Dale had liked the track since the first time he raced on it, and during his 1980 championship season he finished second to Buddy Baker in the Winston 500 in May and third behind Neil Bonnett and Cale Yarborough in the Talladega 500.

Both times, Earnhardt was in position to win on the final lap and lacked the drafting experience of the other drivers to make the right moves. He learned quickly, however, as was evidenced in his last-lap victory over Waltrip in the 1983 Talladega 500, which only deepened his love for the big track.

"I think if someone asked Dale to design the perfect race track, he would recreate Talladega," Richard Childress says. "If it was up for a vote, Dale would probably vote to race at Talladega every week. There really are no great secrets or mysteries to running well at Talladega. It is flat-out racing, and if you know Dale Earnhardt, you know why he is so successful at Talladega. He and the track are a perfectly matched pair. They go together, and that is where he is at his best."

Dale quickly admits his love affair with the track. "I thoroughly enjoy driving a race car, but at Talladega, I thoroughly love to drive a race car. Running in the drafts, the quick speeds, the high banking in the turns, the strategies, setting up to make a pass, all of it makes Talladega racing special. Nothing we do in racing compares to Talladega. It has its own personality. I love it."

Earnhardt's enthusiasm for the Talladega races also gets the rest of the team pumped up.

"I know there are a thousand little things that can go wrong on a race car, those nagging little unexplainable problems that can pull the curtains instantly," crew chief Shelmerdine says. "But one thing we don't have to worry about, and especially at Talladega, is our driver. If we put him in a competitive car that will go the distance, Dale will do the rest. Sometimes I get the impression that Dale thinks he is supposed to win every race at Talladega."

Earnhardt certainly was feeling good about his chances for getting his first victory with the Childress team in the 1984 Talladega 500. Cale Yarborough, who had followed his Daytona 500 victory by winning the Winston 500 at Talladega in May, qualified for pole position with a speed of 202.474 miles per hour, and Bill Elliott, the Ford driver who was beginning to flex his muscles on the big tracks, won the other front-row starting spot.

Dale started third in the 40-car field and pushed his Chevrolet by the front-row starters on the first lap and held the lead for three laps before Buddy Baker wheeled his Ford to the front, setting off an unprecedented string of lead changes that had the crowd of more than 100,000 fans on their feet most of the hot afternoon.

In all, there was a total of 67 lead changes among 16 drivers, and that was just the count at the start-finish line, in what many people say was the greatest stock car race in Winston Cup history.

Going down the stretch of the 188-lap, 500-mile race, Earnhardt and Baker were still battling door-to-door, with each trying to establish a position for the last-lap scramble to the checkered flag. Neither wanted to be the leader entering the final lap, since it seemed almost certain that one of the other stronger cars – if not a crowd of them – would slip out of the draft and slingshot around the leader.

Dale gave way to Baker on the Lap 155. Baker stayed in front for three laps and then yielded the lead to Ron Bouchard. Waltrip drove to the front to lead Lap 163. Baker went back ahead for Laps 164-171. Then it was Bouchard for 172-174, Baker again for 175-181, and, finally, Terry Labonte broke out of a 10-car pack to lead six laps, making him the leader under the white flag. Dicing for position, Dale suddenly shot out of the crowd of contenders, pulled around Labonte, and left the others to decide who would finish second.

"It certainly was one of the most competitive races I have been involved in," Dale said later. "It was just a question of where you wanted to be on the last lap. Everyone was jumping around, and it was a situation where I got in the right place."

Dale's biggest fear was that Baker, who was between him and Labonte, would not wait until the final lap to make his move. "I was glad to see Buddy stay put until I made my move," he said. "Terry stayed in the low groove, and since it was too muddy in the infield for me to do any racing down there, I went on the outside of him."

Baker attempted to follow Earnhardt around Labonte, but was unable to completely clear him, and they began racing each other.

"That let me get away," Dale said. "When I saw them back there, I was so tickled that I didn't know what to do."

What he did was stick his left hand out the window and wave to the fans as he sped toward the checkered flag. "I just kept saying 'Please, Lord, please, please,' " he recalled.

Baker and Labonte, side-by-side, crossed the finish line 1.66 seconds behind Earnhardt. At first, Labonte was credited with second-place, but official photos clearly showed that Baker, on the high side, won the position by a few inches.

Bobby Allison was fourth, followed by Yarborough, Waltrip, Harry Gant, Lake Speed, rookie Tommy Ellis, and Bill Elliott. Five other drivers also finished in the lead lap.

"With about 10 laps to go, I was running eighth in the pack and couldn't get anywhere," Labonte later recalled. "I couldn't creep up one-by-one, but then I caught the traffic just right on the inside and went around everyone. I wasn't sure I wanted to be the leader entering the last lap, but I knew being out front was better than being back in eighth place."

Labonte said he slowed a little on each of the following laps and no one was willing to take the lead from him. So he began working a strategy that he hoped would be good enough to win from the point on the final lap.

"When I took the white flag, I pushed the accelerator to the floorboard, and I might have done it too soon," he said. "I wanted to get a lead and hoped everyone else would start racing each other. But they didn't. They just stayed behind me in a draft until we got to the backstretch. Dale came flying by me and Baker pulled up on me. Dale got away when Buddy and I hooked up side-by-side.

"It was probably the most exciting race I have ever been in. Earnhardt won it, but six or seven others could have won it, too."

Baker, noted as the foremost authority on high-speed drafting, described the race as one of the tightest he'd ever seen from start to finish.

"I have never raced so hard for so long in my whole life," said Baker, who didn't have to see the photos to know he had edged Labonte for second-place. "When they first said Terry had beaten me for the position, I told them to look at the pictures. I could see as we crossed the line that Terry's door post was behind mine. It is like a foot race. You are going like Jack the Bear, but you can tell."

Dale's first victory with the Childress team gave more credibility to his front-running position in the Winston Cup standings and was timely because Waltrip, who had three victories and was fourth in the standings, was complaining that someone might stroke his way to the title.

It was doubtful that Waltrip included Earnhardt in the "stroker" category, though, since he knew first-hand how hard Earnhardt drove. Still, Dale didn't take kindly to any hint that he had been stroking, and Victory Lane provided him a perfect stage for giving a reply to Waltrip, who finished sixth.

"I read in the paper the other day where ol' Darrell said I was stroking my way to the championship," Dale said. "Well, I didn't see any stroking out there today."

Asked if he thought the victory would quiet Waltrip, Earnhardt grinned. "How many years has Waltrip been racing? Has he ever been quiet in any of those years?"

During the post-race press conference, someone made the mistake of asking Dale if he wanted to win the Winston Cup title again to prove his 1980 championship "was not a fluke."

"A fluke?" he shot back. "Anyone who was around in 1980 knows that championship was not a fluke. I had to race Cale Yarborough for the title the entire season, and it took beating him in the final race of the season to do it. This team is working real hard for me to win the title, and our chances at this point seems good. This victory has got to help our confidence and make us stronger. It is a big shot in the arm for us."

Labonte emerged from Talladega trailing Earnhardt in the Winston Cup standings by 65 points. He sliced the lead to 35 in the next race at Michigan International Speedway, and took the lead by 15 points by winning Bristol, where Earnhardt wound up 10th after being involved in a wreck.

The Childress team went to Darlington for the Southern 500 in early September with hopes of refueling their championship drive. But winning only a 20th-place starting position on the narrow old track was hardly a good omen for Earnhardt.

"I started 20th in the spring race on this track, too," Dale said. "Before I could get up to one of the top five positions I had done been through the infield three times. There is a lot of beating and banging going on back in the field with people trying to get to the front. Sometimes you have to shut your eyes to keep from scaring yourself to death. It is so easy to get in trouble at this track if you are running harder than you are supposed to. Darlington is one place where you can get into big trouble without trying.

"It is not that the track is that hard to drive, but they use that slick sealant to keep it from cracking, and the track just never stays the same. If they would go ahead and pave the old worn-out bitch and be done with it, everything would be all right."

The condition of the track's surface would not be the big problem for Earnhardt. His blue and yellow Chevrolet, which had performed flawlessly through most of his first season back with Childress, experienced its first engine failure of the year and finished 38th.

Four weeks later at Charlotte Dale again was the victim of engine failure, and a 39th place finish left the championship for Labonte and Harry Gant to decide.

Noting that he was 267 points behind Labonte, Dale admitted, "This puts me out of the points race. I just hope I can win some races now before the end of the season."

Gant failed to make a strong challenge in the final four races and Labonte, a 28-year-old Texan, won his first Winston Cup title by a 65-point margin. Ironically, both Labonte and Gant, a longtime winner on the Sportsman circuit before getting a late start on a Winston Cup career, had finished behind Earnhardt in the 1979 rookie-of-the-year race.

Labonte claimed the championship with only two victories, the same as Earnhardt, but he had 24 top-10 finishes. Darrell Waltrip posted the most victories, seven, and received several driver-of-the-year awards, but a series of bad luck finishes left him out of the run for the title.

Bill Elliott, whose Ford was the strongest runner down the stretch, finished third in the points. Posting late-season victories at Charlotte and Rockingham, Elliott seemed to be giving his competitors a preview of what they could expect from him in the future.

Earnhardt, who got his second victory of the season in early November at Atlanta International Raceway, beating Elliott by only a half-second, dropped to fourth, one position ahead of Waltrip, in the final standings. He was disappointed, but when the dust settled on the first full season that Earnhardt and Childress had run as a team, they had plenty of reasons to be optimistic about the future.

Despite the two late-season engine failures that proved fatal to the championship bid, the durability factor that Childress wanted had been there. Dale posted 12 top-five finishes, won two races, $616,788, and failed to finish only twice.

Most of all, Dale had convinced himself that he made the right move in returning to the Childress operation, a place where he felt appreciated and where everyone was working toward the common goal of winning.

"My situation couldn't be better," he said. "The atmosphere is a lot like it was at Osterlund Racing when we won the championship in 1980, only it is better. We have got a great bunch of guys. They all know what they are doing, they stick together, and they work hard. I think we have got the best team in racing. I have never seen a crew with more team spirit."

Childress was just as happy with his team's performance and was brimming with confidence as he awaited a second season with Earnhardt.

"We are going to evaluate every aspect of our performances during 1984, make the necessary adjustments, and I feel like we will have a shot at winning every race we go to next year," he said during the winter break.

"I know the competition is going to be stronger, but we will be totally prepared for every race. Everything we did last year was in preparation for 1985, and we are right on schedule. At the end of 30 races, we hope to be the Winston Cup championship team and get our share of what is going to be the richest racing season ever."

Childress was referring to an announcement in December of 1984 by tour sponsor R.J. Reynolds Tobacco Co. that it would add a couple of new bonus programs for the 1985 season, and also increase the points fund by $250,000. One of the new programs was the creation of an all-star race called "The Winston."

Only drivers winning a race the previous season would be eligible. The winner of the 105-mile sprint race, scheduled for Charlotte Motor Speedway, would collect $200,000 from a

$500,000 purse – more than the winner of the Daytona 500 received.

The biggest prize, however, was being posted for a driver winning three of four races in what was being called the "Winston Million Series." The four races were the Daytona 500, the Winston 500, the World 600, and the Southern 500. The reward for a driver winning three of them was $1 million.

"It would be awfully hard, as competitive as the Winston Cup circuit is, for one driver to win three of those races, the Winston all-star race, and the Winston Cup championship," Childress said. "But if any one team did, that would be worth almost $2 million right there. We will be running to get all we can, and I am sure the other teams will be, too."

LIKE FATHER, LIKE SON:
Dale Earnhardt, right, grew
up with racing in his blood.
His late father, Ralph, is a
member of the National
Motorsports Press Association Hall of Fame. Below,
Ralph Earnhardt, left, talks
with Bobby Isaac and
LeeRoy Yarborough in
1963.

Charlotte Motor Speedway

IN THE EARLY DAYS: Dale Earnhardt builds a motor for his Sportsman car in his daddy's garage in Kannapolis in 1976.

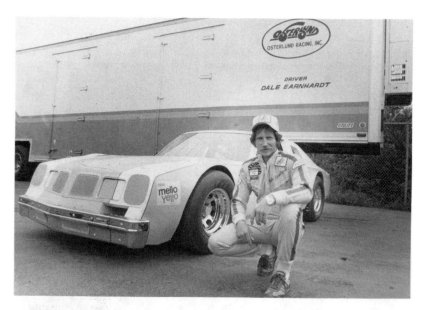

THE BEGINNING: Earnhardt poses with the first car he drove for Osterlund Racing Inc.

RIVALS FROM THE START: Earnhardt, right, and Darrell Waltrip in 1980, when Earnhardt won his first championship.

Jerry Haislip

A WATCHFUL EYE AND A VICTORY: Earnhardt's wife, Teresa, watches a race from the pit, left. Below, Teresa and Dale celebrate after he won a Grand National race at North Carolina Motor Speedway in 1985.

Jerry Haislip

A WAVE TO THE CROWD: Earnhardt acknowledges the fans after a victory at Martinsville Speedway in 1985.

ANOTHER VICTORY: Earnhardt poses with trophy after winning the Busch 500 in Bristol, Tennessee, in 1985.

8

'Heeeere Comes Awesome Bill'

As Dale Earnhardt proclaimed during his rapid rise to stardom, the door is always open for new drivers who have the talent and determination to succeed. But some slip through more quietly than Earnhardt, who won races and a championship in unprecedented quickness.

Bill Elliott, who grew up in Dawsonville, a small town in the north Georgia mountains, attracted little notice in 1976 when he arrived on the circuit. He competed in eight races without giving anyone an indication that eventually he would emerge as one of the brightest stars on the circuit, running at the front of the field with the new wave of talent that dominated the sport during the 1980s.

While there is virtually no similarity in the backgrounds and the driving styles of Elliott, a smoothie, and Earnhardt, the ultimate charger, both were fortunate enough to get desperately needed breaks just when it seemed they might have to give up their dreams. For Earnhardt, it was the opportunity in 1979 to drive for the Osterlund team, which provided him the equipment and manpower to prove his abilities.

Elliott was not that fortunate.

All he got was a comparatively small handout from Harry Melling, who owned a factory in Jackson, Michigan, that manufactured gears and oil pumps for some of the race teams. Elliott received $500 to put Melling's product name on his car at the Charlotte race in October, 1980. It was a one-race deal, which had been secured with the help of Benny Parsons, who was getting full sponsorship from Melling.

Instead of removing Melling's name from the car, which would have required a new paint job, Elliott just left it on the fenders for the Atlanta race in November. He won the outside pole position and ran strong in the race, although a mechanical problem spoiled his chances of winning. So impressed was Melling that he agreed to sponsor the Elliott team, which included Bill and his brothers, Ernie and Dan, for 12 races during 1981.

"We had just about gone through all the money we had, and we didn't know if we could race or not in 1981 until Harry gave us the help he did," Elliott said later. "It wasn't anything like the break that Dale got with Osterlund, but it was enough to keep us racing."

The Elliotts continued to struggle financially, running only 13 races in 1981. The team did not get on firm financial ground until 1982, when Melling agreed to purchase it and let the Elliotts continue to operate the team as if it were their own.

Running 18 races in 1982, Elliott began serving notice of his potential with a trio of second-place finishes and three third-place finishes. Bill and Ernie, who was being recognized as one of the top engine builders on the circuit, convinced Melling to let them run the full schedule in 1983.

"Just don't embarrass yourselves," Melling told them.

They didn't. After four more second-place finishes, Elliott closed the season by winning his first race on the Riverside, Calif., road course.

Elliott was the hottest driver on the circuit down the stretch in 1984, winning two of the final five races and finishing second and fourth in two others.

But no one was prepared for what was to come in 1985, when Elliott would spoil the entire superspeedway season for Earnhardt and the other teams.

All race teams work hard during the winter to get ready for Daytona and the coming season, but none put in more hours than the Elliott brothers, who were motivated for a couple of reasons. Their sizzling down-the-stretch finish in '84 had given them hope of making a run for the Winston Cup championship.

Ernie especially was upset with a rumor that drifted down from the Carolinas, which he accepted as fact.

Cale Yarborough, who had won the last two Daytona 500s in a Chevrolet, was switching to a Ford for the 1985 season. Someone told Ernie Elliott that Yarborough's engine builder, Waddell Wilson, had said if the Elliotts could make a Ford run 202 miles per hour that he could build an engine to make one go 205 miles per hour.

There is no record that Wilson, not one to boast, actually made the statement, and he denied having done so. "I never said anything like that, and I don't know how or where it got started," he said later.

But Ernie didn't bother to check with Wilson when he heard the rumor. He just went to work.

"I felt that it made us look like a bunch of dummies, and it hurt my feelings," Ernie said. "It made all of us work harder, to show we could make a Ford go 205 miles per hour at Daytona, too."

Bill Elliott, who spent Christmas Day working on his race car, winced when he heard his brother's goal. "If he builds an engine to go that fast, I wonder who he's going to get to drive the car," Bill quipped.

The man driving at such a speed when qualifying began for the Daytona 500 was Bill himself.

He blistered the track with a speed of 205.114 miles per

hour, breaking the record Yarborough set the previous year by a whopping three miles per hour and becoming the first driver in the event's 27-year history to put a Ford on the pole. The next fastest car was the Ford driven by Yarborough, who was clocked at 203.814 miles per hour.

It was not a good way for the season to start out for Chevrolet drivers, especially Earnhardt, who was not among seven drivers breaking the 200-miles-per-hour barrier during qualifying.

Richard Childress was among a group of General Motors team owners who lodged a complaint with NASCAR after seeing the two Fords outclass the field. Childress contended NASCAR had bent the rules too far in trying to help the Fords to become more competitive.

"That was fine when they couldn't keep up," he said. "But now it is clear they don't need any special help. I am thinking the Fords won't be that fast in race conditions. If not, everything will be fine. But if they go out there and blow us off in the qualifying races, you can bet I'll be over there in the NASCAR offices."

Neil Bonnett, who had the fastest-qualifying Chevrolet, at 202.584 miles per hour, seemed convinced the Fords would not be that fast under race conditions. "I have a Chevrolet that can flat chew the chrome off their rear bumper," he declared.

However, following the two qualifying races, won by Ford drivers Elliott and Yarborough, Bonnett was screaming as loud as the other Chevrolet drivers. His Chevrolet hadn't been fast enough to run in the fumes of Elliott's Ford, much less do any bumper-chewing.

Earnhardt, who finished ninth behind Yarborough in the other qualifying race, was disappointed, too, but he was not as vocal about his frustrations as Bonnett.

"Everyone says that Ford is making the rest of us look like a bunch of dummies," grumbled Bonnett. "I don't feel like a dummy. We have an excellent race car. The dummies are the ones sitting over in the NASCAR offices. Right now, they have got egg all over their faces."

Darrell Waltrip's Chevrolet finished second to Elliott's Ford, but he was 37 seconds behind.

"I am happy to be that close," Waltrip declared. "I thought I had won the race, because by the time I got to the finish line, Bill was out of sight. I did win the real race. The other cat won the unreal race. But it is just the shape of things to come, boys. The handwriting is on the wall."

The message on the wall told Waltrip he probably would have to go another year without winning the Daytona 500, something he desperately wanted to do before his career was over.

"It is the jewel in my crown that is missing, and that is true for any driver who has never won it," said Waltrip, who was then 38 years old and no longer the brash, controversial figure he had been during his earlier years on the circuit.

"What makes a driver look good at Daytona is a fast car. A good driver with experience can use the draft to maybe keep up, but he is not going to win unless he has a fast car. Even then, there is no guarantee. In 1981, when I won the Busch Clash, I had a car fast enough to win the 500, too. I was leading when the engine blew up.

"A lot of people say I don't know how to win the 500, and my car owner, Junior Johnson, has just about got me convinced that I don't know nothing about Daytona. Go ask him, and he will probably say this is just one track that I don't drive very well. What he won't tell you is that his cars have never done very well here, either. After I qualified at only 197 miles per hour, I went up to Junior and told him, 'Maybe I am doing something wrong. Do you know a different way to hold the accelerator wide open?' I always thought if you ran a car wide open, that was all you could do."

Waltrip figured his only chance to beat Elliott in the Daytona 500 was if Elliott's Ford had a problem. "We know Bill is fast, but we don't know yet if he can stay fast for 500 miles," he said. "I have been here before when I felt I should have won and didn't. Maybe when I feel like I won't win it, I will.

"Even a blind pig can find an occasional acorn. I have enough confidence in myself that I feel I will win this race sooner or later. And it is important for my career that I do win it before I have to quit. More people will remember you won a Daytona 500 before they remember you won seven other races. It gives you more credibility."

Earnhardt felt just as strongly about wanting to win his first Daytona 500, too, but the the media pressure had not yet begun to weigh on him. Waltrip, who had been around a few years longer, was the one who annually caught the heat for having never won.

With Elliott's Thunderbird ruling the track, this was not a year for Waltrip, Earnhardt, or anyone else to get their hopes too high about winning the Daytona 500. A good thing, too.

Elliott streaked to an easy victory while a crowd of challengers blew up more than a quarter-million dollars worth of engines trying to keep pace.

Earnhardt lost the engine in his Chevrolet after only 84 laps. The engine in the final contending Chevrolet, driven by Bonnett, exploded with four seconds left.

"I am just surprised the engine stayed together as long as it did," Bonnett said. "I had the accelerator on the floorboard the entire day. That is the hardest I have ever driven a race car. But I never had a chance of winning. The best I was going to do was finish second."

In all, 14 cars in the 40-car starting field left the race because of engine failures. They included Yarborough's Ford, which lasted only 62 laps.

After the disappointing and frustrating Daytona 500 experience, Dale was more than anxious to get to Richmond a week later. Elliott had proved at Daytona he was going to be tough for anyone to beat on the superspeedways. But short-track racing was a different story. A driver who didn't mind a little bumping and shoving could make up for a lack of horsepower, and that was the kind of racing in which Dale had developed his talents and still excelled.

"Short-track racing will either make you a survivor or a loser," he said later. "It taught me to ask no quarter and give none. If you don't win, you lose. It is as simple as that."

Junior Johnson says Earnhardt never forgot the lessons he learned on the dirt tracks before beginning his Winston Cup career.

"That is where he got his aggressive style. A lot of these guys nowadays don't understand it," Johnson once told interviewer Chris Browning.

"At those dirt tracks, you learn a lot about how far you can hang a car out and still save it. You learn how far you can stick a nose into places and still survive. Earnhardt understands that. He can just outsmart a lot of drivers who didn't come up on the dirt tracks."

Dale says his short-track strategy is simple. "Just give me a car that will run and I'll try to get it to the finish line first," he said. "I love to race. I'm a racer and not a driver, and that is what it takes to win on the short tracks."

The Miller 400 was Earnhardt's kind of race, one in which fender muscle and driver power proved to be the most valuable assets on a windy, spring-like day at the Richmond Fairgrounds Raceway.

After qualifying fourth fastest in the 30-car starting field, Dale was involved in a pit road collision on Lap 93 that left the front end of his car badly crunched. Earnhardt was driving out of his pit when he was forced to swerve to miss Neil Bonnett's car, which was parked partially on pit road while his crew serviced it. As Earnhardt drove wide to avoid Bonnett's car, he and Terry Labonte, who was already coming down pit road, banged together.

Dale had to return to his pit for the crew to pull the crumpled sheet metal away from the right front tire. The front end of the car also had been knocked out of line, but the crew didn't have time to correct that and get him back on the track without losing a lap.

The race for the checkered flag came down to Dale and his friend Tim Richmond, who elected to pass up a pit stop for new tires during the final caution period to stay on the track and retain his leading position.

The race restarted with only 13 laps remaining. Dale immediately charged to the inside of Richmond and the two cars slammed together in the first turn. Dale stayed hard on the throttle to complete the pass and continued on to victory.

Richmond was mildly upset. "I expected that from him. That is his style," he said. "But that is not what beat me. I felt my right rear tire going down just as we took the green flag for the restart and I couldn't barrel into the first turn as hard as I wanted to. That allowed Earnhardt to drive up under me, knock me out of the way, and go on."

Dale was glad that Richmond didn't blame the collision for losing the race. "I didn't do anything that Tim wouldn't have done," he said. "That was just how you are supposed to race on these short tracks, and anyone who says he wouldn't have done the same thing would be lying. We were all out there to win, seeing who could get to the finish line first, and just one of us was going to do it. Tim's strategy was to not stop during that last caution. He thought he could win that way. But my strategy turned out to be right, didn't it?"

Earnhardt, whose two victories during his first season back with Childress had come on the big tracks at Talladega and Atlanta, had to be content with using that aggressive strategy to salvage what he could on the short tracks in 1985.

After Elliott won his second superspeedway race of the season at Atlanta, Dale collected his second short-track victory at Bristol in a performance that most drivers and mechanics had to see to believe.

The power steering on Dale's Chevrolet quit after only 50 laps and he manhandled the car the rest of the way to beat Ricky Rudd by only one second.

"I can't believe he drove the car the way he did with the power steering all the way gone," Rudd said.

Other drivers said they would have parked their cars if their power steering failed. They were amazed that Earnhardt not only drove 450 laps after his power steering failed, but that he saved the car in a spinout with Ken Schrader.

"How in the world can a man keep a car off the wall in a spinout if he doesn't have power steering?" drivers were still asking each other when they arrived at Darlington the next week. Dale had no answer.

"I don't know how I saved the car when Schrader and I got together, but I did it," he said with a grin. "The car was hung out and I kept waiting for it to hit the wall. I couldn't tell you what I did. I guess it was just reflexes."

With Earnhardt and Elliott each having two victories in the season's first five races – Bonnett had won at Rockingham – no one quite knew how to figure a favorite on the Darlington track, which is listed as a superspeedway but has some characteristics of a short track.

Elliott won pole position with a speed of 157.454 miles per hour, but Earnhardt seemed more worried about having to beat David Pearson, the second-fastest qualifier and a 10-time winner at Darlington, and Cale Yarborough, a five-time winner.

"I would hate to have to race either one of them for the victory at this track," Dale said. "Those two guys can come up with tricks that you have never seen before. When I won the TranSouth 500 in 1982, I had to beat Yarborough and I couldn't believe some of the moves he made."

Pearson scored his last victory on the Darlington track in the 1980 TranSouth, the year after he won the Southern 500 in the Osterlund car while Earnhardt recovered from the injuries he had received in the Pocono crash his rookie season.

"Pearson is just one smart driver, a helluva driver," Dale said. "If he is there at the end, he will beat you time and again. He might be getting old, but as long as that son-of-a-gun is still breathing, you can't count him out. If you do, you might find him breathing down your neck."

Neither Earnhardt, Pearson, nor Yarborough was around at the end of the race, however.

Earnhardt, who started eighth, led 130 laps before blowing an engine on the 209th lap. "I had them all covered before we lost a cylinder in the engine," he said. "I never pushed the car that hard, either. I was running a comfortable pace."

Pearson was eliminated by a wreck on Lap 184, and Yarborough was another victim of engine failure.

With those three drivers in the garage, Elliott breezed to his third victory of the season, beating Waltrip by 1.7 seconds. It really wasn't that close either. Elliott, who had won only four times in 136 races before the '85 season, had built a 14-second lead before a final caution flag bunched up the field for the final 18 laps.

Not since 1976, when David Pearson won 10 of 20 starts, had a driver threatened to so thoroughly dominate the Winston Cup superspeedways. The Darlington victory was the third in four superspeedway events, and NASCAR officials finally began to understand what the General Motors teams had warned them about at Daytona.

After the Darlington race, NASCAR president Bill France, Jr., announced a new rule, aimed at slowing Elliott's Thunderbird, would be in effect for the Winston 500 at Talladega. The new rule required the roof line on the Fords to be a half-inch higher and permitted the roof-lines on the General Motors car to be a half-inch lower.

France claimed the move was in the interest of making racing more competitive on the superspeedways, and not in preventing Elliott or other Ford drivers from winning.

"It is not in the interest of the sport for one car to have the advantage that Elliott has showed on the big tracks," France said. "I am not really interested in which make of car wins the races, as long as the competition is close. That is what the fans come to see. We can't have one car lapping the field, like Elliott showed he could do at Daytona."

France said the modifications would equalize the height of the roof line for all cars. Previously, Fords were allowed to be an inch lower. France also admitted that NASCAR had been reluctant to approve the Thunderbird for competition in 1982 because it was a smaller car. "We were afraid the car had the potential to do what the Elliott car is doing now," he said.

If France thought the new rules would bring Elliott back with the others on the track, he quickly learned differently on Winston 500 pole day.

Elliott defiantly pushed his No. 9 Thunderbird around the track at a world-record stock-car qualifying speed of 209.398 miles per hour – almost four miles per hour faster than the Ford of second-fast qualifier Yarborough and five miles faster than the best Chevrolet, driven by Terry Labonte.

A stunned France arrived at the speedway, which his family owns, the next day. Waltrip greeted him in the garage area, and pointed out a string of cars in practice runs on the track. Leading the pack was Elliott's Thunderbird, which Waltrip clocked at 207 miles per hour. He then pointed to Labonte's Chevrolet, which was losing a struggle to stay in Elliott's draft.

"That is the fastest Chevrolet here and he can't hold the draft," Waltrip told France. "If that is how it is going to be, there won't be much of a race. Instead of buying tickets, people ought to stay home and watch the paint dry. This just ain't no fun. This is like being at the dog tracks, when that rabbit comes around the corner, and they say, 'Heeeere comes Lucky.' Dust is flying all up behind him, but Lucky is just a gettin' it. That's the way Sunday will be. Except they'll be saying 'Heeeere comes Bill!' "

General Motors drivers weren't the only ones hoping Elliott

would slow down. Other Ford teams that couldn't get their Thunderbirds to go so fast also asked him to ease off the throttle just a bit so NASCAR would not hit them with another rules change.

Elliott stubbornly refused.

"Would I be a true competitor if I backed off?" he asked. "That would be like telling a boxer to lay down in a fight."

Meanwhile, there was a big debate raging in the garage about the legality of Elliott's Ford. "There are too many smart people in this garage for the Elliotts to have that kind of advantage, legally," Geoff Bodine contended.

Neil Bonnett argued otherwise.

"I'd bet it is the most legal car in the garage area," he said. "I guarantee you that if there was anything not right with that Ford, NASCAR would have found it by now. They have looked at everything on it, and they can't come up with anything that is amiss. I have just got to believe the Elliotts have found something, within the rules, that no one else knows about."

Earnhardt, who seldom becomes involved in garage politics, didn't offer an opinion. But he was not too thrilled by qualifying at 201.583 miles per hour and still being eight miles slower than Elliott.

Everyone knew Elliott, who was now being called "Awesome Bill from Dawsonville," had a fast car and was capable of easily winning the Winston 500. They also knew that would move him to within one victory of claiming the $1 million bonus offered in the Winston Million Series. But no one knew how fast the Elliott T-bird could fly until he was forced to show everything the car had after experiencing an oil leak on Lap 48, resulting in a pit stop that put him five miles behind the leaders.

Elliott, without the help of a caution period, charged around the track, picking up about a second a lap on the front-runners, and finally regained the lead on Lap 145. He led 35 of the final 43 to claim his fourth victory in five superspeedway starts for the season.

As was the case at Daytona and Darlington, Earnhardt wasn't around at the end. He blew an engine in his Chevrolet on Lap 160.

If Elliott's dominance on the big tracks was a source of concern for NASCAR officials, it was a blessing in another area. With the Winston 500 victory, Elliott could win the $1 million bonus in the World 600 at Charlotte, a race annually scheduled for the same weekend as the Indianapolis 500. For the first time in racing history, the NASCAR race was getting as much, or more, national attention as the one in Indianapolis.

Most of that attention was being focused on Elliott, a red-haired mountain boy who was uncomfortable in the spotlight. The constant stream of reporters and television crews was too much for him. He spent a lot of time hiding in his truck, or working under his car. "I had never been in that kind of situation before, and I didn't know how to handle it," he said later.

"People were pulling at me from all directions – sponsors, the media, fans, and all I wanted was to be left alone so I could work on my race car. When it came time for the race, I didn't care if I won or not. I just wanted to get out of there."

Elliott was so disturbed by the circus-like atmosphere that his entire weekend, which included the inaugural Winston all-star race on the Saturday before the 600, turned into a disaster.

Waltrip captured the $200,000 first-place prize in The Winston by beating Harry Gant to the finish line by three-tenths of a second as Elliott's Ford was slowed by a transmission problem. Waltrip won the 600, too, and a brake problem on Elliott's Ford caused him to finish 18th, far from the $1million bonus.

Earnhardt was not a factor in The Winston, but he made a strong and exciting bid in the 600 before his Chevrolet ran out of fuel near the end and he finished fourth.

Making his strongest big-track performance of the season, Dale led a total of 97 laps, including one that was worth $10,000 to the leader. He ran Waltrip down to the edge of the infield grass to collect the bonus.

"I tell you, that boy Earnhardt earned the money, and he showed me that he wanted it awfully bad," Waltrip said. "I just didn't feel like taking that much of a chance so early in the race."

Elliott led 81 laps before his mechanical problems cost him a chance to win the big bonus, which he would try to collect in the Southern 500 at Darlington – on another unwanted visit to the spotlight.

If that was not enough to sour Elliott's mood, NASCAR announced another rules change – reducing the size of the carburetor throttle bore on all cars – to go into effect at the Firecracker 400 in Daytona. NASCAR officials said the new rule was to reduce speeds by five or six miles per hour, and was not designed just to slow Elliott.

Ernie Elliott didn't think the slower speeds would have any effect. "It is just going to cost everyone more money, like most of the rules NASCAR comes up with," he said.

Earnhardt called the new rule "the good, the bad, and the ugly."

"It is good because it will slow down some people. It is bad because it will slow me down and I like to go fast. It is ugly because now I won't have the chance to break the speed records that Elliott has set this year."

Neil Bonnett was another driver who did not appreciate NASCAR's move to reduce speeds. Bonnett, a card-carrying pipefitter before beginning his Winston Cup career, believed race fans wanted to see how fast the cars would go, and it was his job to show them.

"I don't think anyone feels comfortable at speeds over 200 miles per hour, and no one should promise his team owner that he can bring a car back in one piece when racing at those speeds," Bonnett said.

"At Daytona, when I drive my car into the first turn I put my front wheels right down on the apron of the track. Coming out of the turn, the car is right up against the wall. It takes every inch of real estate to get that car through the turns at those speeds in qualifying. You have to commit yourself to the line you're going to take and then a quarter-mile later you find out if you made the right choice. If you've still got the car under you when you come out of the turn, you took the right line."

Bonnett did not complain about the dangers of 200-mile-per-hour racing because he saw it as job security. "A lot of fans think it would be fun to drive one of these Winston Cup cars until they see one coming off the turn sideways, or flipping end-over-end. When I was a pipefitter, I had a big line of people trying to get my job. It is not that way out here on the circuit. It is my job to drive that car any way it takes to go as fast as it will go, whether it is sideways or on its roof. If someone goes 205 miles per hour, I want to go 210. All it means is if I hit the wall, it will be only five miles per hour harder."

Bonnett knew that several drivers, such as Darrell Waltrip, approved of NASCAR's effort to reduce speeds. "But I would hate to see the speeds drop to under 200 miles per hour," he added. "There is a magic in 200. If someone goes 199.999 miles per hour, you don't see much reaction in the stands from the fans. But 200? Everyone stands up and cheers. It is the thrills and chills of auto racing. That is what we are selling out here on the Winston Cup circuit."

The rules change had a strange affect on qualifying at Daytona. With Elliott leading the way, Ford drivers swept the top three starting positions and the pole speed, which Elliott had set at 205.114 miles per hour in February, dropped to 201.523 – not quite as much as NASCAR officials had hoped, since the summer heat also helped to make the runs slower.

The latest change seemed to have a greater affect on some of the General Motors teams, and especially Bonnett's Chevrolet. His had been the best Chevy in the Daytona 500, but Bonnett saw his qualifying speed slide from 202.284 miles per hour in February to 197.113 in the July heat.

Earnhardt was also suffering with the slow disease as he

qualified for the Firecracker 400 at only 195.639, barely ahead of two other Chevrolet drivers, Waltrip and Benny Parsons.

Bill Elliott was pleased with another pole victory, but his brother Ernie, who may have noted something in the engine's performance that he did not like, was not smiling. When someone asked him about the rules change, Ernie curtly replied, "If you want to talk to someone about that, go see Billy France. I have got no comment."

Elliott did not win the Firecracker. The victory went to an unheralded driver named Greg Sacks, who was driving a research and development car for the DiGard team. Elliott's Ford began vibrating and he had to leave the race after leading more than half of it.

Elliott was on the pole again at Talladega, qualifying at 207.578 miles per hour, but the big news for Ford fans came when Elliott announced he was not going to switch to a General Motors product for the 1986 season. Earlier in the week it had been reported that Elliott was entertaining multi-million-dollar offers to switch to either a Pontiac or Buick.

"Please tell everyone we are staying with Ford," Elliott asked reporters. "Ever since that story got out, my telephone hasn't stopped ringing. Hundreds and thousands of people have called, asking that I stay in a Ford. That is what I am going to do, if the creeks don't rise and wash us all away."

Once again, however, pre-race predictions that Elliott would blow away the competition were spoiled by more mechanical problems. Cale Yarborough grabbed the lead when Elliott's Ford encountered engine trouble late in the race.

The most chilling moment of the race came when Yarborough ran over a drive shaft that fell from another car. The piece was knocked up into the air and crashed through the windshield of Dale Earnhardt's Chevrolet, missing him only by inches. "That was the most nervous moment I had the whole day," Yarborough said. "I knew if that thing had hit Dale, it would have killed him."

Earnhardt, who suffered facial cuts when the three-foot piece of metal exploded through the windshield, didn't have much time to think about the danger. "I didn't know what knocked the hole in the windshield, it just happened so quickly," he said. He remained in the race, although barely able to see through a windshield covered by tape.

Dale was more upset by the "slow-down" rule NASCAR had put into effect earlier in the month. His Chevrolet had been too slow at Daytona, and it was just as slow at Talladega.

"That rule is nothing but a bad joke," he said. "The only thing it has done is to cost everyone time and money. They should have left everything the way it was."

Dale's mechanical woes and Elliott's successes on the big tracks had eliminated Dale from the title picture. In fact, when Elliott went to Darlington for the Southern 500 and his last chance to collect the $1 million bonus, the only driver with a realistic chance to make a title challenge was Waltrip, trailing Elliott by 138 points.

As at Charlotte, Elliott sweated under the glare of the media. At his request, to the embarrassment of R.J. Reynolds officials who had posted the bonus to get publicity, two South Carolina Highway Patrol officers were stationed in his garage stall to keep reporters and visitors away from him.

Waltrip, who enjoys attacking a championship opponent by whatever means, tried to put more pressure on Elliott. He didn't mind if Elliott won the bonus. He just didn't want him winning the championship, too.

In the days leading to the Darlington race, Waltrip kept needling reporters about how Elliott wouldn't talk with them. Waltrip's own car was parked near Elliott's roped-off stall, and as reporters approached, Waltrip grabbed a rag and began rubbing a fender. "You all go on now and leave me alone," he mockingly whined. "I want to work on my race car. Go on, now, leave me alone."

For Earnhardt, Elliott's experience was an education. He

saw how Elliott's treatment of reporters created even more pressure for himself. And he saw how smoothly Waltrip dealt with the media and how adroitly he used his barbs to undermine an opponent.

Waltrip and other drivers did not understand Elliott's reluctance to talk about his chances of winning the million dollars. "When you take something out of a sport, you should be willing to put something in it," Waltrip said.

Looking toward Elliott, who was alone with his race car in his stall, Waltrip noted, "He looks more like Lonesome Bill now instead of Awesome Bill. Doesn't he know that real race drivers don't work on their cars? I imagine if Bill does win the million bucks he will show up at the next race wearing a layer of gold chains around his neck and with his own personal bodyguards."

Elliott didn't know what to make of Waltrip's verbal blitz. "He can say what he wants. I just do my job and go on about my business," Elliott said.

Elliott did win the Southern 500 and collected the $1 million, but he admitted he did so by surviving the field rather than running away from it. Cale Yarborough, Harry Gant, and Earnhardt thought they had better cars on that hot afternoon, but all had problems that took them out of contention.

Earnhardt's problem almost became Elliott's, too. The Wrangler Chevrolet, leaking fluids, did a 360-degree spin off the second turn on lap 317 and slid across the track, barely missing Elliott.

"I thought Dale was going to keep the car up on the wall, but it shot down across the track in front of me. I don't know how close I came to hitting it, because I had my eyes closed," Elliott said.

Elliott was close behind Yarborough when the power steering on Yarborough's Ford erupted and sent a cloud of smoke into the air. "I thought Cale had blown an engine and I ducked to the inside to try to miss the oil," Elliott said after the race.

Yarborough felt he would have won if not for his problem. "When the power-steering failed, it felt like I was steering a freight train instead of a race car," he said. "When that happened, there was no way I could race him for the victory. I just had to take a line and hold it through the corners."

Elliott was not sure how much money he would get for himself out of the big bonus. The government would get its share. Team owner Harry Melling would get his share. And he would share some with other team members.

He was "Million Dollar Bill" but he still had problems to handle, not the least of which was championship points race, although that seemed to be going his way, too. Waltrip finished 12th in the Southern 500 and with only eight races remaining trailed Elliott by 206 points.

No one previously had ever squandered such a sizable points lead to lose the title in the final last eight races. But Elliott had to go through a stretch of short-track races, in which he was usually Awful Bill, and his Ford was not the monster on the big tracks that it was during the first-half of the season. He'd had mechanical problems at Daytona and Talladega in July, and the car handled poorly at Darlington, even in victory.

"Things aren't going to get easier for me, even if the pressure of (winning) the $1 million is over with. Everything will probably just get crazier," he said.

Things did get crazier, and they did get worse.

By the time the Winston Cup circuit moved into Martinsville Speedway in late September, Elliott had suffered a string of misfortunes at Richmond and Dover, which had cut his lead over Waltrip to only 86 points.

Waltrip chopped another 63 points of the lead when he finished second to Earnhardt in the fender-banging race at Martinsville.

Earnhardt survived heated duels with Tim Richmond and Waltrip to claim his fourth victory of the season while hard-luck Elliott seemed to get into wrecks with half of the field.

118

Richmond led 98 laps before Earnhardt rammed into his rear bumper in the fourth turn on Lap 442. As Earnhardt drove inside of Richmond for the pass, Richmond turned into the side of Dale's car, almost forcing him into the pit wall along the front stretch. Both drivers continued to steer into each other through the first turn until they had to ease off when Elliott spun in front of them after being tagged by Greg Sacks.

Richmond dropped out of contention after pitting to correct a tire problem and was penalized two laps for changing more than two tires during the caution period. He was furious after the race, the third time he felt Earnhardt had banged around him to win.

"I guess Dale can get away with the rough stuff as long as it sells tickets," Richmond said. "But as far as I am concerned, enough is enough. If NASCAR is not going to police it, we will have to deal with it ourselves."

Dale understood why Richmond was so upset. "I did not mean to run into the back of him, and I can't blame him for being so hot," he said.

Dale also had to use his fenders to block Waltrip from passing following the episode with Richmond. Then, with two laps remaining, Waltrip made a final attempt to get inside and almost spun Earnhardt sideways in the third turn. Dale recovered and pulled in front to deny the pass.

"I had to chop Darrell off pretty good," Dale said. "But he came by and smiled after the race, so I guess everything is all right."

It was a wrong guess, Waltrip said.

"I was smiling because I gained a bunch more points on Elliott, and not because everything is all right between me and Earnhardt. Things got a little out of hand."

With Waltrip within 23 points of Elliott and five races remaining, Earnhardt was among a crowd of drivers becoming convinced that Elliott would not be able to hold off Waltrip for the championship. Dale knew from the experience of his 1980 championship battle with Yarborough how tough a Junior Johnson team could be.

"They really come at you in those last few races. There is not a tougher team to beat down the stretch," he said. "You know Junior and Darrell are going to be tough at North Wilkesboro next week. That is Junior's track, only a few miles from his house."

Dale suggested that Waltrip should ease off the psychological games he had been playing with Elliott.

"Everything is in Darrell's favor right now, if he stops trying to put pressure on Bill mentally," Earnhardt observed. "If Darrell is not careful, he might psyche himself out of the championship. You can go overboard with anything. If Darrell keeps running strong and finishing ahead of Bill and just grins at him, that will worry Bill more than anything. But if he keeps talking and makes Elliott mad, it might just make the Elliotts work harder."

As for his own goals in the final five races, Earnhardt, who was 11th in the Winston Cup standings, wanted to move up at least one notch, putting him in for a share of the season-ending money. And he wouldn't mind winning a couple more races.

Waltrip did take the lead from Elliott by winning at North Wilkesboro as Elliott struggled to finish 14th after losing several laps in the pits because of a burned spark plug wire.

After Waltrip won at Rockingham and Elliott at Atlanta, they went into the final race at Riverside with Waltrip trying to protect a 20-point lead for the championship.

Strange things can happen during the final race of the season when the championship is on the line, and no one knows better than Bobby Allison, one of NASCAR's greatest drivers, who won his only title in 1983, after finishing runner-up the previous two years. During one of those years, he began the final race on four punctured tires. In another, someone dumped sugar into Allison's gas tank. He also had been a victim of psychological warfare.

"A lot of untrue remarks were made to the press by my opponent (Waltrip) that was offensive to my crew, and they would want to know why I was degrading them," Allison remembered. "It is all a part of playing the championship game."

Another strange thing happened to Elliott in the final race. His million-dollar Thunderbird, once the monster of the speedways, was foiled by an eight-dollar part on the transmission that broke on only the eighth lap.

The part that failed had been manufactured in Franklin, Tenn. – Darrell Waltrip's hometown. Butch Stevens, a member of Elliott's crew, charged that the manufacturer may have known it was defective and did not tell anyone.

Waltrip felt insulted by such a suggestion.

But did he sympathize with Elliott's misfortune?

Waltrip giggled.

"It made my job a lot easier. I came here to win the championship anyway I could," he said.

9

Back to the Mountain Top

Dale Earnhardt had to look only at the final Winston Cup point standings following the 1985 season to realize his career seemed stalled. He had made a late-season rally to finish eighth in the points, and he knew that he would have to begin outracing all of the drivers finishing ahead of him – Terry Labonte, Ricky Rudd, Geoff Bodine, Neil Bonnett, Harry Gant, Bill Elliott, and Darrell Waltrip – if he were to maintain his fading status as a superstar.

Although his four victories in 1985 were topped only by Elliott's 11 triumphs, neither Dale nor team owner Richard Childress was pleased. Both had gone into the season expecting to make a strong challenge at the championship and they had come up far short. Dale failed to finish nine of the 28 races, and he did not have a single second or third-place.

Childress was so disappointed by the mechanical problems during the season that he told Dale he would understand if he wanted to drive for someone else in 1986.

"We went into this thing together, and we are going to stay together and make it work," Dale told him.

Childress felt it was going to work, too.

"I still felt we were on the verge of being a team capable of winning a lot of races and the championship, but I didn't want to hold Dale back if he thought he could do better somewhere else."

Dale had listened to offers from other team owners, including Rick Hendrick, who eventually lured Tim Richmond away from Raymond Beadle's Blue Max team to drive a second car for him in 1986. Earnhardt remained convinced, however, that the best situation for him was with Childress, a man he trusted as a friend and respected as a car owner.

"The mechanical problems we had in 1985 were frustrating to everyone, but I knew Richard and the crewmen were working hard to overcome them," Dale said later. "I guess, looking back on it, you could find some things that made it seem like it was a hard decision for me to make. It didn't seem that hard at the time. I knew Richard was a racer himself, and he was committed to building a championship team. It was just a matter of time before things started going our way."

Some things already had.

The Childress team received an important financial boost in 1985 by signing GM Goodwrench as an associate sponsor. That helped Childress to build a new engine room, lay plans for a new, ultra-modern race shop, and add more personnel. He hired Cecil Gordon, another former driver, to be the shop foreman.

"The primary sponsorship we still had with Wrangler was good, but the GM Goodwrench deal came along just at the right time so that we could continue to make improvements and get stronger," Childress said.

The newly-developed muscles were popping out all over the Wrangler-GM Goodwrench Chevrolet when Shelmerdine and the rest of the Childress crew rolled it out for a new season.

Although Dale had run well previously at Daytona, 1986 was really the first year he went there with both the experience and the car to win the 500.

For the new season, General Motors, after suffering a rare beating by Ford on the big tracks in 1985, had engineered its own brands of sloped-back cars that were stout and sleek enough to compete successfully against the Thunderbird. Voicing the new confidence of the Chevrolet drivers was Geoff Bodine, who said, "Mr. Elliott had quite an advantage over all of us General Motors drivers in 1985, but we've got the cars to go after that Ford this year."

The most exotic of the new General Motors cars was the Pontiac Grand Prix 2+2. The Chevrolet Monte Carlo SS, which Earnhardt, Bodine, Waltrip and others would drive, was a little less exciting. "You can put your family in one of them and ride down the highway," Waltrip said of the Monte Carlo. "The only thing you can do with the Pontiac is race it."

The Childress crew worked hard during the winter to solve the engine problems that plagued the team in 1985, and to iron out the handling problems on their newly-designed car.

Earnhardt was excited by the results during the winter testing season, but he, like everyone else, wondered if Bill Elliott's Thunderbird would still have the same advantage on the super-fast tracks that it enjoyed at Daytona in 1985.

Elliott proved to be only almost as fast when qualifying began. He rocketed around the track to win pole position with a speed of 205.039 miles per hour, a fraction slower than the record 205.114 he had posted the previous year – before the two rule changes NASCAR came up with to slow him down.

But unlike 1985, the Chevrolet teams showed that they had a car that would run with the Thunderbird, as evidenced by Bodine's second-fastest qualifying speed of 204.545.

Earnhardt, who seldom revealed the full potential of his car in individual qualifying laps, had a speed of 203.142, for sixth place. But it was in the 20-lap Busch Clash that he would demonstrate just how much improvement his team had made during the offseason.

Starting fourth in the eight-car field composed of 1985

pole-winners, Earnhardt took the lead from Neil Bonnett on the sixth lap and held it through the final 15 laps to beat Elliott by two car lengths.

"I answered a big question today that I had been asking myself all winter," a happy Earnhardt told reporters afterward.

Asked what that question was, Dale grinned. "Whether or not I could beat that Ford. I learned that I could, and I really wasn't surprised either. I felt all along that I had the car to beat. But I had to be concerned about ol' Bill, after the kind of season he had last year."

Elliott, the only Ford driver to finish among the top five admitted he didn't have enough power for Earnhardt. "Dale had my number when it came down to showtime in those last four laps," he said.

Elliott had sped from sixth place to second relatively easily, and most of the 75,000 fans thought he was setting up Earnhardt for a slingshot move on the final lap. Dale thought that might be the case, too. He zig-zagged down the long backstretch on the final lap to prevent Elliott from drawing a straight line on him.

Entering the third turn, Dale kept his Chevy glued to the bottom lane. In his rearview mirror, he saw Elliott's car push high in the turn. "I knew I had Bill beat then. He wasn't going to catch me after that," Dale said. "I really felt I was going to win this race, and I had to keep reminding myself to not get too confident. Sometimes when you are that confident, you go out there and the thing blows up in your face."

Dale reminded reporters that the only other time he won the Clash was in 1980. "I went on from there and won the championship," he said, then added, "That is the plan for this year, too."

Not every Chevrolet driver was as pleased with the new sloped-back model as was Earnhardt. Waltrip rode in the rear of the field through most of the race and admitted his team did not properly compensate for the new body design.

"Everyone tried to tell us the new rear window would make a big difference, but we had to see for ourselves. We set the car up the way we raced it last year and just flat screwed up," he said

It was a familiar story for Waltrip, who was being asked again to explain how he could win three Winston Cup titles and big races at other tracks without winning a Daytona 500.

"Every February I always get excited about coming to Daytona – until I finally get here," Waltrip said. "This year, for instance, during the winter we took the car to the wind tunnel and had the best technology available. We built the strongest engine that we'd ever had, and the driver was pumped up and aggressive. The car was strong in the tests. I mean strong! Then we bring it here for the race and it won't run a lick."

After the last-place finish in the Clash, Waltrip instructed his crew to go to the backup car, a two-year-old Monte Carlo. "It might not be fast, but it at least handles well," he said.

Still, he was not any more confident about breaking his personal Daytona jinx. "Daytona is not my favorite place to race. I repeat: it is not my favorite track. It is the only race track I know that talks to you," he said.

What could Waltrip hear the track saying?

"It says, 'Boy, you tee me off,' that's what. And, it tees me off, too, because I have never won the big race here. I would think something was missing in my career if I never do win the Daytona 500. It is not an obsession, but just something I need to do. Eventually, I am going to win the Daytona 500.

"I just haven't found out yet what it takes for me to do it. I know someday that something is going to happen and I will win this thing. When I do, I'll probably shake my head and say to myself, 'So that's what it takes. I have done all these other things and that is all it takes to win the Daytona 500.' "

Unlike Waltrip, Earnhardt enjoyed racing at Daytona, loved the fast speeds, the tradition, the rush of Speedweeks, and the tingle of excitement around the garage area.

126

It is one of his favorite tracks, and had been ever since he discovered the land of fast cars and wild bars for himself in 1976, when he and a few friends brought a car down from Kannapolis to compete in the 300-mile Sportsman race on the Saturday before the Daytona 500.

The journey was made in his daddy's old one-ton Chevrolet pickup truck, with race car in tow. "There were four of us sitting in the track, and stuff was piled high in the back and covered with canvass. We must have looked like a bunch of gypsies going down the highway.

"We put a case of oil on the back of the truck, and when we got back home we didn't have a can of oil left. Every time we stopped for gas, we put two cans of oil in the engine."

Although he had seen pictures of the Daytona track, Dale had no real idea just how big it was until he saw it for the first time.

"We drove off Interstate 95 onto Highway 92 and it was only a couple of minutes before I saw the race track. We kept driving by, and we kept driving by, and I said, 'Oh, Lord, how big is that thing?' That was a pretty awesome deal. It was just unbelievable a race track could be that big."

The first car Dale brought to Daytona was a Chevrolet Nova that had been built for short-track racing, although he had raced it the previous October at Charlotte Motor Speedway.

"It had pretty much a short-track steering box and set up," Dale said. "I was lost there for a day or two, with the car darting around a little bit. Once we finally got the car so it would go straight, we were in pretty good shape. I qualified about 22nd, and we waxed the car all week long, trying to make it slicker and faster.

"We finished about 13th in the race, and it would have been better except for a bad fuel filter. I had a great time. It was really an awesome experience, with everything going on around us in the garage area. I would be walking around, and there would go Richard Petty, and here would go David Pearson, and then you would see them practicing on the track. What time I wasn't on the track, I was watching them. It was something else."

Not only at the speedway either.

"The whole week was just a blast. We all stayed together in one motel room, and I don't remember any of us sleeping. We had heard stories about Curtis Turner, Joe Weatherly, Buck Baker, all of those guys, and we wanted to see all the places they would go to at night. We partied every night, running up and down the beach, trying to hit every spot. I don't think we missed many," Dale said.

Daytona in 1976 was everything he expected it to be – big, fast, and exciting. It still was in 1986, and the only place where Dale, now happily married, had slowed down was away from the track.

The partying he left to his crewmen, who had earned the nickname "The Wild Bunch." Among that distinguished group was barrel-chested Danny (Chocolate) Myers, who was scheduled to wrestle a bear named Ginger in one of the bars until someone felt sorry for the bear and canceled the match.

"A few years ago, I probably would have wrestled that bear myself," Dale said. "I guess that I have matured beyond that point now."

What had not changed was Dale's driving style. Just as rugged and aggressive as ever, it was becoming a source of concern in the garage and a point of interest by the media.

"I am from the old school," Dale told reporters. "I learned to drive by watching my daddy race guys like Tiny Lund and LeeRoy Yarborough. I was made to fit between a steering wheel and the gas pedal. Some people are drivers. I am a racer."

Dale racked up another preliminary victory in his 125-mile qualifying race, which not only gave him the No. 3 starting position in the 500 but created a minor controversy.

Harry Gant complained that oil dripping from Earnhardt's car covered his windshield and spoiled any chance he had of winning.

"I couldn't see anything except the top of the grandstands through my window," said Gant, who was running second to Earnhardt before dropping back to finish eighth. "That is the first time I have ever had to quit racing for a victory because of something like that. I had to back off because at one point I nearly ran over Earnhardt."

Geoff Bodine said the oil from Earnhardt's car splattered onto his windshield, too, when he drove up to replace Gant in the second position. "But that is not why I did not win the race," Bodine said.

"I could still see through the windshield. I don't have any excuses. I just have to blame myself. I backed off and then tried to get a run on Dale, but I had laid back too long and did not have enough car to do it."

Earnhardt was unaware the oil was leaking from his car. "It could have happened. I just don't know," he said with a shrug.

Dale won his third race in seven days in the 300-mile Grand National on the Saturday before the Daytona 500. He sped across the finish line only one car length ahead of both Geoff Bodine and Darrell Waltrip.

This time Earnhardt outran another controversy that erupted in his exhaust fumes in the race for second place.

"Bodine was a little wild at the end," said Waltrip, who finished third only by inches. "He was picking on everyone. I thought I could get second place, but Bodine's car was too strong. In fact, with that car, Bodine should have won the race. He was just too busy doing other things."

Bodine agreed the last lap was wild.

"Darrell and I banged in the corners and down the straightaways. We both got our cars a little sideways. But that is how you have to race when it comes down to the last lap. You let everything go."

Earnhardt was worried that Waltrip or Bodine might try to slingshot by him on the final lap until they got caught up in the bumping. "I didn't know if I could win the race by being the leader going into the last lap or not," he said. "But I guess Darrell and Geoff got to racing each other a little too strong and let me get away."

The victory put Earnhardt in position to become the first driver in Daytona history to sweep the Busch Clash, a qualifying race, the Grand National race, and the 500.

Looking ahead to the next day, Dale said, "Now comes the big one. It would be great to win that one, too. That is the one we want."

Earnhardt who already had won $126,843 with his victories in the preliminary events, was a co-favorite with Elliott to win the 500. Elliott, who had won the second 125-mile qualifying race, was not as dominant as he had been the previous February, but some observers felt he had not showed the full strength of his Thunderbird.

"Dale's car is handling well enough that he might be the only one who can race Elliott in the corners," mechanic Jake Elder said. "But whether Dale can race him for the checkered flag, I don't know."

Tim Brewer, the crew chief for Neil Bonnett, said Elliott was probably just a little wiser and more discreet this time around. "I think he still has everyone covered," Brewer said.

Elliott clearly saw Earnhardt as a strong challenger. When asked what might happen in a last-lap showdown between the two, Elliott closed his eyes and laughed.

"There might be one helluva wreck at the finish line," he said.

The 125,000 fans who arrived at the speedway expecting to see a duel between hard-charging Dale and easy-rider Bill were disappointed. Elliott, disproving the theory that he had been sandbagging, seldom challenged for the lead and his hopes for a second straight Daytona 500 victory were crushed, along with his T-bird, in a pair of wrecks.

Earnhardt's Chevrolet was as strong as expected, but it never had the chance to race for the checkered flag either.

A much-awaited last-lap showdown between Earnhardt and Geoff Bodine fizzled when Earnhardt coasted into the pits with an empty fuel tank only three laps – 7 1/2 miles – from the finish line.

That allowed Bodine, who finished second to Earnhardt in both the qualifying race and the Grand National race, to win his first Daytona 500 by an 11-second margin over Terry Labonte.

"I thought I was going to beat him until I ran out of gas. But that is racing," Dale said, disappointment showing in his voice. "You win some and you lose some. Today, I just ran out of gas."

Bodine said that when he saw Earnhardt coasting into the pits he began praying the same thing wouldn't happen to him. "I held my breath the rest of the way," he said.

It seemed strange that Earnhardt ran out of fuel and Bodine, who pitted before him, did not.

"I am not sure what happened," said Richard Childress, who had called the shots in the pits.

"We should have won this race, and we had the car to do it. I am not sure what happened that the car ran out of fuel. We were concerned more with tire wear than we were fuel, and maybe that was a mistake."

Gary Nelson, Bodine's crew chief, admitted, "We were lucky, but I will take that."

How much fuel did Bodine have left at the finish?

"Enough," Nelson said with a smile.

After a series of early caution periods, the final 70 laps were run without incident, and drivers had to make their final pit stops for fuel and tires under the green-flag. Bodine pitted first, on the 159th lap, and was on pit road for only 16.3 seconds.

Earnhardt stopped on the next lap, getting tires and fuel in 19.4 seconds, leaving him about four seconds behind Bodine when he pulled back onto the speedway. Dale sliced Bodine's advantage to only a fraction of a second with about 20 laps to advantage to only a fraction of a second with about 20 laps to go, and was content to follow at close range while waiting for the final lap to make his move.

Bodine slowed his car, hoping Earnhardt would take the bait and move to the front. "But he didn't do that, and I really didn't think he would," Bodine said. "My car was a little loose, and Dale was making some maneuvers in the draft to make my car even looser. He was trying to make me use up my tires, and I knew he wanted to try slingshotting around me on the last lap.

"That was his strategy, and I had mine. I won't tell you what it was, but you can bet it would have been a wild last lap if he had not run out of gas. I knew that he was going to make history today or I was going to win and make history for myself. I kept trying to think of something I could do to keep him from beating me on the last lap. It just never came down to that."

Not only did Dale run out of fuel, his engine blew up on pit road as his crewmen frantically tried to refire the engine and get him back onto the track. "The crew had to spray ether into the air cleaner to try to get the engine to fire. It must have detonated and busted the motor," said Earnhardt, who finished 14th – one position behind Elliott.

Waltrip, who finished third, still had not learned what it took to win a Daytona 500. But Dale could tell him that it took more than just having the dominant car.

• • •

At the 1985 NASCAR Winston Cup awards banquet in New York during the offseason, Ricky Rudd had apologized to the black-tie crowd when he was introduced. "My shoes were shined when I got here. But Dale Earnhardt ran all over me when he was coming up here to get his award," Rudd quipped.

The gathering of drivers, wives, sponsors, and NASCAR officials laughed long and hard. But even as they laughed, many knew there was something other than humor in Rudd's remarks. Rudd was only one of many drivers whose car almost had been knocked out from under him by Earnhardt on the race track.

When Pete Rose was chasing Ty Cobb's hit record during the summer of 1985, stock car racing insiders were joking that Earnhardt had collected more hits on the track in a season than either of the baseball stars during their careers.

In three of Earnhardt's four victories in 1985, he had used a fender or a bumper to push aside challengers in the stretch run. Some were calling Earnhardt "NASCAR's resident bully." Others, more bluntly, were calling him a dirty driver.

For the most part, Dale seemed to take the criticism more as a compliment and a tool for intimidation than anything else. He was proud of the fact that he raced hard and won races by doing what he had to do.

When several NASCAR drivers recorded an album, each doing songs writing especially for them, Earnhardt crooned, "Say I'm a hard charger, that's all I ask. Just let me be a hard charger and stay on the gas."

Finally, however, after a violent and controversial finish in the second race of the 1986 season, NASCAR officials decided it was time to crack down on Earnhardt.

With three laps remaining in the Miller 400 at Richmond Darrell Waltrip, who had come from a lap down after an early-race wreck, drove under Earnhardt in the second turn to take the lead. As the two drivers sped down the backstretch toward the third turn, Earnhardt never backed off and attempted to steer his Chevrolet to the inside of Waltrip to regain the lead.

He never made it. His left front fender tagged the right rear fender of Waltrip's Chevrolet and both cars spun out of control. Wrecking with them were the third-place car of Geoff Bodine and the fourth-place car of Joe Ruttman. Although out of contention for the victory, both Earnhardt and Waltrip got their banged-up cars rolling again and in the first turn Waltrip drove into the side of Earnhardt.

Back in the garage area, both drivers presented contrasting

emotions and explanations for the wreck that permitted Kyle Petty to score the first Winston Cup victory of his career. Earnhardt was cool and calm. He said the incident was the result of hard racing. Waltrip, angry and shaken, claimed Earnhardt deliberately spun him out, and demanded that NASCAR officials take action.

"It was a hell of a race, wasn't it?" Dale asked. "I barely clipped the rear of Darrell's car and that spun both of us. I hate it tore up both cars. If I was trying to wreck him deliberately, I could have done that without wrecking myself, too. That is for damn sure. My intention was to drive under him in the third turn. I know Darrell was a little upset with me, because he drove into me after we got going again. Oh, well, you win some, lose some, and crash some."

Waltrip was in no mood to be philosophic.

"Dale knew I had him beat and that he was a sitting duck. I wanted to wait until the last lap before I passed him, but I saw an opportunity and I had to take it. I knew he would be all over me and there would be some pushing and shoving. But I didn't think it would be what it was. It was like a land mine going off. I hurt my neck and my vision was blurred. I want to win as much as anyone else, but I have never tried to hurt anyone."

Waltrip's car owner, Junior Johnson, seemed just as convinced that Earnhardt had triggered the accident to prevent Waltrip from winning.

"Earnhardt just spun Darrell into the wall because he knew he was beat," Johnson said. "There isn't much you can do when you are racing a fool like that."

Waltrip claimed the second incident, when he drove into Earnhardt, was the result of the steering on his car being damaged in the first wreck. "But considering who I hit, it didn't bother me much," he added.

Waltrip said it was time that NASCAR took action against Earnhardt.

"This stuff went on all last year and it is starting again. I would hope they finally do something about it. Just look at the man's track record. He doesn't mind running over anyone. He is not choosy. But I think the magnitude of what he did today was surprising."

NASCAR's immediate reaction, as reported by spokesman Chip Williams, was that the incident was the result of "a racing accident" and no one would be fined or punished.

However, after reviewing film of the incident the next day, NASCAR race director Bill Gazaway said it appeared to be more than "just racing." He fined Earnhardt $5,000 and placed him on probation for the remainder of the season for what the sanctioning body termed "reckless driving."

"There is a thin line between racing hard and racing recklessly, and Earnhardt clearly stepped over that line," Gazaway declared.

Furious, Earnhardt filed an immediate appeal. After hearing his argument, NASCAR agreed to remove the season-long probation, but not the fine.

"It was just a case of hard racing and someone making a mistake," Dale said. "I admitted I made a mistake. I thought Darrell had cleared me. I was trying to get inside of him and didn't have the room that I thought was there. It was not intentional. If you look at my career, you will see that I have never been involved in anything like that before. I never wrecked anyone intentionally and put them out of a race. I might rub some fenders or bump another car, especially on the short tracks, but you see that kind of stuff going on all the time. It is not just me."

Dale vowed not to let the incident affect his driving. "I have got a job to do, and that is to win races and the championship. I am going to try to do that job, and if it takes rubbing fenders, then that is what I am going to do."

A footnote to the Richmond incident was a contention by Kyle Petty that a lucky pair of underwear may have been the real reason for the wrecks that enabled him to win.

Petty was almost three-fourths of a lap behind when Earn-hardt and Waltrip tangled. "I saw the smoke from the wrecks and I figured I might be lucky enough to move up to finish second or third," Kyle said. "When I got around to where the wrecks were, I saw the cars of Waltrip, Earnhardt, and Bodine. I didn't see Ruttman's car, so I figured he had gotten through all right and would win the race. But on my next lap around, I saw Ruttman's car sitting on the edge of the track. I just fell into the victory."

Petty, one of the most superstitious drivers on the circuit, figured his luck was due to the new underwear he had worn.

"Here's what happened," he explained much later. "I go to Richmond and I didn't have any underwear, because I am real bad about packing. So, I had to buy underwear and I put on a brand new pair the morning of the race. That was it. There was no way I was supposed to win that race, but those front four cars crashed and there I was. I wore the same underwear during races the rest of the season, which was the first time I finished in the top 10 in points. I wear them in races the next year, too, and win the Coca-Cola 600.

"After one of the races, I left the underwear on the Wood Brothers race truck. You know, you are hot and sweaty and you get on the truck and throw all your clothes off. I forgot about them and left them on the truck. The Woods get back home, find the dirty clothes, and throw the underwear in a dumpster. I realize the next day that I had left my lucky underwear on the truck. I called the shop and the Woods say they had thrown the underwear away. So, I drive up to their shop, dig the underwear out of the dumpster, and take them home. My wife refused to wash them because they had gotten all greasy and dirty in the dumpster. I put them in Clorox and forgot about them and let them soak too long. When I finally took them out, there wasn't anything left but the band and a little piece of cloth on the side. I still wore them like that the rest of the year. The next season, I got off to a bad start and finally threw them away."

Richard Petty, delighted that his son had scored his first victory, was amused by the lucky underwear story. But he had a better explanation for the unexpected victory.

"One cat, Earnhardt, made a mistake. It should never have happened, but it did and Kyle wound up winning the race," Richard said.

• • •

There was nothing lucky about Dale's first victory in 1986, which came in mid-April in the TranSouth 500 at Darlington. He led 335 of the 367 laps and only Darrell Waltrip, finishing second, was able to stay in the same lap with him.

Dale's biggest concern came when a late caution flag allowed Waltrip to close up on his rear bumper. "After the bad luck I'd had at Daytona, I was just hoping something would not go wrong again," Dale said.

He relayed that uneasiness to Childress, who was standing watch in the pits. "Don't worry. We got them this time," Childress quickly radioed back.

"When the green flag came back out, I just stood on the throttle, kept the car straight, and brought it on home," Dale recalled. "Waltrip hadn't been able to pass me on the track all day, so I didn't think he could do it unless I had bad luck or something."

Waltrip gave Earnhardt his due. "That last caution flag gave me a chance, but it would have taken a miracle to beat Dale today. He was just too strong for everyone, and he deserved to win the race."

The victory gave Dale a perfect opportunity to tell reporters that rumors about him leaving Childress to drive for Junior Johnson were untrue.

"It gets frustrating when you run as well as I have this season without winning," he said. "But I knew it was coming. Overall, it has been a very good year and we are going hard for the Winston Cup championship. We have led more miles than anyone else, and at most races we have had the car to beat. I am happy driving for Richard Childress. I consider it the best team on the circuit, so why go anywhere else? I hope to be here for several more years."

Earnhardt went from Darlington to become the season's first two-race winner a week later at North Wilkesboro. He led 195 of the 400 laps, including the final 145, and finished one second ahead of Ricky Rudd.

The victory left him second in the early-season Winston Cup standings, 23 points behind Waltrip, who was still winless after the first seven events.

"Earnhardt sure seems to be the hottest driver on the circuit right now," Waltrip admitted, "and he has had the strongest car in most of the races. But it doesn't bother me to see someone that hot this early in the season. I can't see how he can keep that up for the rest of the year. When the tables are turned, it could be my team that is right there to take advantage of it."

Ironically, it was starting to look and sound like 1980 all over, when Waltrip had declared early in the season that Earnhardt would not be able to maintain his championship pace. Like 1980, too, Waltrip was planning another team change. The hot rumor was that he would leave Johnson, where he already had won three championships, and become the driver for another new team fielded by Rick Hendrick, who already owned cars driven by Geoff Bodine and Tim Richmond.

The missing face in the crowd of early winners on the circuit was Bill Elliott, who had been so dominant the previous season. Elliott finally made his presence known in qualifying for the Winston 500 at Talladega, when he showed his old, fast form by winning pole position with a record speed of 212.229 miles per hour. He beat second-fastest qualifier Bobby Allison, driving a Buick, by almost three miles per hour. Junior Johnson's two Chevrolets, driven by Waltrip and Neil Bonnett, failed to get one of the top 20 starting spots in the first qualifying session. Earnhardt was 14th.

Elliott's best finish through the first eight races was fifth place at both Atlanta and Bristol. In recounting what had gone wrong, Elliott pointed out that his brother Ernie, the engine builder, had been sick most of the year and his chores were being handled by brother Dan.

"We have had to work very hard to overcome Ernie's absence, but it is difficult to do. Dan does a good job, but he just doesn't have Ernie's experience," said Elliott, who had used an old, rebuilt Ernie engine to make his record qualifying run.

Elliott's Ford was just as fast on race day, but less than 100 laps to the finish line, it dropped out of the lead and went to the garage because of engine failure. That left Earnhardt to battle tough veterans Bobby Allison and Buddy Baker for the victory.

Baker emerged from the final round of pit stops with the lead, followed by Rick Wilson, Allison, Earnhardt, and Richard Petty. Allison drove around Baker to take the lead with six laps remaining and Earnhardt moved up to second place. Hoping to sling-shot by Allison, Earnhardt held his position until the last lap.

He drove under Allison in the third turn to momentarily take the lead. But Allison used the outside groove to move back to the front in the fourth turn, leaving Earnhardt to fight off Baker for second-place.

"I gave Dale three lanes and I took only one," said Allison, then 48. "I knew what Dale would try, but I felt my car was strong enough to beat him back to the finish line if we didn't collide. It got awfully close, and he got ahead of me a little. But he had to go into the third turn awfully hard and his car was out of shape. My car was in perfect shape, and I had the throttle wide open."

Dale knew his only chance was to make an all-out charge into the third turn. "I just got beat. I gave it my best shot and got by him a little bit in the third turn. But he drove right by me again. His car was just too strong."

With Waltrip's Chevrolet blowing an engine and finishing

34th, Dale moved on top of the Winston Cup standings for the first time in the season with a whopping 109-point lead.

Elliott finally got back to Victory Lane in the The Winston all-star race, which was held on Mother's Day at Atlanta International Raceway and attracted fewer than 15,000 spectators. Elliott rolled across the finish line 2.5 seconds ahead of Earnhardt, who spent a frustrating afternoon trying to chase down the Ford and finished second.

"I got frustrated when Bill shot by everyone in the third turn on the first lap, and that's the way I stayed the rest of the day," Dale said in a gloomy mood.

On the first lap, both Waltrip and Earnhardt took the lower lanes into the third turn. Elliott went high and wide. "I had my car wound up and it stayed wound up. When the other two backed off, I wasn't ready to back off," Elliott said.

That statement brought a cry from Earnhardt. "No one backed off, Bill."

"Well, you went somewheres," Elliott drawled.

Earnhardt speculated that NASCAR's return to a larger carburetor earlier in the year may have given back to Elliott the advantage he had in 1985. "I don't know what it is, but I am not going to cry about it," Dale said. "We are just going to go back home and work harder to try to beat him the rest of the year."

A couple of weeks later, Earnhardt enjoyed one of the most satisfying victories of his career by winning the Coca-Cola 600 at Charlotte Motor Speedway. He led only 25 laps but finished one and a half seconds ahead of second-place Tim Richmond.

"I have always wanted to win the 600," Dale said. "I used to come over here to the Charlotte track when I was a boy and watched the races from the infield, while standing on my dad's truck. Then I would go home and stay awake at night, dreaming about winning the race."

It was his first Charlotte victory since winning the 500-miler in 1980. "That was a great thrill, too, but it was not the 600," Dale said.

But he admitted that he hadn't felt good about his chances midway through the longest race of the season. "I had a higher gear in my car, and we were having a hard time getting the right chassis set up, too. But then the gear went to work and ol' Dale went to work, too," he said.

In mid-summer, Waltrip finally confirmed rumors that he had signed an agreement to leave Johnson and drive for Hendrick's new team in 1987. He insisted, however, the early disclosure would not affect his team's efforts to overtake Earnhardt and win a fourth championship.

"This isn't like it was in 1980, when I was involved in that controversy with the DiGard team," Waltrip said. "Junior and I are not at each others throat. We have been successful, and both of us want to win that fourth championship. It would benefit me and him, too."

But, as was the case in 1980, all Waltrip could do was talk about beating Earnhardt for the championship. His verbal needling had been enough to shake Elliott down the stretch the year before when he was able to come from behind to win the title, and he hoped that would be the case again in his duel with Earnhardt.

"Dale just isn't the kind of driver that can win this title. You don't win championships by beating and banging and running over people," Waltrip said.

Replied Earnhardt, "I have read some of the stuff that Darrell is saying about me, but it is not going to work. I ain't the Elliotts. I am not playing that psychology game with him."

Waltrip thought otherwise.

"If he is reading what I am saying about him, then he is playing the game whether he knows it or not," Waltrip contended.

• • •

Geoff Bodine, Bobby Allison, and Earnhardt were in the limelight for the Southern 500 at Darlington on Labor Day weekend. Each had one leg in the Winston Million Series and if

141

either could win the final event he would collect a $100,000 bonus. Earnhardt was hoping the race would come down to a three-way shootout involving the trio on the last lap.

"I think each of us would do everything we had to do to win that money," Dale said. "Allison has put a fender to me a couple of times, but the only times he did was when a race came down to the money laps. Things could get a little physical, even a little wild, if the race does come down to three of us."

Tim Richmond spoiled the potential big pay day for the trio, however, by beating Allison to the checkered flag by 2.3 seconds.

Bodine had looked as if he might collect the bonus until his car ran out of fuel with 14 laps, taking him out of the lead. Dale had seen his strong bid dashed a few laps earlier when he cut a tire and made a green-flag pit stop.

The next race was back at Richmond, the scene of the big crash between Waltrip and Earnhardt in February, and Dale wasn't shy when asked if he would like to have another late-race duel with Waltrip.

"Man, I'd love it," he said. "I think it would give the fans something they were deprived of seeing in February."

Waltrip was not as thrilled about the thought of another such confrontation. He shuddered when asked about the possibility of racing Earnhardt for the checkered flag.

"I don't want to race the No. 3 car under any circumstances. Is that enough said?"

Dale hadn't been in any major controversies since the first Richmond race, but he still was the target of critical remarks from other drivers. Among those complaining was Richard Petty, who claimed Earnhardt had caused him to wreck the week before at Darlington.

"It seems like Earnhardt's brain goes out of gear when he switches on the engine. As a driver he is number one, but he just doesn't seem to have respect for anyone," Petty said.

Any thoughts about an Earnhardt-Waltrip rematch disappeared quickly as Waltrip's Chevrolet developed a fatal transmission problem on the 61st lap, and he was the first driver out of the race. Dale finished second to Richmond by only seven car lengths.

Waltrip rebounded from his misfortune at Richmond three weeks later with a victory at North Wilkesboro that revived his hopes of overtaking Earnhardt for the championship. His third victory of the season pulled him to within 122 points of Earnhardt, and he had clipped off 68 points in the last two races.

"I am pretty sure Earnhardt must be getting worried about me now," Waltrip said. "He sure looks worried to me. I saw him one time talking to himself during one of the caution periods. He should be worried. Look at my team's record. We have always been able to do what we had to do. We have been able to rise to the challenge."

If Earnhardt was worried, he didn't show any signs of it when he arrived a few days later at Charlotte. He laughed when someone told him Waltrip was saying that he must be worried because "when you go up against the best, it has to weigh on your mind."

"Is Waltrip the best?" Dale asked. "How can anyone say who is the best? There are too many great drivers out here, and Darrell is only one of them. The only thing that I am worried about is that I might fall off my tractor while working on my farm."

Dale reminded that his team still had a big lead in the points and was not as vulnerable as the Elliott team had been the year before.

"Bill's team had some wounds, and there was pressure coming at him from a lot of places. Ol' Darrell just poured salt in those wounds. But he's got to cut us to have a wound, and I don't think he can do that. I have got a lot tougher team than Darrell has raced against for several years. We are in great shape and we are doing our thing."

Earnhardt smiled and told the reporters surrounding him,

"Y'all let me know what ol' Darrell says next. I can't wait to hear it."

Dale was even more anxious about what Waltrip had to say after he won the Oakwood Homes 500 to sweep both Winston Cup events at his home track. Waltrip finished ninth and dropped 159 points behind.

Waltrip was never in contention after being involved in a multi-car wreck on the 84th lap. Earnhardt also had problems early and went two laps down because of a couple of flat tires. "I was a lot more than concerned. I was plain worried to death," he said. "I didn't know if I could make those laps back or not. When I made up the first one, though, it put the fire back into my team."

After making up the second lap, Dale got into a crowd-pleasing duel with Tim Richmond. He enjoyed the tight battle as much as the crowd but finally had the sense to call it off.

"I was having such a good time racing Tim that I forgot how much racing was left. I got too high between the first and second turns once and almost hit the wall. I had to tell myself, 'Boy, use some good sense and calm down.'"

Dale backed out, allowing Richmond to build a six-second lead. A few laps later, Richmond blew his engine, leaving Dale to beat Harry Gant to the finish line by 1.9 seconds.

Dale refused to declare the victory had clinched the title for him. He did admit, "It looks awfully good with three races left."

Then he winked. "Go ask ol' Zip (Waltrip) if he's got anything to say now. I don't really think this victory is going to silence him, and I really don't care. It is fun racing with someone with the competitive spirit that he's got. And if he wants to know what I have got to say, tell him that we are going to win the title by trying to kick butts and take names."

Waltrip admitted his title hopes were in serious trouble. "We are not out of the title race, but we didn't do ourselves any good today," he said.

Needing to pick up a bundle of points at North Carolina Motor Speedway two weeks later, Waltrip gained only a handful as both contenders experienced problems. Earnhardt's Chevrolet developed ignition trouble while running second and he finished sixth. Waltrip had a setback during a pit stop while leading the race that dropped him back to third.

Thus Waltrip gained only 15 points and headed into the next-to-last race of the season, the Atlanta Journal 500, trailing Earnhardt by 144 points. That meant Earnhardt could clinch the championship by leading one lap and finishing eight positions ahead of Waltrip.

"I have said all along that I would like nothing better than to win the championship in Atlanta," Dale said. "Then I could go to the final race at Riverside and not have to worry about the pressure of the points."

Waltrip understood that he needed Earnhardt to have an unusual amount of misfortune to keep his own chances alive. "I want it to go one way or another," Waltrip said. "I want to either get close enough to have a serious chance to win the title at Riverside, or I want Dale to go ahead and get it over with."

When reporters asked Waltrip what he would be looking for in the race, his quick reply was, "Smoke."

"I will be looking for blue smoke from Earnhardt's car," Waltrip explained. "If he has an early engine failure and I win the race, I will have the chance to win the title at Riverside, which is one of my better tracks."

Waltrip saw smoke on the 86th lap. But it was coming from his own engine.

After steering his disabled car back to the garage area, he climbed out and threw up his arms, as if to signal defeat, and walked dejectedly to his team truck. He emerged a few minutes later, disappointment still showing in his face.

"The engine just blew up. Engines have been our demise the entire season," he said. "Some people have claimed that I have not been aggressive enough this year. Today I wanted to be aggressive and now I am in the garage area, out of the race and out of the picture for the championship, too."

Waltrip began the race ninth. He had led a lap and was running third when the engine expired. "I figured that Earnhardt was due some bad luck. I thought my car would run strong and maybe I could force something to happen. I guess that I am as disappointed about losing this championship as any of them."

Dale had not seen the smoke coming from Waltrip's car and did not know he was in trouble until Childress told him by radio. "I couldn't believe it," Dale said later. "I kept asking them if they were sure that Waltrip was out of the race. Finally, Richard came over the radio and said Waltrip was leaving the track."

With 26 laps remaining, the Childress crew hoisted a bright red banner in their pits that read: "Winston Cup Champ."

Dale had made no secret that he wanted to win the title "by kicking butt and taking names," as he had put it. With Waltrip making an early exit, he was able to do just that. He went on to win the race with a record speed of 152.523 miles per hour, more than a lap ahead of second-place finisher Richard Petty.

"That is great," Dale exclaimed when told his winning average speed smashed the former mark by eight miles per hour. "When you go to kick butt, kick butt!"

Following the trophy presentation in Victory Lane, Dale went to the press box. He had just begun answering questions when he was called to the telephone.

"I hated to see you drop out like that," he was heard to be saying. "Yeah, we'll go to Riverside now not worrying about the points and race like hell. All right. Thank you for calling."

Dale grinned after hanging up. "That was just ol' Darrell," he said. "Shoot, I thought it was the president."

Dale had begun the race fourth, and it wasn't until Lap 81 that he drove to the front. From then on, he was unbeatable.

"I wanted to drive a smart race, but I wanted to win, too," he said. "I think I did both. You knew that I was not going to lift off the throttle. You pull up on that horse and it doesn't ride as good."

The win was worth $67,950 and the championship $716,000. Dale picked up another $50,000 by winning a couple of contingency programs, and he already had earned $1,073,400 in the first 27 races. But he didn't seem interested when someone added it all up.

"I just count the victories, not the money," he said.

Now, he was back to counting championships, too, and he admitted that the second was more satisfying than the first.

"Back in 1980, I really didn't understand or appreciate what winning the Winston Cup title meant," he said. "I was wild and crazy, young and dumb. But the thing it did was prove to me and others I could compete with the best in the sport. It established me as a driver, and we did it with an unproven driver and an inexperienced crew chief, Doug Richert. Those things made the 1980 championship very special.

"But it seems as if I never got to enjoy being the champion. The next year, Rod Osterlund sold the team during the middle of the season and there was all the chaos that resulted and I didn't win a race that year. The whole situation just fell apart and I couldn't enjoy being the champion like I should have.

"What makes this championship important is that it is the first for Richard Childress. He built this team from nothing, and the glory and congratulations should go to him because it is his work that made the team a winner. He selected the people and gave us the chance to win. Richard never won a race as a driver, and I am happy that I am part of the group that earned his first Winston Cup championship."

Dale's charge back to the mountain top for his second Winston Cup championship wasn't the only big story of the 1986 season. It was also the year in which Tim Richmond established himself as a superstar in much the same controversial and aggressive style that brought Dale to public attention in 1980.

Daring to race not only on the ragged edge, but a few steps over it, Richmond won seven of the final 17 races, including the finale at Riverside, and finished third in the final Winston Cup standings, only six points behind Waltrip.

Called "Hollywood" by his peers, Richmond, who was 31 and had rakish good looks, had given up a promising Indy-car career to join the "good ol' boys" on the stock-car circuit. His first appearance in a stock car was in the summer of 1980, after he had been the top rookie in the Indianapolis 500.

He had won only four races – two for J.D. Stacy in 1982 and two for Raymond Beadle in 1983 and 1984 – before he and mechanic Harry Hyde discovered the winning combination during the second half of the 1986 season.

Richmond, a native of Ashland, Ohio, had been courted in 1984 by a team on the Formula One circuit, but he chose to remain with stock cars. "I would be a fool to leave," he said. "I was born to race cars, and I was born to be a Winston Cup driver."

It was easier for Richmond to adjust to the laid-back style of Southern auto racing than for oldtimers in the sport to adjust to him. He wore fancy clothes, his hair was long and looked as if it had been styled in a New York salon. Pioneer driver Buck Baker once advised his wife, "Find out who does Tim Richmond's hair. It looks better than yours."

Still, Richmond swore that if he had been born 25 years sooner, he would have been the best drinking and brawling buddy that Baker, Li'l Joe Weatherly, and Curtis Turner ever had. Unlike Earnhardt, he had not learned his racing in the old school. But he sure wished that he had.

"I have heard tales about how those guys would drink and brawl all night and race the next day," he said. "I just wish I could get in some kind of time machine and go back to that era to be a driver, or even a spectator. I think Tim Richmond would be better suited for racing in the '60s than he is in the '80s."

Not surprisingly, Richmond's best friend during his early

years on the circuit was Earnhardt, who told him stories of growing up during the good ol' days and watching his daddy compete against some of the legends of the sport.

It was Dale, too, who introduced Richmond to the hell-raising art of drinking moonshine whiskey. "I have become quite fond of cherry-bounce," said Richmond, referring to the Carolina cocktail of clear moonshine and cherries. "Dale and I took a jug of that stuff out on his boat to do some water skiing. The deal was that the guy in the boat would fish the cherries out of the jug and throw them back for the skier to catch in his mouth.

"Dale is a pretty good thrower. I caught enough that I got a little woozy from eating so many cherries and, well, I fell off the skis and nearly drowned myself."

Dale taught Richmond some neat tricks on the race tracks, too. During the 1985 season, he gave his buddy first-hand demonstrations of how to win short-track races with a bump and a bang.

"Tim is an aggressive driver like myself, and I liked that about him," Dale said. "We can beat and bang on each other during a race and still be friends when it is over. I know Tim wants to win as much as I do, and he is capable of doing the same things I do. That can be a problem. Sometimes the race tracks ain't big enough for both of us."

Others weren't as fond of Richmond's aggressiveness. After Richmond's victory at Pocono in July, Richard Petty scolded him because the two were in a skirmish that knocked Petty's car out.

"Except for Earnhardt, maybe, Tim doesn't fit the mold of other drivers who have come on the circuit and become winners," Petty said. "But Winston Cup racing is changing so fast that he might be the new mold. If you talk about Bobby Allison, David Pearson, Cale Yarborough, or Darrell Waltrip, they were all aggressive to a certain point. But we all knew our limits.

"So far, Tim has not found a limit. For instance, during the thing at Pocono, anybody who has got any kind of limit at all would not have caused what happened. It wasn't all Richmond's fault. It started earlier when Geoff Bodine passed him and Tim just didn't back away from him. It was not like the last lap and he was racing for the flag. In fact, he did everything he could to lose the race. He hit the wall, he spun out, and he blew tires. But he had a fast enough car that despite all of those things he won."

Even Hyde, Richmond's crew chief, admitted that his driver was much like a young Earnhardt. "Tim is a lot like Dale in that he can burn the wheels off a car. Even if a car is not handling well, he will drive it just as hard as he can. I have never seen him back off, and I don't want him to back off in the last part of the race. But sometimes he wants to race too much too quick.

"He doesn't want to bide his time. He is awfully competitive. I am trying to get him to look at 500 miles, instead of five."

Richmond admitted he was guilty at times of the charges leveled against him. "I did get upset with Bodine at Pocono," he said. "Maybe I did over-react. Basically, I just went down in the corner and had no room to maneuver."

Earnhardt, who developed a dislike for Bodine during the 1986 season, disagreed. "If it had been me, I might have taken it even farther than Tim did," he said.

Richmond claimed that only a few drivers, such as himself and Earnhardt, were blessed with the ability to drive past the ragged edge. "A lot of guys can't handle a situation like that. Only drivers who have the natural feel of a race car can take it past the limits and maneuver it back. Anyone who drives a car just to its limit is going to get beat."

While Earnhardt and Richmond had the same philosophy on the race track, their personalities contrasted sharply. Racing was not the the ultimate for Richmond, only the means for what he hoped to accomplish. He took acting lessons, and he wanted to model. He loved giving interviews and being in the spotlight. While Earnhardt enjoyed hunting and fishing during his free time, Richmond was always on the go, searching for the next party and the prettiest woman.

"I like the way Tim drives a race car," Harry Hyde said, "but I don't like him being late for practice, or the time he spends with reporters and television people and all that Hollywood stuff. I mean, he will get to the track when he is supposed to get here, but it might take him a half-hour or an hour to get from the parking lot to the race car.

"He does interviews, he signs autographs, and he talks to fans. Meanwhile, I am standing here waiting to talk to him about the race car. But I'll say this. When he does get in the race car, he is one of the most dedicated drivers that I have ever seen. He is as serious as hell. Then, when the car stops and he is out of it, he is hot-damn Hollywood-plus."

Just as Jake Elder had patted Dale on the head and pointed him in the right direction at the beginning of his career, Harry Hyde was showing Richmond how to become a winning driver during the 1986 season.

"This is the best year that I've had in racing," Richmond said at the end of the season. "It was a very positive learning year for me and I have become a better racer in one year with Harry Hyde than I was in the last six."

After beating Earnhardt by only one second in the season-ending Riverside race, Richmond gave notice of his intentions for 1987. "This was my first year with Harry Hyde and finishing third in the points makes me feel almost as good as winning the championship," he said. "But I am telling Earnhardt right now. We won't settle for third again. I am going to win the championship."

Richmond, however, would not be able to attempt to make good on that boast. The 1987 season began without him.

Only a couple of weeks after his victory at Riverside in November, Richmond was admitted to a Cleveland, Ohio, medical center, where he reportedly spent most of the winter battling double pneumonia. Veteran Benny Parsons took his seat in the Chevrolet owned by Rick Hendrick until Richmond could recover.

10

Another Title, Another Controversy

"Ladies and gentlemen....Driving the Number Three Chevrolet built by Richard Childress, from Kannapolis, North Carolina, and a two-time Winston Cup champion, heeeere is Dale Earnhardt...The Intimidator!"

No one made that introduction at the beginning of the 1987 Winston Cup season, but it would have been appropriate.

The fans, crewmen, and rival drivers who grumbled about Dale's hard-charging, fender-rattling aggressiveness in past seasons were about to see more – much more – of the same, and they had to wait only until the first lap of the season's first race, the Busch Clash at Daytona.

Benny Parsons apparently missed a gear as the green flag waved to begin the Clash and Dale had to back off the throttle to avoid hitting him. Ricky Rudd and Terry Labonte tried to shoot around Earnhardt but never made it. Fenders and bumpers popped. Rudd slammed hard into the outside wall and Labonte, who had replaced Waltrip as Junior Johnson's driver, was sent spinning down the inside of the track.

"Dale got into my left quarter-panel, and that triggered the accident," Rudd said afterward. "Dale says Terry pulled up too hard in front of him, and some others say Dale tapped Terry in the rear. All I know is that I paid a big price for someone else's mistake. The car that we were going to use in the Daytona 500 is now history."

Labonte's car also was out. "Somebody – I guess it was Earnhardt – hit me in the rear and spun me around," he said.

Dale said he got sandwiched between Rudd and Labonte ran out of racing room. He managed to save his car, but the front end was knocked out of alignment and he could do no better than finish fourth. Bill Elliott won.

Seeing the crash behind him just as the green flag dropped, Elliott thought the race would be restarted and he got off the throttle and faded to the rear. "I saw the cars spinning and I thought the track was going to be blocked and they would have to restart the race. It was just total confusion on my part," he said.

Waltrip, in his debut race for the Hendrick team, whizzed by Elliott and built a sizeable lead on the first lap. But Elliott shot from the back of the pack and took the lead for keeps on the eighth lap.

Earnhardt, who had swept all preliminary races the year before, went into the 1987 Daytona 500 without any wins. Ken Schrader and Benny Parsons won the 125-mile qualifying races, and Geoff Bodine edged out Waltrip in the Grand National race.

Although Dale's car for the 500 wasn't as fast as Elliott's Thunderbird, he did have a plan he hoped would give him his first victory in the race. He simply intended to intimidate Elliott and not permit him to use his speed advantage.

During the 125-qualifier, Dale flushed Elliott's Thunderbird out of the low groove, opening the way for five cars to pass him on the low side. Asked about the move later, Elliott admitted that he had been intimidated by Dale's move and might be vulnerable in the 500, too.

"Earnhardt came up on me and pushed me closed to the wall, and I have to expect things like that from him. But it was a qualifying race and I already had won pole position for the 500, and there was no need for me to do anything foolish," he said.

What could he do if Earnhardt crowded him into a higher groove during the 500?

Elliott shrugged. "I would probably just let him have the lead and go on. I hope it does not come to that and I can run pretty much by myself and drive my own lines. I don't like group sessions."

Dale laughed about Elliott not wanting to race close to him. "I guess I scared hell out of Bill in that qualifying race, and I don't think he will forget it either. I didn't hit him. I just got up there and got the air off his spoiler and his car got loose.

"But that is how you have to race him on the superspeedways. Bill would be tickled to death to jump out on everyone and just ride. We can't let him do that. You've got to move him. Scare him. You know, mess with his head."

In other words, intimidate him.

But, as often happens at Daytona, neither speed nor intimidation was the deciding factor. Elliott emerged triumphant for the second time in three years when Geoff Bodine ran out of gas three laps from the finish and both Earnhardt and Buddy Baker had problems during final pit stops.

Dale, who passed Elliott for the lead on Lap 183 of the 200-lap race, pitted for only fuel a few laps later and Baker, running second, came in behind him. A problem fitting the gas can nozzle into the car stretched Earnhardt's stop to 10 seconds – about four seconds longer than it had taken Elliott to get a splash of fuel three laps earlier.

The only problem for Baker was that he elected to pit with Earnhardt and not Elliott. "I had the race won and that beat me," Baker contended.

"I got beat in the pits, not on the track," Earnhardt said.

Elliott eased back into the lead with three laps remaining when Bodine, who was trying to stretch his mileage, ran out of fuel. He had won the previous Daytona 500 when Earnhardt had to stop for fuel with three laps remaining.

"Did ol' 'Pea-brain' run out of gas?" Dale asked after the race.

Told that Bodine had, Dale smiled.

"Good,'" he said.

Although Earnhardt left Daytona empty-handed, he had reason to be optimistic about his chances for winning a second consecutive Winston Cup championship. The rule of thumb is that a team doesn't have to win the Daytona 500 to get its season off to a good start. It just has to be competitive, not have a major problem, and get a good finish.

In addition to accomplishing all of those things, Earnhardt felt his Chevrolet had proved it would match up well with the new-model Thunderbirds on the super-fast tracks and that it would continue to have an edge on the smaller tracks, where championships are won.

Best of all, the Earnhardt team came into the season in top form and just as solid as in 1986, while several other teams were adjusting to changes.

It soon became evident that Earnhardt and the Childress crew were bumpers and fenders ahead of everyone else. Waltrip began having problems adjusting to the Hendrick team almost from the start. Labonte was a different kind of driver than the Johnson team had worked with previously. And Parsons, despite finishing second in the Daytona 500, didn't seem to have the desire to beat and bang on the ragged edge with Earnhardt, as Richmond enjoyed doing.

In the strongest start in modern-day Winston Cup history, Dale won six of the seven races that followed the Daytona 500 and rolled up an early 157-point lead over Elliott in the championship standings. The only race Earnhardt did not win in that sizzling two-month period was the Motorcraft 500, which he dominated by leading 195 laps before an electrical component in the alternator vibrated apart. Dale was in the pits for six laps while repairs were made and Ricky Rudd took the victory.

• • •

In the first of his run of victories, Dale led 319 of the 492 laps at the North Carolina Motor Speedway and finished 11 seconds ahead of runnerup Ricky Rudd. At Richmond, in a Miller 400 that was postponed for two weeks by snow, Dale badly damaged his Chevrolet in practice on Saturday. The Childress team worked throughout the night to get it repaired and Earnhardt won a thrilling duel with Geoff Bodine.

After the Atlanta problem, Dale led 239 of 367 laps to win at Darlington, led 318 of 500 laps to win at North Wilkesboro, led 134 of 500 laps to beat Richard Petty by less than a second at Bristol, and eased to victory in at Martinsville when a Geoff Bodine collided with Kyle Petty.

Along this trail of victories, Dale stirred controversy at every stop, accused of unnecessarily running over other drivers to get to the finish line.

Before taking charge at Richmond, Dale engaged in incidents with Alan Kulwicki and Harry Gant. On the seventh lap, in a bid to take the lead from Kulwicki, he lost control and spun in the fourth turn. Dropped to the rear because of the accident, he was charging back to the front when he crashed into Gant, who was running second. Dale had tried to go outside of Gant, then dropped low for the pass just as Gant, too, went low.

"Earnhardt is blind as a bat," an infuriated Gant said later. "He ran all over me. I saw in my rearview mirror that he was not under me, so I steered low. He ran right through the dirt into me."

Earnhardt admitted clipping Gant. "I don't think Harry saw me, and he pulled down in front of me."

The most publicized incident was at Bristol, where a duel for the lead between Earnhardt and Sterling Marlin ended in a hotly-disputed collision that put Marlin out of the race. Marlin crashed into the wall after his car was tapped in the left rear fender. He claimed that Earnhardt had spun him out intentionally. Earnhardt, and others, said it was strictly a racing accident. "I got under Sterling several times before he chopped me off," said Dale, who was being pressed from behind by Geoff Bodine.

Bodine, one of Earnhardt's toughest critics, this time agreed that Dale shouldn't be faulted. "It wasn't anything intentional, and I was just as much to blame as anyone," Bodine said.

Still, the angle of the television cameras made it appear that Earnhardt drove into Marlin, slapping his fender, and crashing him into the wall. NASCAR officials instructed Childress to warn Earnhardt to be less aggressive, and angry fans watching the race on television telephoned the track to complain.

Most outraged was Clifton (Coo Coo) Marlin, Sterling's father, who had been a good racer on the Winston Cup circuit despite never winning a major event. Now, he had seen his son crashing out of what might have been the family's first victory, and in an Associated Press story that was published in hundreds of newspapers, the elder Marlin criticized both Earnhardt and NASCAR.

"I would like to take Earnhardt out behind the barn and beat the hell out of him," Coo Coo said. "Earnhardt is bullying his way through racing. He has set Winston Cup racing back 20 years. I blame NASCAR more than I blame Earnhardt. He only gets away with what NASCAR lets him get away with. NASCAR has just sit around and let this Earnhardt thing get out of hand. If Earnhardt had done this back in the old days, the other drivers would have taken care of it by themselves. He would not have lasted many races. We raced hard and there was a lot of contact, but we didn't deliberately wreck each other."

Junior Johnson, who had complained loudly following the celebrated wreck between Earnhardt and his driver, Waltrip, at Richmond the year before, said it seemed to him that Earnhardt was driving like the old-timers did. "Earnhardt is not doing anything that others haven't done in racing before, and there is nothing wrong with that" Johnson said. "He got his racing style from his daddy, that's all."

The Bristol controversy was still raging when the teams arrived at Martinsville a few days later. Outside of turn three, where fans arrive early and set up RV City on a grassy green knoll during race week, someone had hung a dummy bearing the name "Dirty Dale" at the top of a 20-foot pole.

The dummy remained for the week between a Confederate flag on its left and a United States flag on its right.

Wayne King, who owned Marlin's race team, said he was disappointed – "but not surprised" – that NASCAR didn't come down hard on Earnhardt for the Bristol wreck. "Earnhardt has been driving like that for a long time, and they haven't done anything to him yet. If it takes driving like that for him to win the Winston Cup championship, they ought to just let him have it," King said.

Earnhardt was called into the NASCAR trailer for a talk with Winston Cup director Dick Beaty when he arrived at Martinsville. "Dick just asked me to be more careful in the future," Dale said after the meeting. "You know, I wish that thing at Bristol hadn't happened, too. But you can't go back and change it. You just take things and go on from there. I can't let what other people are saying bother me, or change my style of racing. I was raised to push the throttle all the way down, and to take the car to the front. That is what racing is all about. My hunger to win races is as strong as ever, and the fire is as hot as it has ever been."

Noting the dummy strung up in the infield, Dale said, "I hear boos and I hear cheers, and I don't count to see which one I am hearing the most. I just don't worry about that. I am glad that the fans care enough to boo or cheer. If they did nothing, I would be in trouble. But, you know, the fans need a bad guy, and they need a good guy. They need them all. They are the ones who buy the tickets, and they would be pretty bored if they paid their money and then saw a bunch of damn taxi drivers out here, wouldn't they?"

He offered no apologizes for his aggressiveness and had even made a joke of a few weeks earlier by showing up at a track with a bumper-sticker on his car that read, "If you don't like my driving, stay off the sidewalk." But he didn't much care for the the T-shirts that some fans had taken to wearing. They were smudged with blue and yellow paint, the colors of his race car. "Guess who ran into me at Charlotte Motor Speedway," they read.

Another hot-selling item in the Carolinas, where Jim and Tammy Baker were the center of another kind of controversy, were bumper stickers that read, "God Bless Jim and Tammy, And Dale Earnhardt, too."

But most of Earnhardt's competitors had passed the point of humor. "I think he's catching a lot of criticism now because his car is so dominant this year," said Ricky Rudd. "He is winning most of the races and by wrecking people he is adding insult to injury. I don't know if he deserves all the heat he is getting from the Bristol incident, but some of the stuff, he just runs over people.

"Early in the Bristol race, he plowed into Harry Gant, and it was a lot worse than the deal he had with Marlin. I think the thing with Marlin was that they were just racing too tight, and when you race like that you are going to get into trouble."

Dale thought the outcry against his aggressive style was due in part to him winning so many races. "Everyone is just waiting for me to make that one mistake so they can holler about it," he said. "At Bristol, there were 20 or 30 incidents of people bumping and wrecking and the only one that anyone said something about was the one that I was involved in."

In that argument, Dale was supported by Richard Petty, who had seen fit to criticize Earnhardt's style from time to time.

"Dale is in the limelight now, and if he spits out the window someone will see it," Petty said. "Racing nowadays is a lot different than it used to be back when Dale's daddy was running the short tracks. You could beat and bang each other and nobody was sure exactly what they saw, or who did what to whom, you know what I mean? The deal is that there were no television cameras and instant replays back in those days. They couldn't go back and look at the film and argue about what happened. You just went on racing.

"Now, whether Dale deserves all of this latest criticism, I don't know. It is a two-way street. All of the stuff that he is involved in is not his fault. But he is a very aggressive driver, and he does cause a whole lot of it himself. I was involved in two or three deals with him last year and I felt all were his fault, 100 percent. He tries to take his car to the front, and if some cat is in his way, then it is just tough."

Waltrip, who was not over being wrecked by Earnhardt at Richmond the previous year, again was calling for NASCAR to crack down. "NASCAR had the opportunity to get his attention after he wrecked me last year and then they let him off the hook. Now, they are still paying for that. Nothing has changed. He is still driving the way he always has, running over people.

"And there is a big difference between running over people and being aggressive. I feel that I am an aggressive driver, but I can't remember ever spinning someone out of the lead."

Neil Bonnett, who hunted and fished with Dale, said he got upset with his friend during the North Wilkesboro race. "He bumped me good, and if I could have caught back up with him, I would have turned him sideways," Bonnett said. "That is what makes you so mad. His car is so fast that he can bump you and drive away."

Bonnett was not among the group demanding that NASCAR take action. He had raced against Dale on the Sportsman circuit and knew that aggressive driving was necessary for success. He wouldn't criticize Earnhardt for driving the way he had learned to drive himself, and he didn't feel he needed anyone, especially not NASCAR, to settle his disputes for him.

"If you come to my house and go down into the den, you will see pictures of a lot of race cars. The last year I spent on the short tracks, I won 42 out of 80 races, and all the way around that wall in my den, every car in the pictures won a lot of races, and every one of them has a wheel mark on it," Bonnett said.

"All racing has ever been is fender-to-fender, door handle-to-door handle, bumper-to-bumper. And now a lot of people are saying they don't want that anymore. All of a sudden, we are going to clean the sport up. That is a bunch of bull. I respect Dale because he is a hard racer. You know, like I said, he has beat on me. But our deal is I beat back. If you dish it out, you ought to be able to take it.

"I would much rather take care of my own problems at a race track than to run to Dick Beaty and NASCAR and say 'So and so did something.' If someone does me wrong, I don't go crying to NASCAR. Somewhere down the road, someone else's butt will be in a crack. Instead of running to Beaty, I handle the problem myself.

"One thing about racing, you might have a driver that is 6-foot-4 and weighs 240 pounds and is a weight lifter. But on that damn race track, everyone weighs 600 horsepower and 3,500 pounds. They can do what the hell they want to do. When you get off the track, they might kick your butt good, but on that race track you are always the same."

Earnhardt won his fourth consecutive race at Martinsville because of another collision at the front of the field. But the wreck didn't involve him and he escaped controversy for that victory.

Geoff Bodine seemed to be riding a comfortable lead when he was wrecked by Kyle Petty with only 16 laps remaining. Earnhardt, who was five seconds behind Bodine, took advantage of the mishap to snare the victory. "That old Lady Luck can smile on you or bite you," Dale said afterward. "She sure did smile on me today."

Petty took the blame for the wreck and Bodine good-naturedly accepted. "I don't think Kyle did it on purpose."

Earnhardt could only wonder what the reaction would have been if he had been the one tapping Bodine out of the victory.

After competing at Martinsville Speedway, the smallest and slowest track on the circuit, the race teams go directly to Talladega Superspeedway, the largest (2.66 miles) and fastest track.

The fastest driver at Talladega when qualifying began for the 1987 Winston 500 was Bill Elliott, who won his fifth consecutive pole at the track with a record speed of 212.809 miles per hour.

Qualifying second to Elliott, at 211.797 miles per hour, was Bobby Allison, then 49, who had beaten Earnhardt in a thrilling last-lap duel in the previous year's race. Earnhardt, who qualified fourth, was not looking to engage Allison in another last-lap showdown. He knew from experience how difficult it was to beat Allison in a situation like that.

"I used all the experience that I had to beat Bobby, and I did all that I could to beat him," Dale recalled of the previous year's race. "He did not give an inch. I was the one who had to give. I looked over at him and knew he was not going to give."

Told of Earnhardt's remarks, Allison smiled briefly and shook his head. "Oh, I don't remember it being that dramatic," he said. "You know, my car had his beat, and I knew that I could get around him on the high side of the track. I expected him to keep off me. He knows he better keep off me."

Why was that?

"I think he respects me," Allison replied.

Indeed, that was the case. Like Earnhardt, and his daddy before him, Allison had to work for everything he got in racing, and he made it to the top on his determination and stubbornness. As Earnhardt had done when he walked out on Stacy, Allison had gone from the top to the bottom and back to the top a few times during his career.

But, most of all, Allison loved to race as much as Dale did. In fact, following the second round of qualifying and practice for the Winston 500, Allison flew his own airplane back home to Hueytown, Alabama, then drove to a short-track in Birmingham to compete in a 100-miler.

"That is my idea of having fun," Allison explained.

But there was no fun in what Allison experienced on the 22nd lap of the Winston 500 on Sunday.

His Buick ran over debris on the track, cut a tire and took flight, heading directly toward the packed grandstands. The car slammed into the wire fence on top of a five-foot high concrete wall in front of the stands and ripped up a 150-foot section of the fence before rolling back onto the track.

"It was like a stick of dynamite going off," said Wayne Byers, who had paid $35 for a second-row seat at the start-finish line. "There was this stuff flying everywhere. I never saw the car. All I could see was the fence, and then the fence was gone."

Tightly harnessed into his car, Allison rode out the horrifying accident without serious injury. But for a lap, his 26-year-old son, Davey, a rookie driver, steered his Ford around the track while holding his breath and praying for the best.

"It scared me bad," Davey said. "My heart just sank. It was the worst wreck I had ever seen. I asked the Lord to please let Dad stay on this earth a little longer."

On his next lap, Davey saw his father walking away from his battered car. Then he out-raced Earnhardt to the finish line to get his first Winston Cup victory in only the 14th start of his budding career.

Davey was behind Earnhardt, the leader, following the final caution period. He drove into the lead on the backstretch and quickly opened up a 25-car-length lead. No one pressured him during the final nine laps, and Earnhardt, his string of four straight victories broken, fell back to finish fourth.

"I just didn't have the engine to make a run for it at the

end," Dale admitted. "We broke the engine we wanted to use for this race and we had to put in our Charlotte engine. It just wasn't strong enough for this track. I hate to see the winning streak end, but I really feel fortunate to finish in the top five."

NASCAR officials announced a few days later that the teams would be required to use smaller carburetors in an effort to reduce speeds at both Talladega and Daytona. Later, the sanctioning body ordered carburetor restricter plates that pushed the qualifying speeds at both tracks to below 200 miles per hour.

"It was clear NASCAR had to do whatever it could to make sure the races were safe for the spectators," Earnhardt said later. "I would hate to think what would have happened to the sport if Bobby's car had gotten through that fence and into the grandstands.

"As for myself, though, I wish we could go back to racing at over 200 miles per hour. It was fun, and running at the big tracks has not been as much fun since we had to use the carburetor plates."

Not surprisingly, Darrell Waltrip applauded the move to curb speeds. "I have been saying for five years or longer that NASCAR should do something to slow down the cars," he said.

Earnhardt, who often claimed Waltrip never liked to race at fast speeds after experiencing a bad wreck at Daytona in 1983, quickly dubbed NASCAR's move "the Waltrip rule."

• • •

Charlotte Motor Speedway president Humpy Wheeler says he doesn't recall who had the original idea for what was to become known as "The Winston Shootout."

"A bunch of us got in a room and we were determined to stay there until we came up with something that would make the event interesting and exciting. People say you can't force creativity, but I think you can," he said.

The most innovative promoter in auto racing history,

Wheeler had accepted a mandate to save stock car racing's all-star show, The Winston, which had bombed miserably the previous year in Atlanta. That race had been held on a bad date – Mother's Day – and it turned into a boring race, a romp for Bill Elliott.

Officials of the R.J. Reynolds Co., sponsor of the Winston Cup circuit and The Winston, were quick to realize that something needed to be done. Running the race for a shorter distance under the format of other tour races had proved unappealing to fans. Fewer than 15,000 turned out at Atlanta.

The idea presented by Wheeler's group was to divide The Winston into three segments of 75, 50 and 10 laps. The driver leading the most laps in the first two segments would start on pole position for the final 10-lap shootout. The winner of the shootout would receive $200,000.

Wheeler, who grew up on short-track racing, was enthusiastic about the idea, as were the R.J. Reynolds folks. "It takes us back to the old Saturday night short-track shootouts, where daring, guts, and determination – not a perfect race car – won many races," Wheeler said.

"When we first presented the idea to R.J. Reynolds, the initial reaction was, 'Oh, boy. This could be a stick of dynamite.' We really were a little apprehensive about doing it. It was kind of a hairy thing to do, turning these guys loose for the $200,000. But, I felt like it needed that, and I felt like it was a refreshing pause from the distance races."

"It should be very interesting," said Winston Cup circuit publicist Bob Kelly, who noted that teams would be permitted to work on their cars and make chassis adjustments between the segments. "Basically, the drivers are going to be bunched up to run a 10-lap dash for $200,000. It could come down to who wants it the most."

The drivers who were eligible for The Winston admitted they were impressed with the money. But several didn't seem to care for the format. "It seems a little hokey," said Earnhardt, "but as long as they put up that kind of money, I am going to run for it."

Wheeler didn't understand the negative reaction by some of the drivers, especially those saying the shootout could make drivers too aggressive.

"Maybe we are getting too tradition-bound in racing. If you don't do it the way it has been done the last 25 years, they think you are nuts," he said. "This is not lawn tennis that we are playing. Those last 10 laps could be more fun than turning 20 gorillas loose in Yugos on Interstate 85."

The Winston, scheduled for the weekend prior to the Coca-Cola 600 at Charlotte, also marked the return to the circuit of Tim Richmond, who thought a short race, broken into three segments, would be ideal to begin his comeback.

For the first time, Richmond talked publicly about the serious health problems that had hospitalized him during the winter, and he replied to the rumors that had sprouted during his absence. He denied that he was being treated for AIDS, or that he was battling a problem with drugs.

But he clearly was not his old self. Instead of running to the spotlight, he tried running away from it. Instead of socializing with old friends, he hid in the back of his team truck, saying he was saving his energy for the race. He did say that he felt good being back in a race car. "It is like I have never been away, and it seems like it was only a couple of weeks ago that I won at Riverside," he said.

It was after the final race at Riverside that he had checked into the hospital, too sick even to think about racing.

"I was much more concerned if I would see the outside of that hospital room again," he said. "During the worst period, I thought I would be better off if I went ahead and did die. I am not sure even now that I will ever be 100 percent well again. But the only way I can gauge how far I have come is to go out there and race."

He seemed more amused than angry by the rumors. "That

stuff is funny. It doesn't bother me because I wasn't here on the circuit to hear it. But, I guess all of that stuff is more prominent than I thought."

Bill Elliott won the pole position for The Winston, and Richmond qualified second to get the other front-row starting position. Davey Allison and Earnhardt won second-row spots. That put Earnhardt on Richmond's rear bumper for the start, and Richmond seemed anxious to renew the friendly rivalry the two developed in 1986.

"I had a lot of good, close races with Earnhardt and I am looking forward to getting back to that," Richmond said. "Some people have a problem with the way Dale drives, but I never have. In fact, you could say my style is very similar to his."

Dale smiled when told what Richmond had said. "If he wants to race me, he knows where to find me," he said with a grin. "But Tim might find out that there are more cars than just mine to beat. The Fords of Elliott and Davey Allison are running awfully fast."

Elliott's Thunderbird was fast, indeed, and just as dominant as the year before in Atlanta. He led all but four of the laps in the first 75 lap segment, dropping from the lead only during his mandatory pit stop. He led all 50 laps of the second segment.

Then it was time for "the shoot-out" to be tested. During the intermission before the final segment, the crowd of more than 60,000 fans buzzed with anticipation. Would Elliott, starting from the pole again, be able to run away as he had in the first two segments? Would someone crash him before he even got the chance to take the green flag? Had some of the drivers been holding back something for the last 10 laps?

As the cars circled the track for the start, Humpy Wheeler had an I-know-something grin on his face. "We are about to light the fuse to the dynamite," he said.

As if on cue, The Winston exploded.

Only seconds after taking the green flag, Elliott and Bodine collided in the first turn, with Earnhardt only inches off their rear bumpers. Both Bodine and Elliott spun and Earnhardt drove low to come out of the fray with his first lead of the day.

Furious, Elliott thought Earnhardt had instigated the wreck and sought to retaliate. He bumped Earnhardt on the backstretch, then coming off the fourth turn forced Earnhardt down into the grassy infield between the track and pit road. Earnhardt never got off the gas and still held the lead as he steered back onto the asphalt.

On the backstretch, Earnhardt forced Elliott up near the wall, bashing Elliott's fender, which resulted in a cut tire two laps later, dropping Elliott out of contention. Earnhardt went on to win the race, but on the cool-down lap his car was bumped by Elliott and Bodine also tried to take a shot.

Terry Labonte finished second and Richmond was third. Neither got tangled in the rough stuff.

Earnhardt got most of the blame for creating the incident. Elliott was so upset that he hurried across the track and went to the press box on top of the main grandstand to make sure reporters knew his side. He was certain that Earnhardt had started the fireworks. "He hit the right-rear quarter panel of my car, turning me into Bodine," Elliott contended. "He hit me. The fans saw it. Everyone saw it. What Earnhardt did was just not right. You can't say that is racing. He hit me several times. I was ticked off and, yes, I did hit him back. If a man has to run over you to beat you, it is time to stop. I am sick of it. If that is what it takes to be a Winston Cup champion, I don't want it.

"We are not kids. We are not Saturday night wrestlers. We are racers. The thing of it is, Earnhardt liked to wreck me and several others on the track. I am just tired of it. I had the best car and I feel I should have won the race. To have it taken away from me like that...Well, how would you feel?"

Bodine initially said he didn't know what had happened and seemed willing to take the blame himself. "I thought I had cleared Bill, but I guess I hadn't," he said. After realizing most of the blame was being directed toward Earnhardt, he, too, took some shots.

"I guess we have to blame it on Earnhardt again," he said. "It seems we have been doing that a lot lately. It isn't safe and it isn't racing when you have to run over and knock people out of the way to win a race. There is a sport like that, called demolition derby.

"But that isn't stock car racing. Sure, you race hard and you do everything you can. You even bang with people, but you don't try to kill them, if it is for $200,000 or $2 million. If Earnhardt thinks that is racing, he is sick."

Amazed that he was being made the villain, Dale strongly denied being responsible. "Bodine chopped down on Elliott and then Elliott turned into Bodine," he said. "I saw them hook up and figured they would spin up the track. I stayed low and it proved to be a good decision."

Dale said that Elliott bumped him on the backstretch after regaining control. "That didn't upset me, but in the fourth turn when he knocked me sideways and put my car down in the grass, I did get a little upset. On the next lap, I let Bill know I was a little miffed. I rode his car up to the wall, but I never touched him."

Dale said he understood why Elliott was so frustrated. "I know I would be if I were in his situation. But there was no reason for him to intentionally try to wreck me like he did after the race was over. I have a big, big problem with that, and I certainly expect NASCAR to do something about it. If I had done something like that, they would have me swinging from the flagpole. I am not mad at Bill, and I don't carry a grudge. But if he wants to carry it on, I will stand flat-footed with him and we will get it on."

NASCAR president Bill France, Jr., didn't seem to know quite what to do about the situation. "We want to look at the video tapes of what happened those last 10 laps before announcing anything. But we know we have a problem with what happened after the checkered flag, and we will reply to it," he said.

Of the thousands of words spoken and written in advance about the new format for The Winston, the truest came from veteran Neil Bonnett who predicted, "Whoever wins this thing won't be a gentleman, and you can bet he will get some bad press."

Dale, never mistaken for a gentleman on the race track, got plenty of bad press in the days following The Winston, mainly because of the scorching verbal attack on him from Elliott. But most of the things written and said about his role weren't justified, as NASCAR officials saw when they studied the video replays.

Earnhardt may have done some people wrong, accidentally or otherwise, in other races, but not in The Winston. He drove a great race and deserved to hear cheers instead of the boos he received from fans who were believing the accusations made by Elliott and Bodine.

"The problem is Earnhardt is such a convenient whipping boy because of his reputation," a Winston Cup official admitted. "If he is within a mile of anything that happens, he is going to get blamed for it."

NASCAR officials decided they could not permit the roughness on the track to continue.

"Incidents of this nature simply are not going to be tolerated. It is something that has been going on, and we have got to stop it now," declared Winston Cup director Dick Beaty as he announced penalties against all three drivers involved in The Winston controversy.

Elliott was fined $2,500 and Bodine $1,000 for ramming into Earnhardt following the checkered flag. Earnhardt was fined $2,500 for forcing Elliott's car high on the track. Both Elliott and Earnhardt were required to post $7,500 bonds, and Bodine a $4,000 bond. Earnhardt and Elliott were placed on probation for the next six races and Bodine for the next four.

Earnhardt said he did not believe the penalties against him were justified, since NASCAR officials confirmed that video replays clearly had shown that he was not responsible for the initial wreck. He had admitted, however, that he deliberately forced Elliott high to the wall after Elliott had run him into the infield grass.

Elliott felt his fine was too much, too, since it was the first time he had been involved in a controversy. But he mainly wanted to get the incident over with.

"I am sorry for what I did. It was unsportsmanlike, and I have apologized to all the guys on Earnhardt's crew. I promised that restitution would be made for damage on their car," Elliott said. "What happened in The Winston can't go on, and I ain't going to be after anybody."

Other drivers thought it was unfair to penalize anyone for what had happened. "I can't understand what all the fuss is about," said Neil Bonnett. "You throw that kind of money out there, what do you expect?"

"They came up with the 10-lap shootout because they wanted an exciting finish, and by God, they got it," said Terry Labonte.

Darrell Waltrip did not like the format before the race and liked it even less afterward.

"This proves to me that the more this sport changes the more it stays the same. That finish was 1959 vintage. When it was over, they should have given everyone a drink of moonshine and let them go out and whip each other," he said. "If they are looking for a thrill show, they ought to get Joe Chitwood and Dale Earnhardt."

After NASCAR announced the penalties, Earnhardt invited Elliott to join him for a drive to an isolated corner of the Charlotte Motor Speedway infield.

"Look, we are both running for the Winston Cup championship, and it would be unfair for either of us to let this interfere with that. I am going to race you as hard as I can, and I expect you to do the same," Dale later recalled telling Elliott. "NASCAR is trying to put a cloud over our heads, and that is not fair to either one of us."

Earnhardt told reporters much the same thing when asked if he would become less aggressive because of being on proba- tion. "I can't let that affect the way I drive my race car," he said. "If I did, I wouldn't be much of a champion, would I? Richard Petty has been through a lot more stuff than I have dur- ing his career, and he is the greatest champion in the history of this sport."

While Earnhardt and Elliott seemed to have no problems settling their differences, neither seemed in a hurry to mend their relationship with Bodine, who was still being flippant about the controversy. He claimed he did not know why NASCAR fined him. "I was just trying to tap Earnhardt's car so I could get his attention and congratulate him for winning the race," Bodine said with a snicker.

Of all the drivers in the garage area, Earnhardt disliked Bodine most.

"I really don't like that little pea-brain, no-good Yankee," he had said. "Bodine has been cocky ever since he won the Daytona 500 in 1986. It swelled his head so much that he's got watermelon-head syndrome. All the blood got to his head and cut off the circulation.

"I have thought about inviting him to go deer hunting with me, but I can't ask him with a sincere enough look on my face. I would make him wear antlers. After all, hunting accidents do happen."

Bodine, who won 511 Modified and Grand National races before getting his chance on the Winston Cup circuit, claimed he did not understand Earnhardt's dislike for him.

"All I know is that I stand up to Earnhardt. I don't get out of his way. I am not intimidated by him. I race him like he races everyone else – tough, a lot of pushing and shoving – and I am the one who gets into trouble with NASCAR," Bodine said.

"But I have had to deal with controversy most of my career. When I started out racing in Chemung, New York, my father owned the track and people said the reason I won was that I got special favors. It wasn't true, of course, but that did not stop them from booing."

Bodine later moved from New York to race on the fiercely competitive New England modified circuit, where he kept winning and kept hearing boos. "They booed because I won so much. But I told them, 'You just keep on booing, because that makes me run faster.' I called it boo-power," Bodine recalled with a chuckle.

Most drivers, including Earnhardt, were nice to him when he first joined the Winston Cup tour, Bodine said. "It was really only after I starting running good that things began developing. I really don't know Earnhardt personally, so I can't say if we could ever be friends or not. But I don't like him as a driver, because of the things he does on the track, the way he tries to intimidate people. He is the top dog. He has won races and championships. Still, he does all this rough stuff, and still you see other drivers sucking up to him, and moving over for him on the track. It is like they are saying, 'He is better than I am, so why fight him?' I don't feel Earnhardt is better than me. I feel like I am his equal, and I don't move over for him when I see him coming."

Despite the stern warning by NASCAR, less than a week after The Winston incident, Bodine and Earnhardt hooked bumpers again in the 300-mile Grand National race held the day before the Coca-Cola 600 at Charlotte.

Earnhardt, who had rallied from a lap down, was charging back toward the lead with 14 laps left when it appeared that Bodine tried to spin him out in the first and second turns. Earnhardt had passed Bodine for second place a lap earlier and was gaining on leader Gant when Bodine drove into his rear bumper as the two entered the first turn.

Bodine never backed off the throttle, and he repeatedly

slammed into Earnhardt's car as they continued at speed through the turns. Afterward, Bodine said the incident was the result of bad judgment by both drivers.

"I tried to drive inside of Dale and there wasn't enough room. I thought he would slide up and he didn't. I went in too hard and couldn't stop. None of us are perfect. As Dale as said before, that's racing. We all make mistakes."

Earnhardt was upset, but he declined to comment. "Let NASCAR take care of it," he said. "I talked too much after The Winston and it got me into trouble."

After reviewing video tape, NASCAR spokesman Chip Williams announced that Bodine was being fined $15,000 for rough driving, the biggest fine in the sport's history.

Les Richter, a NASCAR vice president, said the incident indicated that Bodine had not taken seriously the warning issued after The Winston. "If this action does not show results, stronger measures will be taken in the future," he added.

Bodine and his car owner, Rick Hendrick, appealed the fine. "The penalty is so unjustified that it is hard to decide whether to laugh or cry," Hendrick said. "It is impossible for NASCAR or anyone to determine cause or intent from looking at film or tape."

Under the threat of legal action by Bodine, the NASCAR committee formed to hear the appeal agreed that there was no proof that Bodine had intentionally attempted to wreck Earnhardt. The committee lifted the fine and year-long probation.

"Here I am, free again," Bodine quipped upon receiving the news.

The Coca-Cola 600 ran without incident, and was won by Kyle Petty, who was more than a lap ahead of second-place Morgan Shepherd at the finish. Earnhardt, Elliott, and Bodine encountered mechanical problems and finished well behind Petty, while staying out of each other's way.

• • •

Every sport has golden moments preserved in memory and

words. Humpy Wheeler says Dale Earnhardt gave stock car racing a 14-karat memory in the 1987 The Winston when he was forced off the track by Elliott and still came back to win.

"That was the greatest, single movement in NASCAR racing since it started in 1949," Wheeler said. "I have seen a lot of crazy deals, but I have looked at replays of that thing over and over. Earnhardt had lost control of that car, on grass, of all things, which is the worst thing you can run on, and saved the car by staying in the throttle. Everybody else would have gotten off that throttle, hit the brakes, cut left, and let her slide. He didn't do it. Unbelievable!"

Dale provided a few more memorable moments and victories during the 1987 season, as did his racing protege, Tim Richmond, whose return to the circuit was more of the stuff that makes legends.

Richmond picked up where he had left off at the end of the 1986, as he raced to victories at Pocono and Riverside in his first two starts. When he pulled into Victory Lane at Pocono, he was still trying to control his emotions.

"I took an extra cool-down lap, hoping to dry the tears, but when Dale and a few other drivers started congratulating me, the tears just kept coming," he said.

The race seemed to be coming down to a classic showdown between Richmond and Earnhardt until a leaking tire slowed Earnhardt in the stretch. Instead of pitting, Earnhardt rode out the slow leak to finish fifth.

Richmond's second victory a week later was even more convincing as he led 48 of 95 laps. Dale finished seventh, without leading, and he seemed to be having mixed emotions about his friend's success. Dale was glad that Richmond was healthy enough to be back winning races. But he felt that he was being restrained from racing Richmond as tightly as he wanted because of his probation.

"Tim knocked me down the straightaway and cut me off twice at Pocono," Dale said. "But I can't afford to get in trouble. I am having to mash the brakes and drive as if my hands were tied."

Earnhardt, though, was back in form the week after Richmond's victory at Riverside. He ended Richmond's streak by winning at Michigan International Speedway, taking his final lead from Richmond on Lap 130 and holding on through the final 70 laps despite a fuel problem near the end.

Dale had more than his seventh victory of the season to celebrate. With a whopping 304-point lead in the Winston Cup standings, he assured his team a $150,000 bonus for leading the points race mid-season.

Richmond, who finished fourth at the Michigan, also was experiencing mixed feelings about Earnhardt's splendid season. It was the kind that Richmond thought he would have had if not for his physical problems.

"I am sure that Dale and his team had their act together when the season began, but I don't think he would have had a chance if I had been healthy enough to run the full season," Richmond said. "Dale tells me a lot of people have been on him this season, and he can't drive as aggressive as he used to. Well, my style hasn't changed. I have got enough money to pay any fines NASCAR wants to throw my way, and I don't mind paying them, either."

Richmond said he had learned to appreciate his work as something other than a job. "I did not think I would miss racing as much as I did. I guess it is like that with a lot of things. You don't really appreciate them until you don't have them.

"The only strange thing that I've experienced since coming back was that I felt miserable, emotionally, the day after both of my wins at Pocono and Riverside. I really don't know why that happened. You hear stories of a salesman suffering from depression right after he cuts a big deal. Maybe it was the same thing."

Richmond was quiet for a few moments. Then he smiled brightly.

"You know what I think it was? I was probably depressed because I thought about what I could have accomplished if I had been healthy for the entire season. I would be in the hunt for the championship. It would have been me and Earnhardt right down to the wire."

Earnhardt came off of his probation in mid-July at Pocono, and he immediately collected his eighth victory of the season by bumping Alan Kulwicki out of the lead a half-lap from the finish line.

The incident did not stir much controversy, however, because Kulwicki was not one to voice public gripes. "There were a lot of things I wanted to say after the race, but I didn't want to come off sounding like a crybaby," he said later.

He also considered the incident a good lesson.

"I had the lead, and I had the fastest car. I felt that I only had to keep my car in the groove for that final half-lap to get the first Winston Cup victory of my career. I didn't choke, and I did what I thought I had to do to win the race. I know Earnhardt likes to intimidate other drivers, but he didn't get me rattled, even when he bumped into the back of my car a lap earlier.

"On the last lap, he just did this one move that knocked my car out of the groove that I needed to be in to win the race. Going into the tunnel turn, Earnhardt was on the high side of me, and I knew that he couldn't pass me up there. He slowed down and turned left into me with his front left fender."

Kulwicki sighed and shrugged.

"Looking back," he continued, "I should have slowed down, too, and kept him fully beside me. That way, if he had bumped into me, it would not have done much. But at the time, I was not thinking about that. I was just trying to get away from him and win the race."

Other drivers, after looking at video replays of the bump, said Earnhardt's move was one of the slickest they had seen.

"There was only one way he was going to win that race, and that was to bump me out of the groove I wanted to be in," Kulwicki said. "He did what he had to do to win the race. Of all the drivers on the circuit, I think that Earnhardt is the only one who would do something like that to win a race. Everyone knows that Dale is an aggressive driver and I don't want to criticize him publicly for his style of driving. Who can say if he is aggressive or overly-aggressive?

"I just know that he is awfully close to the limit. He is close to overstepping the bounds. But he is so good at what he does. He tapped me just enough to make my car bobble. The whole thing didn't take more than two or three seconds to happen. But, by the time I got control of my car, he was gone. If he had hit my car any harder, I probably would have wrecked, like Marlin did at Bristol, and Waltrip did at Richmond."

• • •

Without much fuss, Dale won his ninth race under the stars at Bristol and rolled into Darlington a week later with a 573-point lead, the biggest 20-race lead that anyone had enjoyed since Richard Petty led Dave Marcis by 573 points in 1975.

Despite the wide margin, Dale and his crew were pumped up and determined to win the Southern 500, a race cherished by drivers for its proud tradition. Before Daytona or Charlotte had major raceways, the egg-shaped Darlington track, three-eighths mile long, was the high-speed playground of legendary drivers such as Buck Baker, Lee Petty, Cotton Owens, Fireball Roberts, Joe Weatherly, and Curtis Turner.

"The Southern 500 was stock car racing back when we were kids growing up," said Richard Childress. "We would keep up with the races at Bowman-Gray Stadium and the other short tracks around the area, but the Southern 500 was the big race that everyone looked forward to. The world stopped on Labor Day and everybody listened to the race on the radio. There was a special magic about Darlington and the Southern 500 back in those days. There are other big, big races on the schedule nowadays, and they are important events. But there is nothing else like the Southern 500.

"Maybe it is just the feeling of pride and tradition that guys like me grew up with in the Carolinas who later got into racing, but the Southern 500 is the one race you want to win."

Dale had won the the spring race at the track three times, but he was still looking for his first victory on Labor Day weekend. "If there ever was a race that fits Dale Earnhardt's style, it is the Southern 500," Childress said. "He wants his name on the list of drivers who have won the race, and we are going to do everything we can to help him get it there."

Although Dale was making a runaway of the points race and had won nine previous races, he had failed to win either of the Winston Million Series races and, thus, was ineligible for the consolation bonus.

Daytona 500 winner Bill Elliott, Winston 500 winner Davey Allison, and Coca-Cola 500 winner Kyle Petty could claim an extra $100,000 if either won the Southern 500 for a second victory in the series.

"Winning this race might be worth more to those three in terms of money, but I want to win it as much, or more, than any of them," Dale said. "And my reasons have nothing to do with money. I grew up like Richard Childress, when Darlington and the Southern 500 was the big race of the year....While some other kids dreamed about growing up and hitting a home run in the World Series, I dreamed about growing up and driving a race car and winning the Southern 500.

"Another thing, everyone on my team wants to finish this season the way we started it. Richard and his guys have worked five hard years to make all this possible, and I don't want to let them down. Anybody who knows anything at all about stock car racing knows the Southern 500 is a true test of a champion. It is the one race we all want to win."

Starting fifth in the 40-car field under rain-threatening skies, Dale followed pole-sitter Davey Allison for the first 58 laps before pushing his Chevrolet into the lead. He was leading when rain brought out a caution flag on Lap 183. Slightly past the halfway mark, the race returned to speed, but it was apparent that heavier rain was on the way.

Richard Petty drove by Earnhardt going into the third turn and held the lead for two laps while fans cheered and applauded in anticipation of seeing "The King" post his first victory since July 4, 1984. But with the clouds becoming darker, Dale pushed the throttle harder and sped by Petty on the backstretch. He opened a comfortable lead before rain ended the race after 202 laps.

"I am mighty proud to win this race, even if it did not go the full distance," he said afterward. "You can win all the spring races at Darlington you want, but the only one that people remember is the Southern 500."

Earnhardt said Petty's charge before the rain came was almost as thrilling to him as for the spectators.

"I could see the fans jumping up and down in the back grandstands when he drove around me. They were going crazy. I even got a little excited myself," Earnhardt said. "I knew Richard was running real good. But when he got by me, he was running a little harder than I wanted to run at that point. I took another lap to settle down and then moved up to race him for the lead."

Tim Richmond, who had won the 1986 Southern 500, was a no-show for the event. His entry was canceled on Wednesday, the day before qualifying was to begin. Monday, following Earnhardt's victory, a spokesman for the Hendrick team released a statement that Richmond was in semi-retirement, and it was not known when he would race again.

No one would say what Richmond's problem was. But it was widely speculated that it was drugs. Members of some teams had complained to NASCAR officials about suspicions of drug use by Richmond after races at Wadkins Glen, New York, and Michigan International Speedway.

At Martinsville in the spring, before Richmond had returned, Dale signed an autograph for a fan wearing a "Say No

181

to Drugs" T-shirt. "You ought to send one of those to Richmond," he told the fan.

Dale had seen a difference in Richmond after his return, and he and other drivers suggested that NASCAR should test drivers suspected of using illegal drugs.

"I am not saying that just because of all the things being rumored about Tim," Dale had said. "If we had tests, and Richmond passed, that would put all of that rumor stuff to rest, wouldn't it? I would like to see Tim back on the circuit, racing again.

"But I want the 'old' Tim back. He hasn't been himself for awhile. Whether fame and fortune got him, I don't know. We are not as close as we once were. He was a great competitor, and he has great talent. But he is not the same as he once was. We used to sit and talk, and drop by each others house for a beer. But we haven't done that in a long time."

Rusty Wallace was another driver concerned that drugs could be a problem in stock car racing, as it was in other major sports. "I am telling you, doing drugs on the race track, you can get killed real quick. It is something this sport can not tolerate," he said. "I don't know if that is Richmond's problem or not. I am not saying it is. But if there is a problem, I feel sorry for him, and I hope he can get it corrected."

• • •

While the 1987 season had been going great for Dale, it had been all downhill for Darrell Waltrip, who never dreamed a season could be so long and frustrating. While Earnhardt had won 10 of 21 races and held a 583-point lead in the Winston Cup standings, Waltrip went into the Wrangler 400 at Richmond still looking for his first victory with his new team.

"It is frustrating. It is annoying. It is aggravating," he said. "I have been in racing long enough that I knew when we entered into this new team that there was a chance anything could happen. But I never, ever, expected something like this. We got off to a bad start, and we have struggled ever since. But

I know this team has the potential to be just as good as any on the circuit."

Waltrip said there was no mystery as to why Earnhardt was having such a great season. "The drivers on the circuit who can beat him have not been able to get up there with him to do it. I have been telling my guys all year that if they give me the car to get up there with him that I can beat him. We have come a long way, and I think this could be the time we do it. I have won six races before on the Richmond track, and the car is working good."

Waltrip made a strong bid, but he still wasn't able to prevent Earnhardt from rolling to his 11th win of the season. Despite an almost constant challenge from Waltrip, Dale led the final 155 laps and coasted under the checkered flag during a caution period.

"The caution caught me by surprise," Waltrip said. "I had planned to pass Earnhardt in the first turn on the last lap. I just didn't get a chance to try. But it would have been tough. I had already tried a bunch of times to get by him."

Earnhardt replied that there was no way Waltrip would have beaten him. "He had tried about 75 times earlier and hadn't been able o get around me. I don't think it would have been any different if he had tried one more time."

The fierce competition between Waltrip and Earnhardt kept the fans on their feet for most of the afternoon. Several times, Waltrip pushed the nose of his Chevrolet ahead in the turns, but Earnhardt managed to regain the advantage off the corners. "I gave Darrell all the room he needed in the low groove. I stayed cool and relaxed and ran my car and let him worry about trying to get around me," Dale said.

NASCAR's Dick Beaty had warned in the pre-race meeting that drivers would be penalized for rough driving. The only incident between Earnhardt and Waltrip came midway in the race on pit road. Each blamed the other, and Beaty blamed both.

"Earnhardt was trying to pinch me up against another car so I couldn't get into the pits," Waltrip charged. "But I got on pit road and he wasn't going very fast. I got up beside him and all the trouble from there on was something he created."

Earnhardt's side of the story was that Waltrip had blocked him from his pit. "He ought not to have been under me. When I started down to get to my pit, he was under me."

Beaty put both drivers at the back of the field because of the incident, and it took Earnhardt, with Waltrip in his wake, 64 laps to get back to the front. His win pushed his Winston Cup championship lead to 608 points.

Two weeks later, at Martinsville, Waltrip finally won in a fender-banging finish against Earnhardt and Terry Labonte.

Dale was in front on the final lap, with Labonte and Waltrip close behind. Labonte tried to get around Earnhardt in the first and second turns, but Dale forced him up near the backstretch wall, giving Waltrip the break he needed.

In the third turn, Waltrip slammed into Labonte, forcing him into Earnhardt, and Waltrip stayed on the gas to pass both. "I shot into Terry, he shot into Earnhardt, and I shot to the victory," Waltrip said happily. "Dale and Terry hung together up high on the track and I was able to get my car inside of Terry's as we went into the third turn. Terry came down to the inside and I tapped him. I don't know how that could make both of them take off like they did."

Labonte said it was easy to explain. "Darrell just ran all over me and Dale to win the race," he said angrily. "Earnhardt had tried to put me in the wall and I pulled in behind him. As we went into the third turn, Darrell never lifted and he ran right over both of us."

Earnhardt was clearly upset, too, but he wrestled to keep his emotions under control. "Just racing, I guess," he said. "I think everyone saw what happened. Darrell ran in there, knocked Terry into me, and wrecked Terry. But there is no use arguing about it now. The race is over, and that's it."

The most heated words came from the crew chiefs. Tim Brewer, in Labonte's pit, said NASCAR should have waved Earnhardt the winner and Labonte second. Kirk Shelmerdine, Earnhardt's crew chief, felt that his team was robbed. "I can stand getting outrun, but I can't accept getting robbed," he said. "But what good is hollering going to do? We could protest, but that would be a waste of time and money. NASCAR is not going to do anything."

After reviewing the incident, NASCAR did exactly that. Nothing. "Dick Beaty said he did not see anything but hard racing, and we can't see where anyone should be penalized," spokesman Chip Williams announced.

• • •

The champagne was on ice and the Winston Cup championship trophy was polished and waiting for Earnhardt and the Wrangler-GM Goodwrench team when they arrived at Charlotte Motor Speedway the week after Martinsville. All Earnhardt needed to officially wrap up his second consecutive NASCAR title was to finish third or better.

"I can't think of a better place to celebrate winning the title than here, only a few miles from where I grew up," Dale said. "It would be a special thrill for me, since a lot of my friends and family would be here to help celebrate. What I really want to do is wrap up the title by winning the race. That is the goal for this weekend."

Bobby Allison won the pole position, but he admitted that Earnhardt was the man everyone had to beat.

"It doesn't take a genius to figure that out," he said. "And there is no mystery why Earnhardt has been so dominant this year either. His team has its act together, and Dale is driving the devil out of the car."

Dale "drove the devil" out of the No. 3 Chevrolet once again, but not to victory this time. After dodging a series of wrecks, Bill Elliott drove away from the other survivors to beat Allison by a couple of seconds.

"My car was the best of what was left after all those wrecks, and that is all it takes," Elliott said in his familiar drawl.

Earnhardt, once three laps down after getting entangled in an early wreck, was close to regaining the lead until a brake problem forced a long pit stop. He finished 12th, passing Elliott and Allison in the closing laps.

"I could see a little grin on Dale's face when he passed me," Elliott said. "But it doesn't matter how good your car is if you are five laps down, does it?"

Dale didn't officially clinch the title, but all he had to do was to claim it was to start the next race.

"Keep the champagne on ice," he said. "We will get the title at Rockingham, but I would rather have gone ahead and done it here. The most disappointing thing is to have a car that good and not win the race."

During the two-week break between Charlotte and Rockingham, Dale went deer hunting. He was relaxed and in good humor when he arrived at Rockingham, joking that he had tighter security than the president of the United States during the break, because his team wanted to make sure he would be able to start the coming race.

"My car owner, Richard Childress, had a member of our crew guarding me every minute. I was out deer hunting the other day when I heard this rustling in the bushes. I thought it was a big buck. It turned out to be ol' Richard. He was just checking to make sure I was all right."

Earnhardt laughed. "The worst part is that Richard had Danny Myers sleeping with me every night, right between me and Teresa. Two or three times a night, Danny would awake me and ask if I was all right. If I was thirsty, he'd nudge Teresa and tell her to get up and get me a glass of water. Man, I can't wait to get this race started so them boys can relax a little bit."

With 11 victories and 19 top-five finishes, Earnhardt had a 525-point lead with three races remaining on the schedule.

"You can look around at other professional sports and see

how difficult it is to win consecutive titles," Dale said. "I think the reason for that is a team gets over-confident and doesn't work as hard after winning a title. But my team didn't allow that to happen this year. We came back and worked even harder, building on what we accomplished last year.

"We had plenty of confidence. You have got to have confidence to be a winner. But we were not over confident in that we knew we couldn't go out and win the title again if we didn't work hard for it."

Earnhardt spoiled his own opportunity to officially wrap up his second straight championship with a victory by hitting the wall in the first turn before the halfway point.

"Bill Elliott was leading and I was running him down when I got a little bit overanxious and crashed," he said later. "It knocked the ball joints out of the car, and I was lucky to come back to finish second to Bill."

In the final two races, Earnhardt lost an engine at Riverside, and finished second again to Elliott in the season-ender at Atlanta, where he and Elliott had a minor collision on the opening lap.

"Yeah, we couldn't let the season end without one more bump," Elliott quipped. "What happened was that I felt I had a pretty good line going into the first turn and I just stayed on the throttle. I gave Dale plenty of room up high, but I guess he liked the groove I had."

Elliott sped out of the bump with the lead, and went on to win by 13 seconds. It was the third victory in the final four races for Elliott, who compared the sizzling stretch run to the 1984 season, which preceded his super season the next year.

"I can't wait to start the 1988 season and see what happens," he said.

Dale was just as eager to get started on what he expected to be a third straight championship season.

"We have just warmed up for 1988, and everyone on the crew is going to be back. The only change will be that our cars will be black and silver since GM Goodwrench is replacing Wrangler as our primary sponsor. The biggest disappointment this year is that we did not win the Daytona 500. But we are going to win that thing yet, and it would be a great way to start off 1988."

The Childress team was just as determined as its driver to keep the championship streak going. "I felt we were prepared to win every time we showed up for a race the last two years," crew chief Kirk Shelmerdine said.

"All of that preparation, along with some good luck and superb, never-quit driving by Dale, got us to this point. We didn't want to be a flash in the pan after winning the 1986 title. We worked harder to get ready for 1987, and I am confident we are not going to disappear into the woodwork in 1988."

Earnhardt, Shelmerdine, and other crewmen credited Childress's leadership for the back-to-back championships.

"Racing is Richard's life. It is the only thing he has ever been involved in," said engine builder Lou LaRosa. "He isn't some rich guy who made his money in business and then decided to dabble in racing. Richard built this team the hard way, and practically every dollar he's made has gone back into the racing operation."

During the 1987 season, Childress moved his operation into a new, ultra-modern, 30,000-square-foot building in Welcome, N.C., just down the road from Winston-Salem, where he grew up. "Richard has put the best crew and the best operation in stock car racing together. He is a very special man, and everyone who works for him knows it," Dale said at the NASCAR championship banquet in New York.

Childress replied by saying the consecutive championships were a team effort, and he praised Earnhardt for more than his flat-out driving ability.

"Dale kept everyone pumped up," he said. "His attitude had a lot to do with the way we bounced back after losing the Daytona 500. He was in the race shop almost as soon as we got back home, reassuring the guys on the crew, just keeping them pumped up, telling them they were winners and if we all worked together we could win another championship.

"Nobody on our team ever got down, and that was a big factor in our second straight title. We all felt we were going to have a good season. But I don't think anyone ever dreamed it was going to be as good as it turned out. I wasn't just good. It was fantastic."

11

'It kind of gets on your nerves'

There is nothing predictable about stock car racing, and certainly no one could have expected the controversies and horrors that would unfold during the 1988 season, one of the darkest in Winston Cup history.

Even before the first car rolled to the starting line at Daytona, the sport was engulfed in dispute.

During the offseason, NASCAR officials, at the urging of several drivers and car owners, adopted a drug-testing policy.

Tim Richmond, who was widely believed to be the target of the new policy, was asked to take a test only a few days before the Busch Clash, for which he was eligible since he had won a pole position the previous season. Two days before the race, NASCAR announced that Richmond had failed the test and would not be permitted to compete.

NASCAR declined for several days to identify the illegal drugs that supposedly had been detected, and it wasn't until Richmond requested, and passed, a second test that NASCAR disclosed the only thing Richmond was guilty of was taking non-prescription cold medicines.

The second test cleared Richmond to compete in the Daytona 500, if he could find a ride, but NASCAR president Bill France, Jr., said Richmond would still have to undergo a physical by the track physician and make available his medical records from the Cleveland, Ohio, hospital, where he had been treated between the 1986 and 1987 seasons.

Richmond, who repeatedly denied that he ever used illegal drugs, indicated he would undergo the physical, but he refused to turn over his medical records.

Pressed to do so, Richmond hired a major New York City law firm and eventually announced he was filing a multi-million-dollar suit against NASCAR.

Meanwhile, new problems were developing on the track, too.

The Goodyear Tire and Rubber Co., the sole supplier of racing tires for the Winston Cup circuit for 14 years, suddenly found itself facing a strong challenge from Hoosier Tire Company, a small, family-owned factory in Indiana that manufactured only racing tires.

At first, Goodyear did not seem to take its new competitor seriously. When it did, only a couple of races into the season, it was too late to avoid an all-out tire war that proved both expensive and dangerous for teams and drivers.

The teams also were bearing the expense, and frustrations, of NASCAR's new idea to keep speeds under 200 miles per hour at Daytona and Talladega. Teams were required to use carburetor restricter plates, which reduced the flow of air and fuel to the engine, and some major teams were claiming to have spent as much as $200,000 during the winter trying to keep the loss of horsepower to a minimum.

The plates accomplished the intended purpose, as evidenced by Ken Schrader's pole-winning speed of 193.823 miles per hour. It was the first Daytona 500 pole won with a sub-200 speed since Ricky Rudd took the top starting position in 1983 at 198.864 miles per hour.

The plates also changed the face of superspeedway racing, and according to many drivers, made it more dangerous. "Plate racing," as it was called, required drivers to race in single-file packs, which invited multi-car crashes. A driver who dared to pull out of line to improve his position was frequently booted back to the rear. Drivers also were reluctant to get off the throttle and brake, even if they saw trouble developing in front of them, because they did not want to lose a fast draft.

Earnhardt, in his new black and silver Chevrolet Monte Carlo SS, opened the new season by winning the 20-lap Busch Clash. He took the lead from Geoff Bodine on the sixth lap and held back a challenge from Davey Allison down the stretch.

"The biggest thing I learned was that Earnhardt is a tough man to beat," said Allison. "But I guess that doesn't surprise anyone."

The biggest concern for Earnhardt during the final laps was that Allison and his father, Bobby, who was running third, might try to hook up in a draft a slingshot around him.

"I figured they might try to pull the 'Alabama Shuffle' on me. You know, it was the Alabama Gang against ol' Earnhardt."

Earnhardt protected his lead by blocking the passing lanes.

"He cut me off every time I tried to make a move," Davey Allison said. "It wasn't anything dirty. We were racing for $75,000, and you do what you have to do."

Bobby Allison added, "The race track is about 30 feet wide, and Earnhardt's Chevrolet looked 40 feet wide."

But even after winning the first test with the new carburetor plate, Dale still didn't like it. He talked about it at length after finishing second to Darrell Waltrip in one of the 125-mile qualifying races a few days later.

"It has slowed us down, but what it took out of there was the throttle response that you had to know how to use. Before, a lot of drivers didn't know how to do that and the cars would get loose on them a lot quicker.

"Now, with this plate, it sort of mellowed the cars out a little bit in the corners. We are still running about the same race speeds, but you don't have that surge of power under your foot in the corners. Guys like Bill Elliott, Geoff Bodine, and myself could run those cars wide open through the corners and a lot of them couldn't. The plate enables a lot of them to get up in there and get all over you."

In his qualifying race, Earnhardt slipped through a massive wreck that involved a half-dozen drivers. He said the crashes were a preview of what could be expected in the Daytona 500.

"I feel like you are going to see crashes like you saw in the qualifying races. You know, Cale Yarborough was second in line, behind Darrell, and he broke loose and crashed. There were five or six cars that went through and never hit anything. Then all those guys in the back crashed. That tells me they were not racing too far off their hoods.

"One reason I got through was I passed a couple of guys during that wreck. It is not courteous to do that, but I was worried about those fools running over me. Sure enough, come back around, and they were all piled up. That is what wrecks you a lot of times. You got to watch out for the guys behind you as much as the ones in front of you. They are racing off their hoods. That was a bad deal.

"Racing at Daytona has changed. I don't know if it is for the better or not. Darrell will probably say it is for the best. You got to be patient. A lot of guys out there will run right up on your tail. I could run up on Darrell's tail anytime I wanted, but it would make you loose. It would make him loose.

"Some of them don't understand you got to ride a half-quarter car length off a car in the corners. You know, give everybody a break. One guy might get loose and that is what causes wrecks. A couple of them shoves it right under you and makes it loose. I learned to draft from Buddy Baker, Cale, David Pearson, Bobby Allison, Darrell, all of these guys.

"You know it takes a little common sense to run 500 miles

and run comfortable. You get up under somebody and loosen them up and it slows both of you down, really. The other guy is going to get out of the throttle if he gets too sideways.

"There hasn't been too much working together out there yet. You get out of line, you think you can draft by somebody. You get out of line and damn if you don't go to the back. I've seen too many of them doing it. Everyone is fighting for that position, you know. It is hard to sit in line and draft along and be patient. You need to be patient."

Waltrip, who had been urging a reduction in speeds for several years, did feel that the slowdown suited his style. And because patience was a key, he thought his chances for winning his first Daytona 500 might be improved, especially after he led from start to finish to win his 125-miler.

Waltrip was feeling optimistic about the rest of the season as well. He had reorganized his team, after winning only once in his first season driving for Rick Hendrick, and he predicted an end to Earnhardt's two-year championship run.

"I guess I am bragging, and I have told Rick Hendrick this, but I feel I am the only guy that can beat Earnhardt week in and week out," Waltrip said. "I know him well enough, and how he drives well enough, and the whole situation, that I feel I would be the best candidate for upsetting his apple cart."

Asked to explain why he felt so strongly that he had an edge, Waltrip chuckled and replied, "It is a lot deeper than on the track."

Deeper than the foot?

"It gets up around the heart," Waltrip said.

Earnhardt won only one pole position during his 11-victory championship season in 1987, and Waltrip said the reason for his success was two-fold.

"His car handles good. It is like in the Busch Clash. He did not have the fastest car, but he got in front and he stayed there. There is a lot to intimidation, too. Over the years, that has been a good tool, intimidation. I guess everyone is intimidated by him at some time or another, me included. He turns you side-ways a few times, it kind of gets on your nerves.

"You see, right now he has got all the confidence in the world. It is sort of like breaking a horse, you know. You got to get a saddle on him before you can ride him, and you got to get him pinned down before you can get a saddle on him. Right now, we've just got him in a corral. He's still running around in there pretty good, and he's hard to get a rope on," Waltrip said.

Both Earnhardt and Waltrip agreed on one thing. It was going to be be difficult for a driver to win the Daytona 500 on his own. "You definitely will need a drafting buddy," Waltrip said. "If you pull out of line and no one goes with you, it is like hitting a brick wall. It is not like it once was, when if you want-ed to get away from someone you just stood on the gas for two or three laps and left him behind. Now you need a buddy sys-tem, and there aren't all that many buddies out here."

Not surprisingly, the two drivers who trusted and admired each other the most, and spent most of the Daytona 500 helping each other in the tricky draft, finished first and second – Bobby Allison and son, Davey.

Bobby sped across the finish line less than a second ahead of his 28- year-old son to win his third Daytona 500, marking the first father-son, one-two finish on a superspeedway in NASCAR history.

"It was really a great feeling to look back and know that I had beaten somebody that I feel is the best young driver ever to come into this sport," Bobby said. "This has to be one of the greatest thrills of my career."

The Allisons' finish was the most heart-warming story of the 1988 season. Sadly, however, it became a part of the sea-son's most heart-breaking story, too. Four months later, at Pocono, Bobby was almost killed in a first-lap accident that ended his career.

That crash also cost him much of his memory, including all recollection of beating his son in Daytona.

Dale Earnhardt cut a tire with 10 laps remaining in the Daytona 500 and dropped back to finish 10th. Waltrip raced the Allisons closely and was a strong contender until his engine lost power in the final laps, and he slipped back to finish 11th.

• • •

The new Hoosier tires attracted little attention in their circuit debut, although Neil Bonnett used them for an impressive fourth-place finish. But the Hoosiers were the dominant tire in the next two races, at Richmond and Rockingham, and carried Bonnett to victories in both.

Earnhardt, after cutting a tire, finished 10th at Richmond and struggled to finish fifth, at the tail end of the lead lap, in at Rockingham, where the top three finishers were on Hoosiers.

"Every car out there on Hoosiers passed me at least once today," Dale complained after the Rockingham race. "I am exhausted as hell."

Although it was suddenly apparent that the brand of tires could now make a difference between winning and losing, the more established teams, such as Earnhardt's and Waltrip's, declared their loyalty to Goodyear, a longtime racing ally.

"I am confident that Goodyear will come through for us," Richard Childress said. "They were good to us in some lean times, and we are going to stay loyal to them now."

Goodyear representative Bill King, following the embarrassment of the two consecutive defeats, promised, "We are going to bring the big guns out."

The comment brought a smile to the face of Bob Newton, whose success on the Winston Cup circuit was coming quicker than even he had envisioned.

"Oh, I am sure the 'big guy' is going to get better. Goodyear brought a new tire to Rockingham, and he will probably have a new tire at Atlanta. But my tires hold up better in the long run, and I think you will see more teams starting to use them. These are million-dollar race teams, and I don't think they will sit around and get beat because they refuse to use the best tire available to them. That would be pretty foolish on their part," Newton said.

As Newton predicted, Goodyear did show up at Atlanta with a new tire, which most drivers – even Bonnett – used. The only competitive driver choosing Hoosiers was Lake Speed, and he went out of the race because of an engine failure after 49 laps.

With racing back to normal, if only briefly, Dale made his return to Victory Lane by leading 269 of the 328 laps. Rusty Wallace was the only other driver to finish in the lead lap.

"People had been asking when I was going to win again, and I was beginning to wonder the same thing," Dale admitted. "We finally got it all back together, and my team showed it can still put a car out there that can dominate and lap the field."

Wallace gave further testimony to the superiority of the GM Goodwrench Chevrolet. "My car ran great, and I almost drove the wheels off the thing. But Earnhardt's car was double strong. He was too tough for anyone to beat."

Earnhardt became the season's first two-time winner when he beat a crowd of strong cars on Hoosiers. He was the only driver on Goodyears who stayed in the same lap with the Hoosier drivers after the first 161 laps. "I wish everyone had used Goodyears. If they had, there is no telling how many laps I would have finished ahead," Dale said.

Dale thought that he would have won the other three short-track events during the first half of the season, too, if not for the cut tire at Richmond, a cracked fuel pump at Bristol, and a leaking tire at North Wilkesboro, which took him out of the lead with only 10 laps remaining.

Despite his rash of short-track problems, Dale was still confident of winning his third straight title. At the break for The Winston at Charlotte Motor Speedway he had huge leads over his strongest challengers – 107 points over Elliott and 122 over Rusty Wallace.

But Earnhardt was not in a particularly good mood for The

Winston. Promotions for The Winston were being centered around the controversial 10-lap finish involving Earnhardt, Elliott, and Geoff Bodine the previous season. A torn Mr. Goodwrench box, a smashed Coors beer can, and a crumpled package of Levi Garrett tobacco were mailed to reporters, a clear suggestion that the trio would be banging fenders again. Coors sponsored Elliott and Levi Garrett sponsored Bodine.

All three drivers registered complaints with Charlotte Motor Speedway president Humpy Wheeler, and Earnhardt refused to participate in some pre-race activities. "I am not going to say anything until the speedway starts promoting the race in a positive manner," he said.

Wheeler apologized, but at the same time he expressed his disappointment in the drivers' reaction. "If Dale, Geoff, and Bill want an apology, I'll reluctantly give them one," he said. "But I would remind them that the very roots of stock car racing is embedded in conflict. What's happened to our drivers?

"Curtis Turner and Joe Weatherly would have laughed at this. Fun used to be part of racing. Today, who is smiling? I know these guys feel some pressure, but that is part of being a star. There are some people in our sport who would like to sanitize racing to the point where we have 40 drivers cut out of the same cookie mold, wearing Brooks Brothers suits and carrying attache cases in the pits. If that happens, I am going to trade my suit for an L.L. Bean outfit and go fishing."

Even with the 10-lap shootout, the Winston generated little excitement. The opening segments were the same ho-hum affairs as the previous year, and Terry Labonte turned the advertised 10-lap shootout into a cakewalk. Starting ninth in the final segment, Labonte blasted quickly to the front and easily led the closing nine laps.

The big story of The Winston was severe problems on the cars that used Goodyear tires. Ricky Rudd's car crashed into the wall after a blowout on the 49th lap. He suffered torn ligaments in his left knee. Earnhardt severely damaged his Chevrolet when he blew a tire and crashed into the wall at the end of the first 75-lap segment. Richard Petty blew a tire and crashed in the Winston Open, a preliminary event which preceded The Winston.

Alarmed by the tire problems, Goodyear officials initially announced the company would not supply tires for the Coca-Cola 600 the next Sunday. "Our Charlotte tires were competitive from a speed standpoint, but our tires caused three accidents and there could have been more," Leo Mehl, Goodyear's director of racing, explained. "Obviously, we can not use the same type of tire that we used for The Winston."

A day later, after a meeting involving NASCAR, Goodyear, and Hoosier officials, Mehl announced that Goodyear was being allowed to bring in its Daytona tire, which had a harder compound, for use in the 600. Although more durable, the tires were considerably slower than the Hoosiers.

Reluctantly, Childress was virtually forced to bolt the faster Hoosiers on Earnhardt's Chevrolet and old guard Dave Marcis was the only one among 40 drivers who used Goodyears to win a starting position. Marcis' speed was 167.385 miles per hour, good enough for only the 38th starting position. Davey Allison, on Hoosiers, won the pole with a speed of 173.594 miles per hour.

• • •

While The Winston failed to live up to Wheeler's pre-race hype, the Busch Grand National Winn-Dixie 300, held the Saturday before the Winston Cup 600-miler, revived old memories and some new hard feelings and accusations. Bodine and Earnhardt, were at it again.

An incident on the backstretch took Bodine out of the lead.

"Bodine came down and pinched me off. I bumped him and turned him around. That's racing, ain't it?" asked Earnhardt.

Bodine initially pretended that he didn't know what happened. "Oh, I don't know. Maybe there was some oil over there that caused us to get together," he mockingly suggested.

Later he became more explicit.

"There is a right way to pass, with a little dignity. It was just a bad move on Earnhardt's part."

Rick Hendrick, Bodine's car owner, was disappointed when NASCAR officials looked at a replay of the incident and said it could not be determined if Earnhardt had deliberately caused Bodine to spinout. "I guess I will have to accept that, for now. But to say I am disappointed is an understatement," Hendrick said.

Bodine dropped a lap down because of the incident, but later in the race he forced Earnhardt's car up high on the track to make a pass and get back into the lead lap. A few laps later, Bodine cut a tire and crashed out of the race. Earnhardt, who blew an engine while in the lead, also wasn't around at the end.

The next day, in the 600, NASCAR officials were not so forgiving when Bodine and Earnhardt went at each other again. The two cars banged together in the second turn. They popped together again and Bodine's car went into a spin and three other drivers, Cale Yarborough, Jim Sauter, and Derrike Cope, got caught in the wreck.

Officials immediately blamed Earnhardt for rough driving and held him on pit road for a five-lap penalty.

"There must be peace and tranquility in this sport, and it is going to happen one way or another," Bill France Jr. later said of the penalty. "We will do whatever it takes."

Hendrick, tired of seeing his expensive cars turned into scrap metal, said it was time for NASCAR to act. "This is getting awfully hard to accept. If NASCAR can't control it, they are going to have an all-out war on their hands, and I would hate to see that happen."

Bodine was in the garage for 69 laps while his Chevrolet was being repaired. "I guess NASCAR must have seen something today that they didn't see yesterday," he said. "Down the backstretch, Earnhardt just turned right into me and put me in the wall."

Dale saw things differently.

"If anyone looks at the tapes, he will see that I did not try to wreck Bodine. I was just trying to race him, and he came down on me twice. I think something ought to be done about Bodine and Hendrick," he said angrily.

Looking for a solution to the discord, Bill France invited both drivers to a dinner in Daytona Beach to work out their differences. That meeting later was written into the script of the movie, Days of Thunder.

France told the drivers that each would be held responsible for any further trouble between them. If either driver spun the other out, both would be ordered off the track and held on pit road for several laps.

"We have got to stop this now, and we will," France declared.

Dale didn't have much to say about the meeting, other than noting that the veal was very good.

Bodine seemed to get more out of the meeting than a good meal.

"This thing between me and Dale has been going on for about three years," he said. "It is kind of silly that it took so long for us to sit down and talk it out. When you have problems and don't discuss them, they compound. That is what happened. I think Dale and I can race side-by-side without bumping each other."

Darrell Waltrip won the 600 for his first victory of the season. He finished only a few feet ahead of Rusty Wallace, who admitted, "I just wanted to get close enough to Waltrip on the last lap to get a piece of his bumper and turn him sideways so I could win."

In addition to the Earnhardt-Bodine incident, which came on the 59th lap, the race was marred by a total of 13 caution flags. Most of the incidents were caused by tire blowouts. Harry Gant and Neil Bonnett were hospitalized after separate crashes. Gant broke two bones in his left leg, while Bonnett was held overnight for observation. Buddy Baker also took a hard crash into the wall after a tire failure. Baker suffered head injuries that were not discovered until about two months later, when he underwent surgery.

Most of the tire problems at Charlotte were with Hoosiers, but Bob Newton explained that teams that had been using Goodyears hadn't properly adjusted their cars for his tires.

Bill Elliott, one of those who crashed on Hoosiers at Charlotte, credited the tires with his victory the next week at Dover.

Elliott, who began the race on Goodyears, didn't move to the front until he switched to Newton's Hoosiers. "I decided about halfway through the race that if I was going to win, I had to make the switch," he said.

Earnhardt, who stayed on Goodyears, finished 16th, five laps down.

Both Elliott and Wallace began to close ground on Earnhardt in the points race after declaring that they would use whichever tire seemed best for each race. "I am a Goodyear man, but our goal is to win the championship. We cannot afford to not reach that goal because we did not use the best tire available to us," Wallace said.

At the halfway point in the season, Wallace was on top of the points race, leading Earnhardt by 87 and Elliott by 97. It was the first time in three years that someone other than Earnhardt had been the leader at that point.

Wallace picked up the $150,000 bonus from R.J. Reynolds for leading at the halfway point. He also pocketed $100 on a bet he won with Earnhardt. "Dale bet me he would be the halfway leader," he said. "We made the bet at Dover, after he lost another $100 on a bet that he would finish higher than me in that race. I framed that $100 bill and put it on my wall at home."

Dale admitted that his team's loyalty to Goodyear probably cost him chances to win more races during the first half of the season, which would have put him in front in the points race. But he didn't question Childress's loyalty to Goodyear.

"We have had a little bad luck with tires during the first half of the season, but I am confident we can bear down and be more aggressive the rest of the way and win the championship," he said.

But tire problems, bad luck, and controversy continued to be the story for Dale during the final half of the season. His only victory came at Bristol.

Both Earnhardt and Childress blamed NASCAR for making a mistake that resulted in a multi-car crash and took them out of a shot at victory in the Oakwood Homes 500 at Charlotte in early October.

Davey Allison was leading Earnhardt when a caution flag came out because of Greg Sack's wreck in the fourth turn. Both Allison and Earnhardt sped into the pits for fuel and tires when they saw the caution flag. They returned to the track holding their lead positions, but NASCAR incorrectly ruled that they had pitted too soon and should be a lap down.

A few minutes later, officials realized their mistake. But instead of returning Earnhardt and Allison to the front, they were put near the end of the lead lap in slower traffic.

When Childress protested, a NASCAR official told him, "You have got 146 laps remaining in the race to make up for our mistake."

Actually, the team had to pay dearly for it much sooner.

On the restart, Allison bumped into Phil Parsons, who crashed into Marcis. then Earnhardt, and all three cars were heavily damaged. "NASCAR created that accident, because neither Dale nor I should have been racing back there," Allison said.

Earnhardt finished 17th and fell 183 points behind Elliott.

"NASCAR screwed us," Childress said, shaking his head with disgust. "That is a heckuva way to lose a championship."

A week later, at North Wilkesboro, Dale collected a new racing enemy as he and Ricky Rudd banged each other out of contention.

With 40 laps remaining, Rudd took the lead as the two collided in the third turn. Dale regained the lead when he spun Rudd in the second turn to bring out a caution flag.

NASCAR penalized both drivers by putting them at the end of the lead lap for the restart, which effectively took both out of contention. They tangled again with five laps remaining as Rudd forced Earnhardt into a wild spin, and again on the final lap when Earnhardt bumped under Rudd to take fifth place.

Both drivers accused each other of instigating the incidents, and Rusty Wallace thanked both for opening the way for him to win. "They were both faster than me," Wallace said.

Rudd blamed Earnhardt for "dirty driving," and added, "If he wants to play this game, he can forget the championship. I have nothing to lose, because I am not in contention for the title, and I am not going to take this crap from him."

Dale finished fifth and dropped 188 points behind Elliott. Not only did he fall farther behind in the points race, he also learned that he was losing his engine builder, Lou LaRosa, to Rudd's team, owned by Kenny Bernstein.

LaRosa, who had built the engines that powered Earnhardt to all of his Winston Cup titles, indicated that problems were developing on the close-knit Childress team. "We have lost the family atmosphere," he said. "The team has just gotten too big, more like a factory."

The pressures and frustrations of the long, difficult season also had an affect, LaRosa admitted. "With Earnhardt, you are expected to win every week, and being the 'Top Gun' isn't always fun. The thrill is gone. I guess, really, I am looking for a new challenge."

Childress and Earnhardt said LaRosa's decision to leave would not hinder the team. "We have other people who can build engines," Dale said. "This ain't no one-man team."

Said Childress, "We hate to see Lou go, because he has done a good job for us. But apparently he has got a really good deal, and we wish him the best of luck."

In 1987, Dale had gone to North Carolina Motor Speedway needing only to make a lap to clinch his second consecutive Winston Cup title. Now, a year later, he was left to watch the title showdown between Bill Elliott and Rusty Wallace.

Wallace, who dropped out of the Winston Cup lead after the Bristol race in late August, made a flat-out charge to beat Elliott down the stretch. He came from two laps down to record victories at both Charlotte and Rockingham and went into the final race of the season at Atlanta trailing Elliott by 79 points.

A self-described "hell-raiser from St. Louis," Wallace was so confident that he was even fantasizing about how he would win the title.

"Here is how it is going to be," he said. "It is the last lap, and Bill and I are racing through heavy traffic. I get spun around but still manage to cross the finish line backward, one foot in front of Elliott. The car flips on its roof and bursts into flames. My crew comes running out to the car, but no one can find me. Then, when the smoke clears, everyone sees me sitting on top of the car and I say, 'Boys, by my calculations, we have just won the championship by one point.' "

Meanwhile, Elliott was dreaming of a milder conclusion. All he wanted was a nice, safe drive and he would have his first Winston Cup title. And that is exactly what happened.

Elliott clinched the title by 24 points, stroking his way to an 11th-place finish while Wallace drove his heart out, leading 174 of the 328 laps and winning the race by three seconds over Davey Allison.

"I can't believe it. I did all of that and Bill just rode around and he gets the championship," said Wallace, who didn't hide his bitter disappointment. "I am a terrible loser, and that eats the crap out of me, that he could win the title by just sitting back there and easing along."

Elliott, who didn't lead a single lap and was never any higher than seventh, admitted he had taken the conservative route. "All I had to do to clinch the title was to be around at the finish, and I did what I had to do. I have won a lot of races in my career, but I had never won the championship and that is all I wanted to do when I came to the speedway this morning."

Elliott, however, understood Wallace's disappointment. He had experienced many of the same bitter frustrations in 1985, when he dominated the circuit with 11 victories but let the title slip from his grasp down the stretch.

"I really believe you have to lose one of these championships before you win one," Elliott said. "I lost the title in '85 and I think going through that helped me to win it this season. So I have been through what Rusty is going through now. He threw everything he had at me, and it wasn't enough."

Earnhardt, who led 49 laps, finished 14th after falling two laps behind late in the race.

"It was not the season we wanted, or expected," he said, "but I know a lot of drivers on the circuit would be satisfied with it. We were a little disappointed from the halfway mark on. The tire thing was a big disadvantage for me, and I will always believe that the five-lap penalty at Charlotte in May was unjust.

"But you have to overcome those things and do the best you can. No one ever gave up, and we are determined to come back next year and do better. Our goal is to be champions again."

Earnhardt, who had wanted to join Cale Yarborough as the only driver to win three consecutive championships, said 1989 would be the starting point for a new effort to accomplish that.

"Winning the championship is getting more difficult, because the competition is getting stronger," he said. "Look at Elliott. Look at Wallace. Then look at the rest. You can't say that Darrell Waltrip, Terry Labonte, Ricky Rudd, Ken Schrader, or Alan Kulwicki won't be in the championship hunt next year. But we know what it takes to win the championship and, believe me, we will be doing all we can to win it in 1989."

CELEBRATION: Dale Earnhardt hoists the trophy after winning the Goodwrench 500 at North Carolina Motor Speedway in 1987.

Jerry Haislip

Jerry Haislip

TOUCH AND GO: Earnhardt and Morgan Shepherd engage in some short-track banging during the 1986 season.

Jerry Haislip

A BANNER VICTORY; Earnhardt enjoys his first Southern 500 victory in 1987.

Jerry Haislip

IN FRONT; Earnhardt keeps the Wrangler Chevrolet in front of Darrell Waltrip in 1987 race.

THE JUNKYARD DOGS: Earnhardt's pit crew (l-r): Danny Myers, Kirk Shelmerdine, Will Lind, David Smith and Cecil Gordon.

THE CREW AT WORK; Earnhardt gets a quick four-tire change and a full tank of gas from the GM Goodwrench crew.

Jerry Haislip

HAPPY FANS: Earnhardt's fans show their support.

Jerry Haislip

READY TO GO: Earnhardt awaits the start of the race.

Jerry Haislip

VICTORY WAVE: After taking the checkered flag, Earnhardt gives a wave to the spectators.

Jerry Haislip

FRIENDLY FEUD: Mark Martin (bottom) and Earnhardt had a tight, clean battle for the 1990 Winston Cup title.

Jerry Haislip

ANOTHER TITLE: In 1990, Earnhardt won his fourth Winston Cup championship.

12

'Tim Richmond was a helluva racer'

During the first nine years of the 1980s, Dale Earnhardt and Darrell Waltrip rolled up victories and championships on the Winston Cup circuit with distinctively different styles. Waltrip, the master strategist, and Earnhardt, the intimidator, were entering the 1989 season determined to settle who could claim bragging rights as "driver of the decade."

The two rivals had won three championships each during the '80s, and each was expecting to make the final year of the decade his best yet by winning a first Daytona 500 and a fourth championship. But those were about the only similarities between the silk-and-polyester Waltrip and the denim-and-leather Earnhardt.

Waltrip, a college graduate, was credited with helping to change the good ol' boy image that stock car racing once had. A smooth operator on and off the speedways, Waltrip was as comfortable hosting a television talk show as he was behind the wheel of a race car.

Earnhardt, a high school dropout, was a throwback to the old days of the sport who had gotten his style by watching his daddy bang fenders with other pioneers of the sport during the rough-and-rowdy 1960s.

Not surprisingly, Waltrip's mouth and Earnhardt's foot created considerable controversy for each. Waltrip was stock car racing's most outspoken driver and earned the nickname "Jaws" because of it.

Earnhardt's aggressive style had involved him in feuds with many drivers, including Waltrip, with whom his most widely known incident had been the late-race wreck at Richmond in 1986.

Now the two appeared headed for another collision in the race for the 1989 Winston Cup championship, and even before arriving at Daytona to begin the new season they began firing verbal shots at each other.

Waltrip suggested that Earnhardt's career had peaked in 1987 when he won 11 races and his third championship.

"Waltrip peaked as a driver several years ago," Dale responded.

Both offered evidence to support their contentions. After scoring back-to-back titles, Earnhardt slipped to third place in the points and won only three races in 1988, the fewest for his team since 1984.

Meanwhile, Waltrip had not made a serious bid for the championship since leaving Junior Johnson's operation in 1986, and had won only three races in two years with his new team.

Richard Petty, the dominant driver in the 1960s and 1970s, liked Earnhardt's chances for winning a fourth championship to close out the decade.

"Dale is a better driver than he was two or three years ago," Petty explained. "Before, he was a diamond in the rough. Now, he is a polished stone. Darrell has got more of a conservative approach to what he does. Dale is more of a gambler. The way racing is nowadays, you have got to charge every lap and no one does that better than Earnhardt."

Rusty Wallace was determined to take the spotlight from both of the circuit's established superstars, and he had good reason to believe he should be the title favorite. He had come on strong at the end of the 1988 season, losing the title to Bill Elliott by only 24 points. There were other advantages, too, for Wallace, a Pontiac driver.

"I really think we can start the season as hot as we left off in 1988," he said. "Ford has a new model Thunderbird and the Chevrolet teams will be switching models, from the Monte Carlo SS to the all-new Lumina, in the middle of the season. Maybe we can get a good jump on all of those teams."

Waltrip pointed out that the Childress team had a new engine builder, Eddie Lanier, the replacement for Lou LaRosa. "If the new guy falls in there and everything goes well, and he can get some confidence that everything is going to be all right, then everything probably will be," Waltrip said.

"But if he goes in there and the first time he blows up an engine and Childress is looking at him, and Earnhardt is on his case, then there will be another engine man coming in there. That is when you have problems. If they can pick up the pieces and parts that were left there and continue to have durable engines, then everything is going to be fine. But it is hard to get all the pieces together and keep them together."

Waltrip said he always uses Daytona as a barometer for the season. "You don't have to win the Daytona 500, as Dale and I both have proved, to have a good season. But if you go there, change a lot of motors, flog and crash, it is hard to come out of there with much spirit. If you sail through there without any major problems, you feel like you have your act together and you are ready to go."

While all teams were pumped up for the new season and headed to Daytona with high expectations, most also were a little apprehensive about what was in store because of the tire situation. Goodyear had developed and tested a revolutionary new radial tire that it planned to debut in Daytona.

The radials were faster and supposedly more durable, and Goodyear was hoping that they would rid the circuit of Bob Newton's Hoosier tires, which had created the painful and costly tire war in 1988.

The fat, squatty radials also gave the race cars a different feel than did the old, standard bias-ply tires, and Newton, who did not have the facility to build radials, predicted that the tires wouldn't work on the fast, high-banked tracks.

Goodyear officials contended that they would work and that 25,000 miles of testing during the off-season had proved them superior to the bias-ply tires. Earnhardt, who tested the radials, said the new tires were so durable they might change race strategy.

"You might not have to pit as often for tires, especially during the late stages of a race, because the radials are not going to wear out as quickly as the others did," he said.

Although most drivers privately were saying they did not feel as comfortable on Goodyear's radials, only Neil Bonnett, Davey Allison, and Morgan Shepherd declared their intentions to use the bias-ply Hoosiers.

The radials did not get off to a good start, and neither did Earnhardt, when the Daytona track opened for the first day of practice. Dale badly damaged his car during an early afternoon practice session when a right front tire exploded and almost blew the hood, fender, and nose off the the car.

Dale was shaking his head as he looked at his damaged Chevrolet. "I swear I didn't hit anything, but it sure looks like I did," he said. "The front of the car is tore up pretty good, and both tie rods are bent."

He thought that he must have run over debris that cut the tire. "I felt a vibration and the car started to slow down right before the tire blew," he said. "I am just glad it happened on the straightway. If the tire had blown in the turns, it would have wiped the car out."

Later in the session, stunned Goodyear officials knew they

had a major problem when Bill Elliott's Thunderbird blew a tire and crashed into the fourth-turn wall. Elliott, the defending Winston Cup champion, suffered two broken bones in his left wrist.

"The tire just blew," Elliott said. "There was no warning, no signal. The thing just blew."

Bob Newton did not like seeing anyone get hurt, but he felt that his prediction that the radials were not suited for super-speedway racing had proved to be right. "No one believed me when I said that. Mine was a voice in the wilderness. But I think some people might have been a little premature in suggesting the radials were going to run me off this circuit," he said. "Radial tires were one of the best things ever to happen for street cars, but they were never built for the purpose of stock car racing. If what happened here doesn't kill the idea that radial tires can be successful in NASCAR, then someone needs to have his head examined."

Reluctantly, Goodyear Racing Director Leo Mehl decided to withdraw the radials from the Daytona 500. He insisted, however, that they would prove successful before the end of the season.

"We had radials on more than 100 cars in practice on Friday, and most of the drivers were pleased with them," Mehl said. "Many of them do not want us to withdraw the tires from this event. The reason we are doing so is because we can not be absolutely certain if there is a problem with the tires or not. It is a matter of taking a risk of hurting someone else or pulling the tires."

Goodyear representative Bill King claimed Newton was only "blowing smoke" when Newton said the radials would never work on the NASCAR circuit. "He would like for them to never work, but the radials are still the race tires of the future, and you will see them winning races before this season is over," King said.

Goodyear supplied a backup bias-ply tire for the Daytona

500, but Ken Schrader used Newton's Hoosiers to win the pole with a speed of 196.997 miles per hour. Earnhardt also was on Hoosiers for a fourth-fastest speed of 195.529 miles per hour.

Earnhardt had more bad luck with his Busch Grand National car, which he wrecked during a practice session. His car shot into the air on the front straightaway and rolled toward the grandstand fence before crashing back onto the track.

"I am all right, just a little sore and $35,000 poorer," Earnhardt said wryly, as he pointed to his demolished Chevrolet.

He admitted that he lost control of the car after failing to heed a flagstand signal to slow down because of an unsafe condition on the track.

"When you see that red flag, you had better get off the throttle, and I didn't," Dale said. "A veteran like me ought to know that, too. I just wanted to stay on the throttle for another 100 yards to complete a hot lap for a spark plug check. I guess someone had blown an engine and I must have gotten into the oil. I really don't know, but I can't blame anyone but myself."

Dale finished third in his 125-mile qualifying race when he made a late pit stop for fuel and both winner Terry Labonte and second-place Sterling Marlin went the distance on a single tank of gas.

Schrader won the other qualifier by leading all but 10 of the 50 laps, and most drivers were thinking he would be the one to beat in the 500. Dale disagreed.

"Schrader won the pole and he looked awfully strong in the qualifying race, but I still feel that I am the guy everyone is going to have to beat," he declared. "I can't wait for the race to begin because I know that I will be tough."

Both Schrader and Earnhardt were tough in the 500, but the man dancing and laughing in Victory Lane when the race ended was Darrell Waltrip, who finally had successfully ended his long quest to win the most prestigious event on the circuit.

Waltrip took control in the final laps by staying on the track when Schrader and Earnhardt pitted for fuel only 11 laps from the end. Using the draft and a slower speed to conserve his fuel, Waltrip completed the final 132.5 miles on a tank of gas. He said he realized he had won the race when he reached the third turn, about a mile from the finish line.

"I could have coasted the rest of the way, if I had to," he said.

When Waltrip slid out of his car in Victory Lane, he began screaming, "Thank God, thank God, I won the Daytona!"

Then he looked at the crowd around him. "Are you sure this is Daytona. Are you sure I won the Daytona 500? Don't lie to me, now."

Everyone assured Waltrip he had won, but in the garage area, away from the wild celebration going on in Victory Lane, not everyone was sure just how he had managed it.

"I felt sure Darrell was going to have to stop for gas," Dale said. "I would like to see his gas tank."

Richard Broome, the team manager for Schrader, said, "I never thought we would get beat by a car getting better fuel mileage. I never thought Waltrip could go all the way at the end without running out."

NASCAR officials determined that Waltrip's gas tank was the legal size, holding no more than 22 gallons, as prescribed by the rules. "He only had a little gas left in there," one inspector said. "It was so little that I would drink all of it for five dollars."

Earnhardt, who had come out of his final stop with the lead, finished third after Schrader passed him with five laps remaining. Now that Waltrip had learned what it took to win a Daytona 500, he had to wonder even more how much longer it would take for him to find the magic button to call up a championship.

Waltrip collected other victories at Atlanta, Martinsville, and Charlotte during the remainder of the first half of the 1989 season. But Earnhardt, with two victories and a steady stream of top-five finishes, held a 124-point lead over Rusty Wallace, a three-time winner, and a 157-point edge over Waltrip in the championship standings at the midway point.

Dale's first victory was in the First Union 400, where Goodyear finally made a successful debut of the radial tires. A few weeks later, Newton took out advertisements in several racing publications to announce that he was withdrawing his Hoosier tires from the NASCAR circuit.

Dale's second victory was a milestone as he posted the first win of his career at Dover Downs International Speedway, nicknamed "The Monster Mile." Driving a new Chevrolet Lumina, Dale led 454 of the 500 miles despite a skirmish with Schrader in a run for a bonus posted for the halfway leader.

Six laps from the halfway point, Schrader drove inside of Earnhardt and bumped him out of the lead. He held to collect the $10,000 bonus and then relinquished the lead back to Earnhardt.

"I wanted that 10 grand," Schrader said. "I got under Earnhardt and asked myself, 'What would Dale Earnhardt do in a situation like this?' Then, I just knocked hell out of him and went on."

Dale admitted that Schrader's roughness caught him by surprise. "I felt like punching him in the nose," he said. "I was giving Kenny plenty of room to make the pass. He got a little rough and I got out of the way. I didn't want to do something foolish and end up hitting the wall, so I just let him go. But I have got a memory like an elephant. I will mark that incident up and somewhere down the road I might slip and get into him."

For the most part, however, Dale built his lead in the point standings without controversy during the first part of the season. The man bending fenders and igniting tempers was Wallace. He created the loudest uproar in The Winston at Charlotte when he spun out Waltrip in the final 10-lap segment.

Waltrip had opened a quick lead at the beginning of the final segment but Wallace drove his car deeper and harder through the turns to close the advantage. Finally, as the two were about to complete the ninth lap, Wallace slipped under Waltrip just enough for the two cars to make contact. Waltrip's Chevrolet spun down through the grass and Wallace emerged with the lead and the victory, worth $240,000.

Waltrip was the angriest he had been since Earnhardt wrecked him out of the lead at Richmond in 1986 for a lot less money.

"Wallace just knocked the hell out of me," said Waltrip, who wound up seventh and won only $22,000. "I hope Wallace chokes on that money."

Waltrip remembered that a year earlier, when Wallace placed second to him in the Coca-Cola 600 at Charlotte, Wallace had commented afterward that he was just trying to get close enough to Waltrip in the final laps to spin him out.

"He got that chance today, and he lived up to what he said he would do," Waltrip said. "A lot of guys let greed overcome speed. It is an ugly way to win."

Suddenly stock car racing fans had discovered another villain to dislike and Wallace was flooded with boos when he arrived in Victory Lane. "I know Darrell is upset, but what happened was just hard racing," he said. "I would be upset, too, if I were in his place, but you have got to drive your guts out and do everything you can to win in a race like this. It is not a race for the faint-hearted."

Waltrip came back the next week to win the Coca-Cola 600. Wallace, who was again loudly booed in pre-race introductions, wasn't around at the finish as his Pontiac blew an engine during the final 100 laps.

"I don't like to use the word vengeance but this is one of the most satisfying victories I have ever had," Waltrip said.

• • •

During that summer, Tim Richmond, who had quietly settled his lawsuit against NASCAR before the season began, was the subject of tragically new rumors. Inside the huge race-car

222

transporters that lined the garage area at Talladega Superspeed-way in late July, the same questions were being asked time and again: "Is it true? What do you know?"

The usual reply was a shrug of the shoulders, a blank expression, or a sad shake of the head. At Pocono the week before, rumors had begun floating through the garage that Richmond was either dead or close to it. Most members of the racing fraternity had suspected for months that he was dying from AIDS, but no one could furnish any proof. Richmond had not been seen around the circuit since the drug-test controversy at Daytona in February, 1987.

Shortly before the Pocono race, a spokesperson for a West Palm Beach, Florida, hospital replied to inquiries by saying Richmond was in the hospital and in serious condition but the nature of the illness could not be disclosed at the request of Richmond and his family.

A week later, hospital officials refused to say if Richmond was still a patient. It was as if Richmond, one of the brightest stars on the NASCAR circuit, had fallen off the face of the earth. Former business associates and a few friends who had been in touch with him confirmed, however, that he was dying from AIDS.

Dale Earnhardt, once the closest friend Richmond had on the circuit, had not talked to him since Daytona in 1987. Dale said he would like to know how to contact Richmond to offer help or to just let him know that he cared.

"I met Tim when he first came into this sport," Dale said. "We got to be good friends. I invited him up to my place on Lake Norman, and he bought a place near me. We used to kick around a lot together. He was dating this girl from Ohio, and I went out with them a lot."

Earnhardt was silent for a few seconds before shaking his head and continuing. "I don't know what happened to Tim. When we were going around together, I never knew him to use drugs. We drank beer and some whisky, but I never knew him to do drugs. Maybe I was just naive, because I don't know anything about that funny stuff.

"Whether it was fame and fortune that got Tim screwed up, I don't know. I wish that I were still closer to him so I would know what happened."

Dale recalled that he had stood by Richmond during the controversy at Daytona. "I told him if there was anything I could do to help that he should tell me. He said everything was all right. I told him to just shoot straight with NASCAR and to come back racing. He said he was being straight."

He also said that he had no knowledge of Richmond's personal life in recent years. "I don't want to know. It is none of my business. Tim Richmond was a helluva racer. I enjoyed racing against him. As far as I am concerned, he never did anything wrong, and there was just no reason for him to drop out of the sport.

"He never conquered this sport, because you don't do that unless you win a championship. But, man-to-man, he was as nice to me as anyone could be. I just never had a big problem with him. It is just hard for me to believe that someone can go from where Tim once was to where he is now, wherever that may be. He screwed up somehow. I wish that it was different. I wish that I could talk to him, to see if there was anything I could do. I wish that he was still out here racing with us. I just hope and pray all the stuff that we are hearing is not true."

Two weeks later, on August 13, Tim Richmond died in Good Samaritan Hospital in West Palm Beach, Florida. He was 34. It was not until 10 days later that the family authorized his doctor to confirm that cause of death was AIDS, which he said had been contracted through heterosexual activity. He said Richmond could have carried the disease for several years and it was not detected until he checked into the Cleveland hospital in December, 1986.

"All of this makes me admire the man even more," said Buddy Barnes, a former mechanic for Richmond. "Tim Richmond was tough. He could have sat there with his disease and done nothing. But he came back in 1987, knowing he was dying, and he won two races. He wanted to prove to himself and the world that he could do it, even if he did have AIDS."

• • •

Both Darrell Waltrip and Dale Earnhardt arrived in Darlington for the Southern 500 in early September with special reasons for winning. Waltrip had become eligible for the $1 million bonus offered in the Winston Million Series by winning two of the three previous events, the Daytona 500 and the Coca-Cola 600, and he could collect the rich bonus by winning his first Southern 500. Waltrip also was losing ground in the points race with Earnhardt and Wallace, and a victory could refuel that bid, too.

In addition to wanting to strengthen his lead in the Winston Cup standings, Dale had a more personal reason for wanting to win. On the Saturday night before the race, his father, Ralph, was posthumously inducted into the National Motorsports Press Association Hall of Fame in Darlington, and Dale wanted to dedicate the victory to him.

He did just that after leading the final 63 laps and posting a record average speed of 135.462 miles per hour. That broke Cale Yarborough's former record of 134.833 miles per hour, which ironically, had stood since 1973, the same year that Ralph Earnhardt had suffered a fatal heart attack.

"It was worth more than a million dollars to me to have my daddy inducted into the Hall of Fame, and I hope someday that I can join him there," Dale said in Victory Lane.

"Going back to the motel after the induction ceremonies Saturday night, I kept thinking how great it would be if I could win this race. I didn't want to get my hopes up too much, but I felt really good about my chances. Everything that I have been able to accomplish in racing, the championships and the victories, I owe to my daddy. My only regret is that he is not here now to share what I have accomplished. I have always known what a great racer and father he was, and I was glad to see others give him the credit he deserved."

Waltrip, who lost his opportunity for the $1 million bonus by twice hitting the wall, finished the race 22nd, eight laps down. He said he let the pressure of the big money get to him.

"I lost a lap when I got the car in the wall the first time. Then, I tried too hard to make the lap up, and like a dummy I got into the wall again," he said.

Dale's third victory of the season left him with a 73-point lead over Wallace in the Winston Cup standings. Mark Martin, although winless on the circuit, slipped into third place, 133 points behind Earnhardt, while Waltrip faded to fourth, 224 points down.

In addition to being close in the Winston Cup standings, Earnhardt and Wallace, both flat-out racers, had developed a friendly, if not close, relationship.

When it became apparent during the summer that they could be in a late-season showdown for the championship, Dale suggested to Wallace that the two refrain from getting into a war of words in the media about who was going to triumph.

Because of that understanding, Dale was miffed when Wallace won at Richmond and declared confidently that he was going to win the championship. "There is no stopping me now," Wallace said.

Dale repeated his earlier victory at Dover a week later and fired his own verbal shots at Wallace, who struggled to finish seventh and fell 102 points behind with six races remaining.

"We did have a truce, but Rusty broke it last week," Dale said. "Well, he had better start getting ready to accept second place money in the championship race. We are going to have him in this same position at the end of the season."

Wallace saw the verbal sparring as nothing serious and voiced confidence the run for the title was not going to destroy their friendly, if competitive, relationship.

"We both want to win this title awful bad, but our friendship will survive, without a doubt," he said. "If we don't get close to each other on the track, we won't have a problem. I know that he's not going to back off for me, and I am damn sure not going to back off for him, friends or not. I mean, neither one of us is going to take any crap from the other."

Strangely, although Earnhardt and Wallace both were running at the front most of the season, they had not gotten into much tight racing together.

"It is funny," Wallace observed. "I have always managed to find myself on one end of the track and Dale on the other. I hope it stays like that the rest of the season. But as close as we are in the points, I can see some problems developing."

The next stop on the circuit, Martinsville, offered just the kind of track to lead to problems. Dale, who hadn't won a pole position in two years, got the front spot under freak circumstances.

During the early morning hours on pole day, Hurricane Hugo blew up from the coast to cut a vicious trail through the heart of the Carolinas. Several drivers and crewmen awoke to find their homes and property damaged by the storm and Dale was among those who assumed, incorrectly, that qualifying at Martinsville would be postponed.

Dale finally got word that it was on, but by then it was too late to get to the track on time. Richard Childress asked Jimmy Hensley, a Grand National driver who knew the tight Martinsville track as well as anyone, to qualify Dale's car.

Dale arrived just in time to see Hensley put the Lumina on pole position with a speed of 91.913 miles per hour.

Unfortunately, the car did not perform as well on race day, and with 50 laps remaining Dale was struggling to stay in the same lap with Wallace, the leader. Darrell Waltrip, running second, smiled brightly when he saw the two drivers begin banging fenders and drifting high toward the wall off the second turn.

Waltrip aimed his Chevrolet to the inside of both, and

hoped they would stay up high. "I knew it was going to be a heck of a pass or a heck of a mess," Waltrip later recalled. "Then it just seemed like a big wave opened up. I shot through and everything was fine."

Well, not everything was fine. A friendship had been severely bruised, and the Winston Cup championship contenders were about to take the gloves off.

Wallace, who finished fourth after Waltrip went on to win, claimed that Dale, who wound up ninth, had tried to wreck him on purpose. "He ain't going to win the championship that way," Wallace said angrily.

Waltrip said he was sitting back, waiting for the fireworks to start. "I knew Dale was desperate to keep Rusty behind him so he could stay in the lead lap, and I was very surprised to see Rusty trying to pass him on the outside. Someone would have to be a very trusting soul to try to pass Earnhardt on the outside in a situation like that."

Dale, whose points lead over Wallace slipped to 75, left the speedway quickly and without comment, leaving crew chief Kirk Shelmerdine to explain that a blistered tire had caused Earnhardt to lose a lap at the midway point.

"Considering everything, I guess we came out of it okay," Shelmerdine said. "I guess we should be happy, but we're not."

Wallace got over his anger quickly and was talking championship again when qualifying began at Charlotte. "We are in the stretch of races that compliments both my team and driving style," he said. "Last year, I won at Charlotte, North Wilkesboro, Rockingham, and Atlanta, and I think my team can handle that again."

Dale smiled slightly when someone told him of Wallace's boast. "I ain't no slouch on those tracks either," he reminded. "But Rusty ought to know that any of those tracks can reach out and bite you, no matter how good you think you are."

But it was Earnhardt who had to deal with misfortune.

With the All Pro 500 only 13 laps off the starting line, a

standing-room-only crowd of 140,000 fans watched in near-disbelief as Earnhardt steered his powerless Chevrolet to the garage because of a broken cam shaft.

Richard Childress could only shake his head at such rotten luck. "It is not anyone's fault. Apparently a piece of metal just snapped, and a cam shaft is something you can't fix at a race track. If there was anyway to get the car back in the race, we would," he said.

There wasn't much for Dale to say either. "You can't drive a car if it ain't running, and it don't run with a broken cam shaft," he said with a shrug. "Anybody can have trouble, but this was the wrong time for something like this to happen. Nobody beat us today. We just beat ourselves, I guess."

Wallace finished eighth behind winner Ken Schrader to make up a whopping 110-points on Earnhardt and move to the top of the championship standings for the first time during the season. He had a 35-point lead.

"I was sorry to see that happen to Dale," Wallace said with a straight face. "I would much rather beat him on the track than with him in the garage. It is going to be a dogfight right to the last race now."

Wallace's Blue Max team celebrated only briefly after the race and team manager Harold Elliott reminded everyone to stay calm, that there were still four races remaining. "I just hope that we didn't gain enough points to get ourselves in trouble," Elliott said. "I mean we can't relax just because we are on top. When we were behind and trying to catch up we were pulling out all the stops. We had to run hard and punish the car and hope everything worked out. We can't back off that now. If we start trying to be conservative, we will wind up losing the championship because of it."

Dale and the Childress crew were to learn that championships can be lost, too, by being too aggressive. The bitter lesson came in a last-lap wreck with Ricky Rudd at North Wilkesboro that spoiled a chance for Dale to reclaim the points lead.

Rudd, who had tangled with Earnhardt in the same race a year earlier, pulled inside of Earnhardt in a duel for the lead on the final lap. Moments later the two cars slammed together and spun in the first turn, opening the way for Geoff Bodine to snatch the victory.

Angry fans of both drivers hurled cans and other objects onto the track, and Earnhardt's crew had to be restrained as it made threatening gestures and remarks toward Rudd and his teammates. Both drivers accused the other of causing the collision, which NASCAR officials saw as only a racing accident.

Dale, who had dominated the race before his car began slowing in the final 10 laps, finished 10th and Rudd ninth. Had Earnhardt held on to first place, or even finished second, he would have taken the points lead from Wallace.

Instead, Wallace finished seventh and padded his lead to 37 points.

Dale had led 342 of the 400 laps and had no serious challenger until Rudd came on strong in the stretch. "NASCAR ought to fine Rudd and make him sit out the rest of the season," Dale said, bristling. "He just spun me and took us both out. It is just a pretty bad deal."

Rudd, who could afford to be more calm since he wasn't in the title race, accused Earnhardt of driving into him. "I had gotten under him cleanly. But I guess he didn't want to give up the lead. I think both of us came here to win today."

Bodine had a clear view of the incident, but wouldn't point a finger at either driver. "Ricky made a super move to get under Dale cleanly, and Dale tried to hold his ground. It is just tough to get two cars, going that fast, through the first turn at the same time."

Rudd said if the incident cost Earnhardt the championship, he could blame only himself. "I hate losing the race, but Dale had $1 million on the line in the Winston Cup championship race, and he may have thrown that out the window. It just amazes me that someone thinks he can run over people and push them out of the way to win races like he does. But sometimes it comes back to haunt you, and I guess this is one of them. He just likes to intimidate other drivers, but I am not going to move over for him, especially when we are racing for the victory on the last lap."

Dale had led the championship standings most of the season without getting into controversy, but now he couldn't seem to avoid it. And his title hopes were slipping away as it grew.

In the next race, at Rockingham, Dale came out the loser in a fender-banging duel with Wallace and found himself 109 points behind with only two races remaining. Meanwhile, Mark Martin drove to his first victory at the track and closed to within 19 points of Earnhardt.

Wallace, finishing second behind Martin, took the blame for the incident involving him and Earnhardt on the 428th lap. "I went into the third turn and the rear end of my car got out from underneath me and I spun up into Dale," he said. "It was nothing intentional on anyone's part. We both went down in the corner like two hard-heads and neither one of us backed off."

Dale's car took its most serious damage when struck by Sterling Marlin after Wallace had tapped it into a spin. Wallace was trying to stay in the lead lap, and Dale was trying to keep from going two laps down at the time of the incident.

Wallace had problems of his own in another collision two weeks later at Phoenix, but Earnhardt was not involved. Wallace appeared headed for a victory that would virtually clinch the title for him when he was bumped into a collision with the wall by Stan Barrett, who blamed the incident on brake failure.

"I couldn't believe it. Here I was about to win the race and clinch the title and the next second I was headed for the wall," Wallace said.

He wound up 16th, while Martin was third and Earnhardt sixth behind winner Bill Elliott. That left Wallace with a 78-point lead over Martin and a 79-point lead over Earnhardt to take into the season-ending race at Atlanta.

Wallace, who had bitterly criticized Elliott for stroking to the title in the final race the previous year, now had to decide his own strategy. He had learned at Martinsville and Rockingham that sparks could fly when he and Earnhardt got to racing too close. Would it be better to leave the hard driving to Earnhardt and Martin in the final race and, for once in his life, enjoy a nice, soft drive to the championship?

"That is exactly what he should do," advised Elliott. "I know Rusty gave me a lot of heat last year for not racing hard in the last race. Still, I did what I had to do to win the title, and that is what he should do, too. If you are running on the ragged edge and something around you happens, there isn't much you can do. But if you are pacing yourself, you might maneuver around something like that."

Wallace thanked Elliott for the suggestion, but said he did not know how to take a conservative approach to driving a race car. "That is just not my style," he said. "I don't know how to stroke. If I start laying off and get back in the field, I get myself back to where a lot of trouble happens. I would probably get in a wreck or something crazy would happen. Man, my idea of winning this championship is coming off the last turn sideways, smoke boiling off the tires, and just say, 'See, I told you I wasn't going to stroke.' "

One thing was certain. The only chance Dale had to win the title was to drive wide open for the full 328 laps and hope that Wallace had problems and Martin finished behind him.

That is what happened, too.

Only Wallace did not have enough problems.

While Earnhardt led 294 laps and won easily, Wallace struggled to finish 15th, three laps down, and won the championship by only 12 points. Martin, who blew an engine, wound up third in the standings, 122 points behind Wallace.

"I don't care how sloppy it looked, or that I barely held on to win it. I couldn't be happier," declared Wallace, who did a little dance on the hood of his car at the start-finish line.

Wallace lost one lap by pitting for fuel under a green flag. Another was lost when he felt a vibration and pitted to change a right front tire. He lost the third when a lug nut came loose on the left rear wheel and he had to make an extra pit stop.

"I drove my guts out and if anyone thinks I was stroking, he is only fooling himself," Wallace said. "I was having all of those problems and I kept thinking, 'Man, I can't believe all of this stuff is happening to me.' It was scary. Hair-raising."

Only 27 of the 42 cars were still running at the finish, and Dale said the dropouts probably cost him a chance to win the title. "If a few of them, especially those Fords, had stayed in the race and finished between me and Rusty, I would have won it," he said. "If I could have worked on them cars and got them back in the race, I would have done it."

Dale was aware that Wallace was having problems and was not among the leaders on the scoreboard, but he did not realize how close he had come to salvaging the championship until the end. "I told my team before the race that I would run as hard as I could and then we would look to see where we stood in the title race when everything was over," he said.

"I did all I could do, and just came up a little bit short. I stood on the gas all day long. I didn't give the car a bit of rest, and it was good enough to stay under me."

Indeed, more than 80,000 fans who had come to see if Earnhardt could take the title from Wallace witnessed one of racing's most spectacular performances. Dale began the race determine to lap the field in the first 100 miles, and he might have done it, if not for caution flags.

Dale and his black Chevrolet cruised the wide, sweeping turns of the raceway with the ease of a gull chasing the wind. When it was over, and he had done all he could, and still had come up 12 points short, Dale displayed a champion's class by quickly putting old feuds and new disappointments behind him.

The broken cam shaft at Charlotte, the wreck with Ricky Rudd at North Wilkesboro, and the collision with Wallace at

Rockingham had left Dale in a situation too difficult to overcome. If he had been more cautious at North Wilkesboro or
Rockingham, he still could have overcome the mechanical failure at Charlotte to win the title.

"I have made mistakes in my racing career and it seems like
I have paid for them dearly," he admitted. "But there is no use
crying over them now. The season is over. The only worry that
I have right now is getting to my airplane and flying over to
Alabama, where I will be out hunting deer when the sun comes
up tomorrow morning."

Meanwhile, Richard Childress and his crew got up Monday
morning and went straight to work on the 1990 season. "Everyone on our team knows he is a champion, so I don't have to
worry about team morale," Childress said. "We will be ready
when the green flag drops at Daytona in February. We have
already started getting ready.

"We ended this season in a great way, and we are going to
come out running wide open next year. We didn't win the title,
but knowing that we kicked them pretty good in the last race
and knowing what we've got to do next year is not a bad feeling."

Childress said anyone would be foolish to blame Dale's
aggressiveness for allowing the championship to get away from
him in the last five races.

"Dale Earnhardt did not lose this championship," Childress
said slowly and firmly. "When anything happens, it is a team
effort. If the motor breaks, if the car doesn't handle right, anything that happens is a team effort. By finishing second, the
whole team finished second. It wasn't one person or one race
that cost us the title."

Crew chief Kirk Shelmerdine agreed with Childress. "It
was pretty disappointing to lose the title by such a small margin. We have lost some races by inches, but we have never lost
a championship like that," he said.

"Coming that close does make it a little harder to take. But we have to feel good about the way we won the final race. Dale just drove his butt off. He always does that."

Finishing second wasn't what the Childress crew had wanted, but even it had its rewards, such as the $400,000 the team collected at the NASCAR banquet in New York. "We got a little bit of the pie, but next year I guarantee you we won't settle for anything less than the big piece," Shelmerdine vowed.

Dale was planning on drinking some of Wallace's champagne in New York, too.

"Rusty and I got into a few scrapes and we are probably going to be in them for the rest of our careers because we both race so aggressively," he said. "We are going to rub fenders and carry on, but we can sit down and talk and still be friends."

13

'I'll bet Richard Childress is throwing up'

When stock car racing began to be a multi-dimensional business, Richard Petty says, he started losing the grip he'd held for so many years as King of the Winston Cup circuit. As the sport grew, more demands were placed on Petty's time, and before he realized what was happening, he was seeing his race car only during races.

"Used to, when I was winning races and championships, I was totally dedicated to just racing," Petty says. "I am dedicated now, but I can't be totally dedicated because so much other stuff is going on. Used to, racing was number one and there wasn't no number two. Now, number one is pretty close to number two, and three is close to two, and so on. I used to not have the responsibility of the shop, of getting the money to race, of looking after the sponsor, or the responsibility of making the deals and making sure they were carried out. All I did was drive the race car and work on it. Then, all that time I had for the race car got gone."

Petty believes the time demands and private business activities that shorten a race driver's day are not much different than they are for other athletes. "Football players begin their careers 100 percent dedicated to football. Basketball and baseball players the same way," he says. "Over time they build themselves into being something and then they are making endorsements, they are making money from this and that, making personal appearances, and trying to start some private business up.

"The first thing they know, they still love the sport but the dedication is not there. Not because they didn't want it to be, but because they had so much other stuff to take up the 24 hours. You know what I mean?"

When Petty was at the top of his sport, winning 27 races in 1967 alone, he didn't do much but race and talk about racing. "Now I am in a situation where I spend three or four hours a week in the race car and the rest of it is gone. The way the structure of all sports is today, money is generated as much outside of a particular sport as it is inside. It is not all greed and trying to get richer either. Time is demanded of all successful athletes. Fans are lined up to take your picture and get your autograph. You have to do something for the sponsor and spend time with the media.

"I am not the only one like that. All of them get into the same thing. Earnhardt gets into it, and he probably handles it as good as anybody can. It is not that they set out to get it. It is just the way it is."

Like Petty, when Dale began his career all he wanted was to race. The race car was all he cared about, and it consumed his thoughts or deeds 24 hours a day. It wasn't that simple any more. Dale's time was in demand by many others. He had his own businesses, such as his Chevrolet dealership, and a business manager to book his numerous personal appearances.

What had not changed since the time Dale began his career was his racing. That remained his top priority. He was determined to keep it that way.

"It is hard to have time for business because of racing, and I am fortunate that my wife Teresa can do a lot of that," Dale explains. "I never try to take time away from racing for business. If I have to take it away, I take it from business, because business came from racing. At the time racing becomes second, and my racing is going to suffer, it will be time to quit.

"When business starts taking priority over racing, that is when you need to sit back and look at what is going on around you, and decide why you are there and where your money is coming from. Everything that Richard Petty has got, and that I have got, come from this racing. I don't see either one of us surviving without it."

As Petty noted, Earnhardt balances the pressures on his time as well as anyone, and he has seemed to adjust comfortably to his celebrity.

Even the disappointment of losing a close championship battle in 1989 didn't change the fact that Earnhardt's career was better than ever.

"The short hours and demands of my time get me down sometimes but I am enjoying this part of my career and life a lot," he said. "I still enjoy about 99 percent of my racing as much as ever. I have won races. I have won championships, you know, and I don't have to go out and talk and boast, like one or two of them do. I didn't do that when I won my first championship either. Man, I was green as a gourd back then. I didn't realize what was going on around me when I got out of that race car at the end of the 1980 season and was the Winston Cup champion. I wasn't out there jumping up and down and hollering about winning the thing.

"Then, in 1981, I was too busy trying to sort out the new cars and later on that year Osterlund sold the team. I didn't have time to bitch about nothing. I was too worried about where my butt was going to land.

"I think you are never too confident about your ride or your position in racing. So many guys out there now are not really sure if they have rides from year to year, or what they would do if something happened to the ride they have now. I am sure. I am confident if something happens to this ride, I could get a ride somewhere else.

"That does not scare me anymore. It used to scare me, up to about 1985 or 1986. It worried me that if something happened, I didn't know if I could get another good ride. Now, I feel there would be someone wanting me. That is what I am saying."

Dale certainly had reason to feel secure in his job. And he never felt more confident about his chances for winning the Daytona 500, when he arrived at the speedway in February to begin the 1990 season, and a new decade on the Winston Cup circuit. He qualified his No. 3 Lumina third fastest in time trials, and he charged from the back of the field after a final pit stop to win his 125-mile qualifying race.

Michael Waltrip summed up the feelings of other drivers by saying, "Earnhardt has got to be the favorite to win this race. He has won every practice session we have had."

During a meeting with the reporters a couple of days before the 500, Dale was feeling good about the way Childress, Shelmerdine, and the other crewmen had the car running. But he knew from experience that he couldn't afford to be overly confident.

"I feel real confident because Richard and the rest of the guys have given me a great car, and it makes me feel good that the other drivers think I have the best car," Dale said. "But I have been this confident before, like in 1986, when I run out of gas and Geoff Bodine won the race. I had won the Busch Clash and a qualifying race, and then I lost the Daytona 500 because of gas mileage. But, like I say, the whole team is confident. We have always run good in this race and we want to prove that we can win it. I believe it is just a matter of time before we do it."

Asked if he had gotten over his disappointment about losing the championship by only 12 points to Wallace, Earnhardt shook his head.

"Not at all," he replied. "You know, we went to Atlanta for the final race last year sort of thinking about all the bad luck we'd had and I drove that race trying to make up for every bad race and every mistake that I had made during the season, which included dropping my guard on some people I thought I could race with. I just drove with a mission, to go win and try to make up for everything. I came close to making it up and winning the championship, and then we lost it by only a few points.

"That only made me madder about the mistakes I made and the other things that happened during the year. So, nah, I ain't got over it. It is going to take a little more time than just the winter to get over losing the championship."

Dale grew more confident of winning his first Daytona 500 when he drove to victory in the Grand National race on Saturday. It was the third time he had won that race, his eighth victory at the Daytona track, although none had come in official Winston Cup events.

"Winning the Grand National race is a good omen. I will see you all tomorrow, after the Daytona 500, same time and same place," Dale told reporters. "Victory Lane."

Another disappointment, even more devastating than the close championship defeat, was waiting the next day, however.

Dale dominated the 500 from the start, and his Chevrolet was running so strong with 75 miles remaining that Harold Elliott, team manager for Rusty Wallace, predicted the only way Earnhardt could lose was for someone to shoot out his tires.

Actually, there was another way and Dale found it on the backstretch of the last lap. Only a half-lap short of what should have been one of the greatest runaway victories in the race's history, Dale encountered one of the race's most heart-breaking defeats.

His powerful Chevrolet ran over part of a bell housing that had dropped off Rick Wilson's car a lap earlier. The debris cut a tire. Suddenly, Dale was wrestling the steering wheel, keeping the car from crashing into the wall in the third turn, and a stunned Derrike Cope drove under him to claim the victory.

Somehow, Dale regained control and steered his stricken car at speed under the checkered flag to finish fifth.

"Say this about Dale Earnhardt," Richard Childress said later. "He knew the tire had blown before he got to the third turn, and he has not backed off yet. He was still trying to beat them."

Ironically, Dale had been regarded as such a heavy favorite that in his race-day column Daytona sports writer Godwin Kelly wrote, "Top Gun (Earnhardt) could probably win on three wheels."

But even the best driver – and many were saying Dale was that – couldn't roll to victory on a flat tire. So for the longest time after the race was over, Dale sat in his black Chevy, alone with his grief, before finally emerging to face reporters.

Then he was told he would have to wait a few moments because CBS was interviewing the winner, Cope, in Victory Lane.

"To hell with Derrike," Dale said in a near growl. "He didn't win the son-of-a-bitch. I gave it to him."

The television crew finally arrived, but Earnhardt was asked to stand by for another moment.

"To hell with CBS, too," Dale said softly.

Yet he wasn't speaking in anger, and he had no ill feelings for Cope, who simply had the good fortune to make the best of Dale's bad fortune.

When CBS finally was ready, and David Hobbs held a microphone in his face, Dale was composed. He even tried to force a faint smile when asked to explain what had happened.

"Well, David, I run over some debris and cut a right rear tire only a quarter-of-a-lap away from victory. There isn't much you can do about something like that."

To other reporters, Dale went on to explain, "The car was running real good and I was just sitting there, hoping to get to the finish line, and I didn't make it. You know, you got to get the checkered flag to win this one, and it has eluded me every year so far. I felt good today, and then I ran over something on that last lap. I heard it hit the bottom of the car and then – bam! – the tire went out. I knew the tire blew out and I knew that I wasn't going to the bottom of the race track, so I just drove it high, trying to stay out of the others' way and keep the car straight. I wanted to come back to the line with something, and I did."

Dale took a rag and tried the wipe the grime, sweat, and disappointment from his face.

"I was sitting there, and no one could get by me. Derrike wins the race, but I beat them all day. He didn't outrun me. He just lucked into it."

He shook his head and rubbed his eyes, as though trying to awaken from a nightmare.

"Damn! I was so close," he said. "You know, the crew, the car, myself, we did all we could do. I'll bet Richard Childress is throwing up. We tested good and the car did what we wanted all day. Everyone knows what car was dominant, and they know the car that was here to beat."

Was it his biggest disappointment in racing? someone asked.

"Well, it was today," Dale replied with a sad laugh. "I might think about it awhile and come up with a different one. Maybe Osterlund selling the team in 1981. But, I tell you, this was the biggest buildup and the biggest letdown that I have ever had in racing.

"There ain't nothing you can do about it either. I mean, you can't kick the car, cry and pout, lay down and squall and bawl. Just got to take it and go on. We have got to go to Richmond this coming week and be just as strong up there. We just run a little bit short of luck today, by about a quarter-lap or so."

Turning to walk away, Earnhardt concluded, "Damn, I still can't believe that happened. That is about all I have to say."

If losing the 1989 championship by only 12 points would take longer than a winter to get over, there was no telling how long it was going to take to get over this disappointment.

Childress, who was watching the final lap on a portable TV in the pit, saw his driver's car bobble as the tire exploded, and he heard the chilling scream of shock from the huge crowd.

"I will wake up in my sleep night after night seeing that black number three car going toward the wall in the third turn," Childress said afterward. "It was like a bad dream. There is no way in the world to describe how this makes you feel. We have lost races at the finish line before, but this is the worst possible way to lose one. We had them all covered today."

The Childress team had not become the best on the Winston Cup circuit by sitting around and licking their wounds. There was nothing they could do now about the cut tire and crushing defeat in Daytona, but there was much to be done about the remaining 28 races and the Winston Cup championship.

"Everyone else had better look out now, because we are pissed off and more determined than ever," crew chief Shelmerdine warned.

• • •

Darrell Waltrip says the Winston Cup season is divided into two parts, and at the end of the year people ask only two questions: Who won the Daytona 500? What happened the rest of the season?

And who won the Daytona 500 generally has no bearing on what happened the rest of the season, as witnessed by the fact that no one had won both the Daytona 500 and the Winston Cup championship in the same season since Richard Petty in 1979.

No one thought Derrike Cope was up to the task in 1990, either. The favorites included both Earnhardt and Waltrip, as well as defending champion Wallace and Mark Martin, who had come on strong during the 1989 stretch.

Some informed observers believed Wallace would not be a

factor in the title run because he announced before the beginning of the season that it would be his final run with Raymond Beadle's Blue Max team, which already was in serious financial difficulties. Wallace was faced with putting together a new team and meeting the demands of a new sponsor, Miller Beer, while crewmen on his team had to make their own plans for the future.

Even so, Wallace, who swept both Richmond races en route to the title in 1989, confidently predicted he would overcome the distractions and disruptions to win his second straight title. "I won the championship last year by leading as many laps as I could and driving every lap as hard as I could," he said. "That was the same way Dale Earnhardt drove when he won his titles, and I don't think anyone can win the championship without doing that."

Waltrip thought otherwise. He predicted a season-long battle by one group of drivers, such as the aggressive Earnhardt and Wallace, and another group with more conservative styles, such as himself and Mark Martin.

"Boys, it is the wild versus the mild," said Waltrip, who also would decide to leave Hendrick at the end of the 1990 season to form his own team.

"I am not willing to take some of the chances that other guys do. My strategy is not to tear up cars or to get into controversial situations. I don't like to race that way, and I think I can win the title without doing it. I just don't believe in leading at any cost. I would just as soon win a race by leading only the last three feet. That is fun, too."

The championship race would come down to a pair of drivers with sharply contrasting racing styles, as Waltrip predicted. But neither Waltrip, who broke his leg during a crash in practice at Daytona in July, nor Wallace would be among the survivors when the stretch run began on Labor Day weekend at Darlington.

Anyone looking closely could have picked out the lead

players in the new title derby from the results of the Richmond race the week after the Daytona 500.

Earnhardt came back from wrecking his car in final practice on Saturday to finish second to Mark Martin, whose second career tour victory was tarnished by a controversial decision by NASCAR following post-race inspections.

Winston Cup Director Dick Beaty announced that an illegal carburetor spacer was discovered on the Jack Roush Ford that Martin drove across the finish line three seconds ahead of Earnhardt's Chevrolet. Martin was fined a record $40,000 and penalized 46 points.

It was the loss of points that bothered Roush team manager Steve Hmiel the most. "If this championship race is as close as last year's, and we are involved in it, this thing could wind up costing us $1 million," he said. "I can not believe we are being penalized so much for a simple mistake that provided us with no advantage. It was just a misinterpretation of the rules. We assumed if you could weld a piece on, as the rules allow, that it made no difference if you bolted the piece on. It was an unintentional mistake on our part, and we are being asked to pay a big price."

The two-inch spacer, which holds the carburetor off the manifold, had been extended by a bolted half-inch piece of metal, which would have been legal had it been welded.

Beaty did not know if the illegal spacer provided Martin any advantage, and other engine builders agreed with Hmiel that the alleged infraction would not have helped Martin in any meaningful way.

Martin and the Roush crew did not get any sympathy from Childress's team, which was suspected of informing NASCAR inspectors about the illegal part.

"If it wasn't going to help them any, why did they go to the trouble of doing it?" Kirk Shelmerdine asked. It was a good question that had no good answer.

Dale rolled to his first victory of the season by winning in

Atlanta, and followed that with another victory at Darlington. The back-to-back triumphs provided him with an early-season, 78-point lead over veteran Morgan Shepherd, who was off to his best start in Bud Moore's Ford.

But Dale wasn't in any mood to celebrate the Darlington victory after learning that his best friend on the circuit, Neil Bonnett, had suffered a complete memory loss from injuries in a multi-car crash. For several days, Bonnett didn't even recognize his wife and children. He later recovered most of his memory but doctors advised him not to return to driving a race car.

The man catching the heat for the Darlington wreck was Ernie Irvan, a newcomer on the circuit. He had replaced Phil Parsons as driver of the Morgan-McClure Oldsmobile for the Atlanta race and responded with a most-impressive third-place finish.

Benny Parsons warned Irvan not to get too pumped up at the tricky Darlington track, but Irvan, whose nickname was "Swervin' Irvan" was still trying to race the leaders hard despite early problems that put him 10 laps down.

He was trying to make up one of those laps when he and race leader Ken Schrader banged together to begin the string of wrecks that included Bonnett.

Irvan's aggressive driving reminded many of the way Dale had charged onto the circuit 11 years earlier, and there were other similarities between the two. Although a California native, Irvan had landed in Concord, N.C., only a couple of miles from Kannapolis, Dale's hometown, after deciding to seek a career in Winston Cup racing.

Irvan raced on many of the same minor league short tracks that Dale had raced on in his younger days and people were always telling Irvan that his pedal-to-the-metal style of driving reminded them of Earnhardt when he was at that stage.

"Being compared to Dale is the highest compliment there is, but I did not pattern my style after him," Irvan said. "I never saw Dale race except on the Winston Cup circuit. I have always been aggressive. It gets you into trouble sometimes, but it wins you a lot of races, too. I am sure that I am going to continue being aggressive but in a couple of more years I should have more finesse, too. That is the way Dale is now."

Some people mistakenly believed Earnhardt had helped Irvan to get a start on the Winston Cup circuit since he had sponsored one of Irvan's cars for a couple of races.

Dale didn't like talking about Irvan because of what happened at Darlington and pointed out he really was helping Mark Reno, who owned the car that Irvan drove early in his Winston Cup career.

"I do sort of hold Ernie responsible because Neil is out of racing, although I probably shouldn't think like that," Dale said a few weeks later. "That is part of racing, but Ernie was in a position that he should not have done what he did. Here was a guy 10 laps down racing the leaders. It could have been worse than it was, you know. I was happy to see Ernie get a good opportunity in the Morgan-McClure car this year. Then he goes to Darlington, gets in that deal and turns me sour toward him.

"Running competitively doesn't make him King Richard. He's got an opportunity to go a long ways if he just uses his head and keeps his nose clean and doesn't put too much pressure on himself to get that first Winston Cup victory. You can drive your ass off, and everything is great. But you have to realize that you are doing it with 40 other guys and you are going to do it 30 times a year, year after year. Ernie just needs to calm down a little bit. He will be all right if he does that."

Tony Glover, the respected crew chief for Irvan's team, was delighted to finally have a driver with the talent to take a car to the front. "When you are racing people like Earnhardt and Wallace, I don't see how you can be too aggressive," he said.

For his part, Irvan seemed genuinely amused that people were saying he was too aggressive and needed to calm down.

"I watched Earnhardt run right over Bill Elliott's door at Charlotte, but is anyone now saying he is too aggressive?"

Irvan asked. "I think being aggressive has got me where I am. Some guy down the street complains that I am too aggressive. Well, that is his opinion, but I have raced this way all my life. I have got a fast race car and my team owner wants me running at the front of the field. My sponsor likes that, and Ernie Irvan likes that, too.

"Dick Beaty told me the other day that five years ago Dale Earnhardt was the guy everyone blamed stuff on, and right now I am the scapegoat. But I would much rather hear people saying I am too aggressive than that I am too easy."

Earnhardt and Irvan had their first showdown on the track at Michigan International Speedway. Irvan seemed to have the faster car, but Earnhardt used his skill, daring, and experience to come out with the victory.

Later in the season, Irvan won the first Winston Cup race for both him and his team at Bristol, just a hill or two over from the team's home base in Abington, Va.

• • •

Charlotte Motor Speedway was one of Dale's best tracks in his early days of Winston Cup racing and it played an important role in launching his career. His National 500 victory in 1980 helped nail down his first championship, and he swept both major races at the track in 1986 en route to his second title.

But in recent years, Dale was having problems at his "hometown track," as he liked to think of it. The broken cam shaft in the October race in 1989 proved fatal to his championship expectations, and more problems were awaiting him at Charlotte in his championship bid in 1990.

Dale seemed back on the good side of the track when he won pole position and led from green to checkers to become the first two-time winner of The Winston All-star race in May.

For the first time the event was divided into only two segments, one for 50 laps and one for 20 laps. Drivers liked the change, saying it reduced the enormous amount of pressure they felt in the old format.

Dale finished the final segment less than a half-second ahead of Ken Schrader, who laughingly told Earnhardt in Victory Lane, "If I had caught you, I would have knocked you out of the lead."

"Don't forget, I had a steering wheel on my car, too," Dale reminded him with a grin.

The strong performance by the GM Goodwrench car in The Winston established Earnhardt as a solid favorite for the Coca-Cola 600. Since he had won the Winston 500 at Talladega, in May, Dale also could remain in contention for the $1 million bonus in the Winston Million Series by winning the 600.

Dale was hoping his strong victory in The Winston was an omen that his stretch of bad luck at Charlotte was over. But the track proved to be up to old tricks.

Dale blew a tire and pounded the wall on the 102nd lap of the 600, just beyond the quarter-way mark. The car was badly damaged, but the crew made extensive repairs to get Earnhardt back onto the track to salvage what Winston Cup points he could.

Despite losing 103 laps in the pits, Dale finished 30th and retained a 21-point lead over Shepherd in the standings. But it was a hard and muscle-pounding day, and it took a couple of days for him to get over it.

"I was running pretty good in that ol' wreck," Dale said the next weekend at Dover, Del.

"I never got lapped again after I went back onto the track, but, let me tell you, it was a chore driving that thing. It was like arm-wrestling all day with someone. I didn't have a left front spring on the the car and it was going bam! bam! bam! all down the straightaways, and the safety belts were just digging into my gut. I told Kirk over the radio that my daddy had built me a wagon when I was 10 years old out of a front wishbone from a '37 Ford that rode better than that beat-up race car did.

"About two o'clock Sunday night I got sick as hell. Started throwing up and every thing. I was sick for about a day and I was drinking stomach medicine and stuff, tying to get straightened out. I had to shoot a McDonald's commercial on Tuesday, and about Tuesday night I began feeling halfway decent, although my gut is still sore. But, come November and they start adding up them championship points, we might be awfully glad we got that car back out there and finished the race."

Encountering a miserable stroke of bad luck for the second straight week in the Budweiser 500 at Dover Downs International Speedway, Dale and his crew again showed their determination to do whatever was necessary to win the championship.

Early in the race, a cam shaft broke in his engine – the same problem that had resulted in a last-place, title-costing finish in the October race at Charlotte the year before.

This time, though, Dale coasted into the garage, grabbed a handful of wrenches and helped the crew to remove the engine and replace the broken part. It was the first time in NASCAR history that such a repair had been made at a race track.

Shortly after the halfway mark in the race, Dale jumped back into the car, flipped the ignition switch, and smiled when he heard the engine thunder back to life. He shook his fist out the window and shouted, "Let's go racing!"

He received a loud cheer when he drove back onto the track. He finished 31st after the engine gave out for keeps later in the race.

"We had trouble, but we still didn't give up, did we?" Dale asked afterward. "We gained 15 points by going back out there, and I lost the title last year by only 12. So, yeah, you have to say it was worth all that effort."

• • •

A couple of weeks before the Winston Cup teams headed back to Daytona in early July, the long-awaited movie "Days of Thunder," starring Tom Cruise, was premiered in Charlotte. The film featured real racing footage from several Winston Cup races and supposedly would be the first high-dollar, serious effort by Hollywood to capture the excitement and drama of NASCAR racing.

NASCAR suggested that drivers give the movie good reviews since the sanctioning body thought it would attract more fans and sponsors to the sport. Team owner Rick Hendrick, who had invested time, money, and cars in the movie, also urged his drivers, Ricky Rudd, Darrell Waltrip, Kenny Schrader, and Greg Sacks, to say nothing but good things about it.

Overall, the movie was received kindly by the racing fraternity, but Dale had no plans to see it or to beat the publicity drum for it. One of the thinly-veiled characters in the film supposedly was based on him. "My son said he went to see it twice, and walked out in the middle both times," Dale said.

Dale and other drivers objected to the movie showing race cars being built in a dirt-floor shop instead of the ultra-modern, multi-million-dollar garages that house the major teams. They also didn't like all the banging and crashing in the movie.

"If we beat and banged each other like that at Daytona and the other big tracks, we'd kill half the field," Geoff Bodine said. "The movie is just not very realistic."

But when the Pepsi 400 got rolling on a hot morning, fans watching on television might have mistaken the real race for the movie. Greg Sacks, a stand-in driver and technical adviser for the movie, started on pole position in a Hendrick car.

"We are going to see if we can stir up a little thunder of our own," he had said before the race.

He did, too, as he helped to create a massive wreck that looked to be straight from the movie. Sacks was caught in the middle, between Richard Petty, down low, and Derrike Cope, up high, and the trio beat and banged a couple of times as they sped through the third and fourth turns. Cope and Sacks made contact on the frontstretch and Sacks's Chevrolet slapped the rear of Petty's Pontiac. All three cars went spinning in front of the rest of the field.

When the smoke cleared, 22 cars had been wrecked. "Three idiots wrecked us all," said Bodine, who got caught in the crashes. "Some of those drivers must have seen the movie and thought they were in it."

Dale was at the front when the sheetmetal began popping and was not involved. He went on to an easy victory, beating Alan Kulwicki by almost two seconds for his first Winston Cup victory at Daytona.

"This isn't anything like winning the Daytona 500, but it is a race that I had never won before, and it feels awfully good," he told a cheering crowd as he celebrated in Victory Lane.

• • •

After winning at Talladega in late July, Dale went to Darlington a month later in a tight championship battle with Martin. A victory in the Southern 500 would give him the $100,000 consolation bonus for winning two of the four races in the Winston Million Series.

"If it had not been for cutting that tire on the last lap, we would be running for $1 million," crewman Will Lind reminded. "We have that cut tire mounted on the wall back at our garage. It is going to be worth $1 million if we do win this race, or that is how much it will have cost us. Maybe if we win the race, we'll set that tire on fire and dance around it when we get back home."

As he had at Talladega, Dale gave another repeat performance to win the Southern 500 for a sweep of the two Darlington races.

Darlington was still a difficult track, Dale noted, offering a dented fender as evidence after a slight encounter with the wall. "You saw the old gal slap me when I tried to get a little fresh with her," he said with a grin. "She didn't knock me to my knees, just kind of slapped my wrist and make me respect her. I tell you, she's still plenty tough."

Dale had proved his toughness, too, as he man-handled his Chevrolet, which had developed a vibration, down the stretch to prevent Ernie Irvan from making a challenge. The vibration became so bad that both of his hands were numb when he steered the car to Victory Lane, where he received the $100,000 consolation bonus.

"Coming so close to that $1 million just makes that nightmare at Daytona even bigger," he said. "But we know we should have won it, and we know we'll have another chance to collect the whole bonus next year."

The Southern 500 victory brought Dale to within 26 points of Winston Cup championship leader Mark Martin, an Arkansas native, who had been on top of the standings since early June.

The week after Darlington, Dale closed the gap to 16 points at Richmond by winning the Miller 400 in a head-to-head confrontation with Martin, whose Ford crossed the finish line only one second behind him.

Martin was second and Earnhardt third behind winner Bill Elliott at Dover, and they switched finishing positions behind winner Geoff Bodine the next week at Martinsville. Martin, whose polite and quiet mannerisms contrast with his fierce competitiveness behind the steering wheel, was becoming a more stubborn title opponent than expected.

If no one had taken Martin's quest for the Winston Cup title seriously, it became a different story at North Wilkesboro, where Earnhardt's title hopes the previous year had taken a fatal jolt in the last-lap collision with Ricky Rudd.

This time, there was no controversy. Just a shocking finish and a realization in the racing fraternity that Mark Martin and Dale Earnhardt were going to take the title fight all the way to the wire.

About halfway through the race, Dale was riding out front without a serious challenger. Martin, after repeated pit stops during a caution period for a chassis adjustment, was in 12th place with a wall of traffic separating him from Earnhardt.

Martin's Ford responded well to the chassis work, however,

and as the race entered the final 100 laps Martin had sliced through the field to move into second place, trailing Earnhardt by seven seconds.

Following a final round of pit stops, Martin drove past Earnhardt and into the lead with 38 laps remaining. The move was so clean and unexpected that Martin's car owner, Jack Roush, was amazed to see his driver in front as the cars sped down the frontstretch.

Martin won by almost four seconds and continued to lead Earnhardt by 16 points in the standings with only races at Charlotte, Rockingham, Phoenix, and Atlanta remaining.

The championship race was as tight as anyone could remember, and no one could recall a more sportsmanlike run for it.

Amazingly, Dale had not been party to a single squabble in the heated battle with Martin. Although he tried to goad Martin into running stronger, that strategy didn't work. Martin and his team seemed to know their limits, and were following a well-developed plan that they thought would carry them to the championship.

"Instead of trying to show we are the biggest men on earth by trying to bump and grind, like at Darlington when we didn't have a very good car, we try to race smart," Martin said. "I didn't try to race side-by-side with anyone at Darlington because I was afraid I would wreck. And we did awesome. We finished sixth with a 20th place car. We were smart, and that is why we have kept the points lead."

Meanwhile, owner Jack Roush thought he saw a weakness on the Earnhardt team at North Wilkesboro, and again at Charlotte, where Dale was not running very strong in practice.

"You don't see the Childress team working on the car very much, even when it is not going good," Roush observed. "Their mechanics seem to stand around, not doing anything to the car unless Earnhardt tells them what to do. It is as if they are willing to let Earnhardt, by himself, beat our entire team."

Dale responded by saying that Roush was trying to drive for Martin the pits, telling his driver everything to do on the track. "Jack ought to take the leash off Mark and let him run his own race," Dale said. "Every time Mark and I get close on the track, Jack tells him to back off."

While their statements were strong, Roush and Earnhardt each had immense respect for each other, as was showed by an incident at North Wilkesboro, where Earnhardt's and Martin's cars were parked side-by-side in the garage. Dale recommended that Roush use a different set of springs on his car. "I don't want you messing up," Dale told him. "I want us to stay close in this championship race."

Did Roush take Dale's advice?

"Actually, we put on the springs that he suggested and, yes, the car did run a little better with them," he later said with a smile.

• • •

Earnhardt never had a full opportunity to show Roush and others how strong his Chevrolet might have been at Charlotte, as the speedway's jinx clobbered him and his title hopes once again, this time on pit road.

Less than a third of the way into the race, Dale was taking advantage of a caution period to get new tires when Ernie Irvan and Alan Kulwicki crashed while racing down pit road. Crewman Will Lind had just changed Dale's right rear tire and was moving around to the left side when Irvan's car spun wildly into the rear of the GM Goodwrench Chevrolet. "If that had happened five seconds earlier, I would be dead," Lind said after the crash.

As it was, the only fatality seemed to be Dale's championship hopes. Not realizing how badly damaged his car was, Dale went back onto the track only to hit the fourth-turn wall on the restart and bring out another caution flag. He sped out of a pit stop with lug nuts loose on both left side wheels but didn't get far. Both wheels spun off at the end of pit road.

"The car wasn't handling right after Irvan hit it, and it got out from under me and spun around and hit the wall," Dale said later. "Then we had that miscommunication in the pits. I thought we were going to change two tires and the crew was getting ready to change four. It was just one those deals, circumstances you can't do anything about."

Dale rode out his problems to end up 25th, his worst finish since mid-June, behind winner Davey Allison, who took control when Bill Elliott began having tire problems. The only good news for Dale was that Martin, slowed by engine problems, finished 14th.

Even so, Martin picked up another 33 points on Dale, stretching his lead to 49 points. "I can't believe that I gained that many points, the way my car was running," he said.

Neither team was able to do much two weeks later at Rockingham. Martin failed to win one of the top 20 starting positions in first-round qualifying and Earnhardt barely made it, getting the final spot.

In the race, both experienced handling problems and finished two laps behind winner Alan Kulwicki, Earnhardt 10th, Martin 11th. Neither led a lap for the second consecutive race.

With only the two races at Phoenix and Atlanta remaining, Martin held a 45 point lead, probably enough to carry him to the championship. Everyone knew that Earnhardt was going to be tough to beat in the last race at Atlanta, where he had won the previous two races convincingly. But Martin seemed to have an edge on the relatively flat track at Phoenix.

Jack Roush was having a tough time coping with the open weekends that fall between each of the final three races on the schedule. "It is maddening on Saturday and Sunday when there is not a race. I am just driven crazy with concern over the things that might happen in that next race that I might not be able to deal with," he said after the Rockingham race.

"I am like that old race announcer who used to talk about the leading cars in the Daytona 500. During the last laps, he would say the drivers hear every little sound, feel every little vibration, and every little quiver, and get nervous about it. Well, I am feeling those vibrations and quivers. I am nervous about a lot of things, just holding on and hoping we can maintain the kind of poise and durability we have had during the season."

Poise and consistency were the main assets of the Roush team. They had stayed at the top of the points standings despite having won only two races to Earnhardt's eight. Ironically, the team's only major blunder had come at Richmond in January, when Martin got his first victory but was denied the full benefits of winning because of the error with the carburetor spacer.

It had cost the Roush team 46 championship points, which seemed even bigger with the showdown for the title loomed. "I would feel much more comfortable with our position if we had a 91-point lead," Roush acknowledged.

His team was in only its third season, and he thought that if a more established team had made the mistake, the penalty wouldn't have been so severe. He also doubted that NASCAR would have made the same call near the end of the season with the title on the line.

"I look at the penalty as paying my dues in joining the exclusive NASCAR community," said Roush, whose teams had won championships on racing circuits. "If those 46 points cost me the championship, that $1 million will be just more dues that I have had to pay."

• • •

That Dale was in position to win another Winston Cup championship was not nearly as surprising as how he had managed it. Or, more to the point, what he had not done.

While chasing Martin in the standings since early summer, Dale hadn't been involved in any controversies, nor had he been accused of laying a fender or bumper to Martin. Many observers predicted before the Charlotte and Rockingham races that the "old Earnhardt" would resurface and attempt to force the closest title run ever into a brawl, in which he no doubt would have the edge.

Dale had opportunities in both races to let his car slip a little in the turns while racing Martin, but he did not allow it.

It was not going to happen in the final two races either, Dale declared the day before he and Martin went to the starting line at Phoenix.

"I think under different circumstances you would be seeing me lay some sheetmetal on Martin," he admitted as he relaxed in the rear of his tow truck. "But it all goes back to the two races at Dover last year, when Mark and I raced each other real hard for the victory both times."

Earnhardt won both Dover races by only slight margins.

"Here was a kid who was hungry for his first victory, and he could have had it in either of those Dover races if he had spun me out to take it," Dale recalled. "My team could hear his crew on the radio telling Mark to do whatever he had to do to pass me. But Mark never put a fender on me. I don't know if he was scared, or what, but it is paying off for him now.

"If he had tried to spin me out in those Dover races, I certainly would be putting some sheetmetal on him. But he showed me respect, and he is going to get that same respect from me in this championship battle."

The gentlemanly manner in which the championship battle was being waged was unusual, and it gave racing fans a different look at Earnhardt. Many critics had claimed Earnhardt was a successful driver only because he intimidated others. At times, it seemed that Earnhardt and his black-and-gray clad crewmen took delight in polishing their nasty-as-we-want-to-be reputation, too.

But no one could complain about Earnhardt's driving this season, and Dale conceded that he found himself enjoying the title run with Martin more than any other.

"The crews are not involved in name-calling, and Mark and I have been able to race each other close without any controversies," Dale said. "All of the attention has been on racing, not a lot of other stuff."

Martin was not surprised to learn that his clean racing at Dover the previous season had set the tone for the championship battle. "I have never had a problem racing Dale," he said. "I have always raced him the way I wanted to be raced, and that is how he has raced me."

Dale joked that he was afraid he might be spoiling his reputation as "The Intimidator," but he turned serious when he said there still could be an incident between him and Martin.

"I am going to race Mark hard, and I am going into the hole just as deep as I can if we are side-by-side," he said. "If things get tight, we might trade a little paint, and we might bump a little. But it will be racing. I am not going to take him out deliberately."

Dale went into the Phoenix race hoping to whittle Martin's lead enough to have a chance to race for the championship at Atlanta.

He surprised himself and everyone else by leading the final 262 laps of the 312-lap event, while Martin, who pitted for fresh tires with 10 laps remaining, finished 10th.

Dale gained 51 points on Martin, sending him into the final race with a six-point lead.

"That is what we wanted to do, notch down his lead and get it close going to Atlanta," Dale told reporters after the race. "It doesn't make me feel any better or prouder of my race team to go down there leading. But, now, Mark will have to go to Atlanta and run the battle. I think we can race him down there and be competitive.

"The Atlanta track has been real good to me, but, still, Mark has run good there and sat on poles there, and I think it will be an ideal place to end the championship and it will be a good race."

Being on top of the standings wouldn't change the way his team would approach the race, Dale said. "Richard Childress and the guys still want to go there and sit on the pole and go out and win the race. We will take the same car that we won there in the spring. We'll stick with our same race plan.

"I hope it will be like today. I ran seemingly hard to probably a lot of people, but I was comfortable the whole time. I wasn't running out of control, and that is how I would like to run at Atlanta, comfortably fast. We've done it there in the past and if we can get a good test in there next week I think we can go back and have a good shot to do the same thing," he said.

Earnhardt admitted he had been surprised when Martin made a late pit stop for tires and fell back to finish 10th. "He had sat there, along about fifth place all day and I thought that was where he was going to finish. Maybe when they pitted it was a misjudgment because of experience. Maybe not. They had to feel they could better themselves with the pit stop to get tires. He was trying to do all he could do to get all he could get, and maybe it back-fired on him,"

Martin was satisfied that the late pit stop was the right strategy at the time. "I really believe it was the racer's thing to do and nine out of 10 of the others would have done the same thing if they had been in our position. I told my crew the tires were worn out and I needed to stop and they said, 'Okay, come on.' I double-checked on the radio before I made the stop and Jack said to come on. If anyone didn't want me to stop, they could have told me to stay out. But I was in the situation where I already had lost some spots and we needed to do something to get them back."

Among those trying to console Martin was Darrell Waltrip's wife, Stevie. "Let me remind you of something," she said. "In 1979 we took the lead from Richard Petty in the next-to-last race and lost it in the final race. So, you can still do it."

Martin smiled. "Thank you," he replied. "We sure tried hard today. We'll just have to go beat them at Atlanta."

• • •

The pressure was on Martin and his team, though, and during the round of testing between Phoenix and Atlanta, the Roush crew made a startling decision to borrow a car from Davey Allison to run at Atlanta. Many observers saw it as a desperation move, and an indication that the Roush team knew it didn't have a chance with its own equipment.

Martin conceded that driving one of Allison's cars was a risk, but it was something the team felt it had to do to have a chance of beating Earnhardt for the championship.

"We would not do this if we still had the points lead, because there are always risks with anything new or different," he explained. "After the swing in points at Phoenix, we just feel we have to take some risks to find an advantage so we can flat outrun Dale Earnhardt on a race track where he has a real good record."

The Allison team, headed by mechanic-owner Robert Yates, had decided not to use the car themselves in the Atlanta race because it had a new chassis design which was not race-proven on large tracks.

The "rental car deal" was the talk of the garage area when the Atlanta track opened for practice and qualifying. It proved to be a major distraction for the Martin and the Roush crew-men, who were having to explain time and again to reporters why they had made such an move, and the glare of the spotlight got even hotter when Martin was scheduled to qualify.

When given the signal to begin his run, Martin flipped the ignition switch and nothing happened. As the bewildered Martin sat on pit road, his mechanics swarmed over the car and located a problem in the electrical system that they quickly solved. Once on the track, Martin had another problem – not enough speed. He qualified only 11th while Earnhardt was sixth behind pole winner Rusty Wallace.

Dale refused to criticize the decision by the Roush team to borrow a car, but clearly he and his mechanics thought it would be an advantage for them. Others thought so, too.

"Earnhardt and his bunch has got Martin and his crowd

261

right where they want them," Richard Petty said. "If their own car was good enough to get them this far, it should have been good enough for the last race, too."

Darrell Waltrip thought borrowing the Allison car might have been a wise move, but he felt it should have been handled more discreetly.

"What difference does it make if he drives his car or someone else's?" Waltrip asked."They are all alike. If someone has got one that is real good and you like it, I say drive that car. Let's put this thing in perspective. If you are playing in the Super Bowl and you can go borrow Joe Montana to be your quarterback, would you do it?

"I don't blame them for borrowing a car that they thought was better. I might have done the same thing. But I wouldn't have told anyone about it. It all would have been 'rumor has it....' "

Although Martin had lost the points lead, he had not lost his sense of humor. A couple of days before the final race, Earnhardt was making the rounds of radio and television stations. At one stop he was asked if he would take a call from a fan.

"I like talking to fans," Dale said. "Put him on."

"Dale, I was just wondering if you are going to be conservative in Sunday's race?" the caller asked.

Dale said that he intended to run wide-open, flat-out all the way.

"But, Dale," the caller said. "I really think you should be conservative."

Dale tried to explain again that he would not change his driving style to try to protect a slim six-point lead. "I am going to run it wide open, take it to the front, and stay there," he repeated.

"Dale, do you know who this is?" the caller inquired.

"No, sir. I don't,"

"This is Mark Martin, and I really do think you should back off a little bit in Sunday's race."

Martin and Earnhardt laughed about the gag the rest of the week, but Dale's declared plan of charging from start to finish was no laughing matter for the Roush team.

"We know what Dale is going to do, and we know that we need to lead a lot of laps and finish ahead of him to have a chance at the title," Roush said. "We will run every ratio of gearing, every degree of timing, run the leanest possible carburetor setting to get whatever advantage we can, with very little regard to risk."

Dale ran just as hard as he had promised, and he finished third, behind winner Morgan Shepherd and Geoff Bodine, to wrap up the championship.

Martin struggled through an assortment of problems to finish sixth and wound up losing the title by 26 points. He offered no excuses and admitted, "I got beat by the best, and I am not embarrassed to lose the title to Dale Earnhardt."

Graciously, he did not mention the 46 points that had been taken away from his team following the Richmond victory. When asked about them, Martin shrugged his shoulders and replied, "I don't want to comment on that. Those points are gone and the season is over. We did the best we could and just came up a little short."

Despite Dale's failure to win, the race had gone according to plan for him. "I wanted to win the race and the championship, but I am satisfied with just the title," he said.

Dale collected five bonus points for leading a lap when he passed pole sitter Wallace on Lap 44. In rocketing to the front, he made a couple of dare-devil passes, then settled down to a more comfortable pace.

"Our strategy was to get those bonus points early and then to just be consistent and hope we had a chance to win the race at the end," he explained. "I had a chance to win it, too, but on that last pit stop, I didn't get a good match of tires and the car didn't handle as well. When I saw I wasn't catching Shepherd or Bodine, I concentrated on finishing third, which I knew was good enough to win the Winston Cup title and the manufacturers' championship for Chevrolet."

The win by Shepherd actually gave Ford a tie with Chevrolet in the standings but the title went to Chevrolet based on its 13-11 edge in season victories – nine of them by Earnhardt.

If circumstances had been different, Dale said he might have gambled on his last pit stop to try for a 10th victory. "We thought about making a chassis change on that last stop. If we had and it had worked, we may have won the race. But if we had missed it, well, you know. Winning the race was worth about $75,000 and the championship paid $1 million, and I could get that by running third."

But it wasn't the money, Dale insisted, that counted as much as the prestige of winning a fourth title, an accomplishment that separated him from others like Cale Yarborough, David Pearson, and Darrell Waltrip, who had won three titles.

The only driver ahead of him in title victories now was Richard Petty, with seven, and catching "The King" became Dale's next goal. "I would like to do that, and I feel I have another 10 good years, at least, to win championships. But if I win seven or eight titles, I will never be King Richard, or even King Dale. There is only one king in this sport and that is Richard Petty."

Other than his late father, Dale respected nobody in racing more than Petty, the sport's greatest winner, Dale's role model in learning to accept defeat graciously. Early in his career, Dale had been notorious for short answers, or none at all, when things went wrong. He worked hard to change that, and he gave Petty credit for showing him how to deal with disappointment.

"Richard has always represented our sport well with the press and the fans. He is the one I've always looked up to. Even if he has a bad day, he gets out of the car and smiles. He signs autographs, and he talks to the fans and the media. He is 'The King,' and it makes me proud to do something that only 'The King' has done in our sport."

Dale had been aware that some of Bill Elliott's crewmen were in a pit road accident late in the race, but it wasn't until after leaving the track that he learned the accident claimed the life of right-rear tire changer Mike Rich.

There had been two similar pit road incidents during the season, one at Talladega and the other at Charlotte in which Will Lind had cheated death by only a few seconds.

"The drivers have to be safer on pit road, and NASCAR needs to make changes. I don't want none of my guys hurt, and I don't want to hurt anyone," Dale said afterward.

The wrappings were put on the championship season at the annual NASCAR Awards Banquet, a black-tie affair held at the Waldorf-Astoria in New York City. The season had been worth $3,083,056 to Dale and the Childress team, which broke the previous motorsports record for single-season earnings, $2,383,187, set by Bill Elliott in 1985.

After accepting the championship trophy, Dale paid tribute to Mark Martin and the Roush team. "In a way, I hated to see them lose because they worked so hard," he said.

The evening was made special for Dale by the presence of his mother, Martha, who was making her first trip to the banquet to see her son honored. She looked on approvingly as her son brought up a personal matter.

"My dad has always had a place in my heart through all of my racing years. I grew up idolizing him. I stood up on the back of a truck on a tire and every turn he took, I took, and it burned right into me what I wanted to do. I never dreamed I would be four-time champion of NASCAR. I have had help from people who were friends of my daddy and people he raced against. He is still in my heart. I remember him, and I miss him dearly."

14

'That is the reason
he is Dale Earnhardt'

The 1990 season left no doubt that Richard Childress had put together the best team in stock car racing. Maybe the best of all time. Dale won his fourth Winston Cup championship, he became the first repeat winner in the all-star race, and he won the International Race of Champions Series.

The GM Goodwrench team dominated the fourth annual Copenhagen/SKOAL All-Pro Team, which was announced during the winter, by placing nine members on the first team, four on the second team, and one on the third.

Kirk Shelmerdine was named to the All-Pro team as crew chief and front tire changer. Others receiving first-team honors were jackman David Smith, tire specialist Will Lind, bodyman Bobby Moody, engine builder Eddie Lanier, assistant engine builder Danny Lawrence, general mechanic Cecil Gordon, and driver Dale Earnhardt. Lind, John Malloy, Dan Kingen, and Gordon received second-team honors, Danny Myers third-team.

If there had been a car-owner category, Childress would have been a sure bet to have won that, too.

Since retiring as a driver in 1981, Childress had built a team that had become a blueprint for others, and the core of its strength was the dedication of his crewmen, who had stuck with him through the years.

Seated behind a big desk in his office, Childress admitted he did not know of another team that had experienced fewer turnovers in the past 10 years. The only major defection had been by engine builder Lou LaRosa, who had been replaced by Eddie Lanier.

"I have done every job that every man on our team is doing when I was driving and running my own shop," Childress said. "Back then, I was driving the truck to the races. I built engines. I mean I did every bit of it. I know what those guys are going through, and I treat them like I would want to be treated.

"I could retire and live real easy from what I have been offered for this race team. But to me, winning and staying involved is worth more than the money. I think those guys on our team look at it the same way. I know Dale has been offered big money to go drive somewhere else. But again, it goes back to wanting to be winners."

Childress treats his team members like winners, too, and that is reflected in their bank accounts and working conditions. Childress set up the first profit-sharing plan in stock car racing, and crewmen receive a large share of the money from winning the championship. Childress took every team member and their wives to New York for the championship banquet, at a cost of more than $50,000.

"I started the profit-sharing in 1987 after our second championship," he said. "I put in 15 percent of every man's salary and that is the maximum you can pay under the law. This year, we are putting in the maximum again. Last year they didn't get that much. It just depends on the kind of season and the profit of the company. Winning championships is where those guys make their real money, and it is where I make mine. It brings those sponsors on board."

Money aside, Childress believes the main reason he hasn't lost many team members is because they are treated as professionals. "When we go to the track and have trouble, no one complains that the engine is bad or the car isn't handling," he said. "I tell these guys that it is a team effort and if one area is off at this or that track, I expect everyone to help carry the load. That is the way we do it. We don't ever blame anyone. It is a team effort through the whole deal.

"Another thing is we try to stay ahead of everyone else. We were one of the first teams to have a computer system. Now, go to Daytona, everyone has it. So, we have to try to get something one step better. We went down there to test and I saw a lot of things on other cars that we had last year. But that is just part of racing. We have got to come up with other stuff just to try to stay ahead."

Childress was the first team owner to buy an airplane big enough to fly key team members to the races. "We try not to burn everyone out and let them have as much of a normal life as possible. If we are going to Dover, we can work all the way up that evening, leave here, and get to the motel in time to get a full night's sleep. After the race, we are back that night and ready to go to work on Monday morning. It is an expensive thing, but it is an extra perk. I have had several car owners ask me how I can justify an airplane. My reply is that I don't know how you can justify not having one. Now it seems everyone has got a team airplane."

Childress raises prize-winning Angus cattle as a hobby, and he has used that as a way to get across to his team the importance of winning. One of his bulls won first place in a national show while another did not do nearly as well and wound up being the guest of honor at the team's Christmas party.

"I had him cut up into steaks," Childress said. "I told the guys, 'This is what happens to losers.' "

The first opportunity for reporters to get an inside glimpse of the forthcoming Winston Cup season is during the popular Charlotte Motor Speedway tour in January. The tour includes banquets, seminars, and visits to several race team shops within driving distance of the track.

The Childress team was the object of great attention during the 1991 media tour. Childress received the coveted Flock Brothers Memorial Award for racing excellence from Charlotte Motor Speedway president Humpy Wheeler at a banquet held at the Speedway Club. His driver was a topic of discussion by a panel of "legendary" drivers that included Hall-of-Famer Ned Jarrett, who noted, "Earnhardt is so good, it is kind of scary."

Reporters attended a luncheon at the Western Steer restaurant in Lexington, only a few miles from the Childress shop, and were told that the restaurant chain would be an associate sponsor of the GM Goodwrench car in 1991 and was naming one of its steaks for Dale. The huge cut of beef would be called, "The Intimidator."

Someone wanted to know if there would be menu selections named for other drivers.

"Yeah. Chicken and shrimp," Dale quipped.

After the luncheon, the tour moved to the Childress shop with its fan museum. "Because of insurance rules, we can't let fans go back to where the cars are being built," Childress said. "But they can get a close-up view, and even climb into one of our race cars at the museum."

Visitors also can see what was left of the tire that Dale cut and blew out on the final lap of the 1990 Daytona 500. It is hung on the wall like a million-dollar trophy.

According to "Little" Bud Moore, one of the reasons that big-time racing was not attractive to Dale's father was the public relations demands being made on the drivers even back during the 1960s.

"Ralph told me that racing was getting into an era where the car owners were looking for a new breed of race driver to represent the companies and factories sponsoring their cars. You know, people don't really understand now that this was going on in the sport even back then. Ralph admitted to me that he was not able to adapt to it. I think he made a couple of trips to talk with Pontiac, and he told me he just never really felt comfortable, you know, with the image and the whole thing that it was going to take to be able to do that, and I think that was a big reason he never took a factory ride on what is now the Winston Cup circuit," Moore said.

When Dale began his career, however, he learned quickly the importance of having a sponsor. And when he made it to the Winston Cup ranks and got the sponsorship of Wrangler, and later GM Goodwrench, he realized that representing those large companies was part of his obligation, and he worked to become good at it.

That he has succeeded was evident in the way he fielded questions during the media tour.

"What was the most satisfying part of the 1990 championship year?" he was asked.

"I think the whole year was satisfying, even the Daytona 500. As bad as it was at the end, it was satisfying to go down there and dominate the race. Even though we lost, what happened was something we couldn't do anything about. I am proud of the whole season. The guys worked hard when we had problems at Charlotte, and we replaced that broken cam shaft at Dover. It was fun getting in there and changing that cam shaft as a team, and when that thing cranked, you know how excited we were about that.

"All of the victories were great, especially the Southern 500, when we had a vibration in the car at the end. I had hit the wall earlier in the day, too, so I was not being too good to the race car and it still won. To come back in the points and have the turnaround at Phoenix, and to beat Mark at Atlanta, all of that was great. We won the championship as a team. It wasn't one guy that stood out all year long. If one guy stood out, it was

Childress, the leader, who kept it all together and everyone working together."

"Is there anything some other drivers do that drive you nuts on the track?"

"Well, there are different drivers that have different characteristics you might not like. There is nothing you can't live with. I race and get along fairly well with all of them, even the guys I don't seem to get along with – even Bodine. We pick back and forth, but I've got to race him 29 times this coming season. I am going to race him one-on-one, just like I am going to race Richard Petty, Rusty Wallace, Darrell Waltrip, or anyone else. I am not going to approach him any differently. I am just going to race a little more cautious with him."

"How long was it before you were able to look at that cut tire from the Daytona 500 and not feel sick about it?"

"It hasn't bothered me since the first time I saw it. That is just one of those things. It is like the next week was Richmond. Life goes on. It is just like that war over there now. After it is over with, we are going to pick up the pieces and go on. That is how racing is. You know, you got to pick up the pieces after the race, go home and fix it, and go on to the next race. Mentally, you got to do the same thing. If I had let that tire and one race work on me like a lot of people think it has, we wouldn't have won the championship in 1990."

"What is your strongest point and weakest point as a driver?"

"The strongest point about my driving is the drive inside of me to win. The aggressiveness, the eagerness, the drive to win, you know, is there and it always has been there, and it is burning as hot as it ever has to win. I don't want to run second. The weakest point? I try not to have weak points."

"As a team, what kind of emphasis is there on going back to Daytona and dominating like you did last year?"

"Well, Eddie Lanier, our engine builder, Kirk, and the others have worked hard to go back and be even better, and the tests proved we were running as consistent or better than last year. We feel we are in better shape. I know everyone is going to be asking the question if what happened last year has anything to do with it, and really it doesn't. We have had some losses down there in past races that we felt we should have won. But, this will be the 1991 Daytona 500, and it won't have anything to do with last year. If we come down to the same situation, leading the race going down the backstretch on the last lap, it might go though my mind. But I don't think it will hamper the way we approach the race. We are going to go in there with a positive attitude that we are going to win. I feel that way now, and I don't think there is a man on our race team who doesn't feel that way."

During the meeting with reporters, Childress was asked about Ned Jarrett's remark that Earnhardt might be the best stock car driver ever.

"I think if you look back over the decades of NASCAR racing, Dale can do things with the car that other people just can't do. Everyone has seem him drive, and I think his driving speaks for itself."

Dale interrupted to add, "It all goes back to the support and confidence this race team gives me to go out there and be able to drive the car. I have confidence that the team is behind me in any situation. I have had conflicts with different drivers over the years and I have got out of the race car and told Richard what happened, my side of it, and they have supported and stood behind me the whole time."

"Rick Hendrick says anyone who wins the championship this year has to beat the Number Three car," a reporter told Dale. "What do you think of that?"

"It makes me feel good to see a team thinking they have to beat us to win the title. That sort of says you are the best, and it makes you proud. I am glad they are talking about us. Before the start of last season they weren't, and this year they are. It just makes me feel good.

Dale and his team were still receiving great attention from reporters when they arrived at Daytona in early February, and Dale gave them more to write about after an almost unbelievable performance in the Busch Clash.

For the first time, the 50-mile sprint race for pole winners from the previous season was being split into two segments of 10 laps each, and the starting order for the final segment would be in reverse order of how the drivers finished the first segment.

Some believed the new format was designed specifically to prevent Earnhardt, back in the Clash again after failing to qualify the previous year, from turning the nationally televised race into a romp, as he had in The Winston in 1990.

The format was a major concern for Dale, too. He didn't know if it would be better to deliberately finish back in the field during the first segment to get a better starting position for the last segment, or to try to win the first segment and take his chances in the second segment.

"I want to win both segments," he said. "But I don't know if it is possible for someone to start dead last in the second segment and have enough time in only 10 laps to get back to the front of the field, no matter how strong his car might be. I don't think King Kong could do that."

Well, King Kong might not be able to do it, but Dale Earnhardt was another story.

He began the first segment sixth in the 14-car field. He moved around Geoff Bodine on the second lap to take the lead and held it to the finish with hardly a challenge. When Bodine spun his car on the final lap, a lot of people were saying he did so on purpose so he could finish last and have the pole for the final segment that determined the overall winner.

Dale, of course, would start last. He had proved that he could go from sixth to victory, and now the question was if he could go from 14th to the front in a 10-lap dash.

Not only could he do it, but he astounded even veteran

observers by making it look easy. He needed only two laps to take the lead, and once there, he received challenge.

"All week long we had thought about this thing and the strategy we were going to use," Dale said after the race. "We kept thinking maybe we should just sit back and not try to win the first segment. But that is not how this team races. We are a go-for-it team, and we try to win every race we are in. That is what we are here for.

"After winning the first segment, I thought it was going to be almost impossible to win the second one. When it began, I was high on the track through the first and second turns and down the backstretch I was sort of boxed in. I really didn't want to be there, but I wasn't sure which lane was going to do what. I went in the third and fourth turns, saw an opening, and slipped down into it, got into the bottom lane, and the car picked up momentum. The car really worked good on the bottom and I just kept passing cars until finally I got behind Geoff Bodine, the leader. He must have known I was coming, because he moved down on the track as he came off the second turn. Down the backstretch, I drafted up behind him and moved under him going into the third turn. I couldn't believe that I was back leading the race, going from the back to the front, in only two laps."

If Dale had not already put an intimidating hold on his rivals with such a display of power, he gave them something else to think about. "We have got a car that is even better than this one that we are going to use in the Daytona 500," he warned.

The groans in the garage area were loud and mournful. Most did not think that Earnhardt had showed everything he had in winning the Clash, and they did not want to hear that he had a better car for the big race.

"He is baaad," Bill Elliott drawled. "You got to understand that. Anyone who can come from last to first at this place in two laps has got to be baaaaad."

Mark Martin, whose Ford finished closest to the GM Goodwrench Chevrolet, was surprised by how fast Dale had blasted through the field. "He had not showed that kind of speed in practice. I think the bottom line is that he was just playing around with us. I couldn't even get a strong enough run to take a shot at passing him."

Darrell Waltrip was not eligible for the Clash, but he didn't have to be on the track to understand the situation. "It tells me that this is going to be a long week for the rest of us. But I don't think anyone who saw what he did here a year ago, or in the Pepsi 400 here last July, should be surprised."

Away from the track, Dale's strong showing in the Clash provided material for jokesters.

"Did you know Dale Earnhardt is going to switch from his Chevrolet to a Ford?" a radio talk show host asked his audience. "No, really, he is. He went to see his doctor last week and was told that he is going to have to slow down."

The one that got the most laughs was tied to other events.

Iraqi leader Saddam Hussein supposedly went into his private office in an underground bunker and could be heard asking, "Mirror, mirror on the wall, who is the baddest of them all?"

Suddenly, Hussein's body guards heard the sound of glass being smashed and their enraged leader emerged demanding to know, "Who is this Dale Earnhardt?"

Dale and his Chevrolet weren't providing much laughter for his competitors, however. When the new Lumina that the team would race in the 500 was rolled off the truck Monday morning, whispers began spreading through the garage area that car looked a little too sleek, and an inch or so too narrow.

"I guess we are going to keep putting up with it until Earnhardt finally wins the Daytona 500," Geoff Bodine said.

Was Bodine insinuating that NASCAR was allowing the Childress team an unfair advantage?

Bodine shrugged, as if to say, "You figure it out," and walked away.

The whispers eventually reached the ears of Winston Cup Director Dick Beaty, whose job is to make sure that the rules are enforced equally. Beaty was infuriated by the allegations. He called for an immediate inspection of Dale's car and invited all other teams to attend. The car proved to be perfectly legal, as all could see when Beaty fit the templates on it.

"I knew the rumors going around the garage were not true, and I wanted anyone from Ford or anywhere else to see for themselves that the car was right," Beaty explained.

Childress, Shelmerdine, and the other GM Goodwrench crewmen wore huge, I-told-you-so grins as they rolled the car back to its stall, following the unprecedented inspection. "The fact other people are claiming the car is not right makes me feel good," Childress said. "You know, it keeps them all searching."

• • •

The age-old question in stock car racing is which is most important: car or driver? In most cases, the car gets the credit. No team ever has been accused of winning because it had an "illegal driver."

Stock car racers are proud. None wants to admit that any other is better, so if he gets outrun it must be because someone else had an unfair advantage with the car.

Former racers view the sport from a different angle, however, as television commentator and former Daytona 500 winner Benny Parsons learned.

"Oh, I see racing much differently now from the booth than I did when I was sitting in one of those cars," Parsons says. "When I was a race driver, I just felt all drivers were born alike and equipment made all the difference in the world. I mean, there was no difference in driving ability. But, after a couple of years in the booth, there seems to be a difference. I still think race car drivers, 95 percent of the time, are the same.

"There is something that makes Dale Earnhardt the way he is. There is just something there that some people don't have. He was tough to race against. Oh, Lord, yes, he was tough.

Everyone one else, you get position on them and, you know, you feel like when you go into the corner that they are going to give you the position and you go on.

"But not Earnhardt. I mean, you just had to race him every inch of the way. When you see that sucker behind you, and he is outrunning you, you know you are going to be hit, too, if you don't move over. I was intimidated by him, and so were most people.

"He has got that win-win type of attitude about him that great drivers need. As someone, probably George Steinbrenner, said, 'Show me a good loser and I'll show you a loser.' I have made that statement before in my life. Obviously, I don't say it with the same emphasis as I once did. You get older, that becomes a little less important, winning at all cost. But, obviously, when you are starting out, or when you are trying to build a resume in this business, winning is the only thing. Everything now is bottom line, which has become the catch phrase of the 1980s and 1990s. When it comes to race car drivers, that definitely is the bottom line – winning."

Parsons saw a different Dale Earnhardt during the 1990 season.

"Dale has matured. It is almost like looking at dark and daylight, comparing Earnhardt now to the Earnhardt of five years ago. I mean nothing made any difference to him back in those days except winning. Now he realizes there are situations where he is better off to take what is handed to him than to try to go out and take something that is not there. The classic example is the thing that happened on the last lap in North Wilkesboro with Ricky Rudd in 1989. If he had taken second place instead of trying to take something that wasn't there, he would have five titles now instead of four."

The only thing missing in Earnhardt's resume at the beginning of the 1991 season was a Daytona 500 victory, and his performance in the Busch Clash indicated that he might be on the verge of getting it.

"As far as Dale's career is concerned, it matters not if he ever wins the Daytona 500," Parsons said. "But to Dale Earnhardt, it obviously matters a great, great deal. He will never, ever be content until he does win the Daytona 500. When he sits and looks at the trophies he has won, for winning this race and this championship, all of a sudden he is going to see the qualifying-race trophies, the Busch Clash trophies, the Grand National trophies that say 'Daytona' and that glow is going to go away and there is going to be a sick feeling in his stomach because he doesn't have the Daytona 500 trophy.

"In this business you remember your losses so much more than you remember the wins. It is terrible. Someone says, 'Do you remember in Victory Lane when this happened?' and I say, 'No.' But I do remember getting beat on that last lap, or wrecking, or something. I remember all of that."

• • •

Dale showed the strength of his car during the 125-mile qualifying race on Thursday, four days before the Daytona 500, when he took the lead from Ernie Irvan on the first lap and led to the checkered flag. The only question seemed to be if he could go the distance without stopping for fuel, and he proved that he could.

"I worked the draft with Irvan, and I didn't use the throttle real hard at times," Dale said afterward. "I sort of feathered it, but not much. I drove up high on the banks and conserved all the fuel I could. When I drove to Victory Lane, there was still some fuel pressure showing, so I must have had enough left to go another lap or so if I'd had to."

Davey Allison, who had won pole position a few days earlier, also led from start to finish in the other qualifying race. Allison did not win a pole during the 1990 season and did not compete in the Busch Clash, which meant he had not gone head-to-head with Earnhardt under racing conditions.

Bill France, Jr., who wears two hats at Daytona – as head of the speedway and head of NASCAR – was worrying that Earnhardt's Chevy was strong enough to spoil the Daytona 500 on Sunday. From what he and everyone else had seen in the Clash and qualifying races, Allison might be the only driver who could prevent a runaway.

On a visit to the garage area, France asked Allison's crew chief, Jake Elder, if he felt Allison had a chance to outrun Earnhardt in the 500.

"I told him that if we could just run with Earnhardt, you know, stay in his draft, that we had a chance of beating him," Elder later recalled. "I said if you can't run with him, you ain't got no chance to beat him. If he runs hard every lap, and we are sitting there watching him, we will probably make him use up his right front tire. I am hoping that is what will happen. We want to draft him. I don't want Davey leading. I want to be behind him and maybe Dale's right front tire will go away quicker than ours, and who knows, the last 10 laps if we run him hard and we've run him hard for 40 or 50 laps, Davey will be able to take the lead and go on."

Elder knew everything seemed in Earnhardt's favor, however. Dale was confident; he had horsepower, and he had a car that handled well. "When he has those three things, he knows what he can do, and he is going to be hard to beat," said Elder, who guided Earnhardt to the rookie title in 1979.

"It is like I told Billy France, when Dale is right, and I have worked with this man, so I understand him, I said when Dale Earnhardt is right, he is in a class by himself. I know Davey is coming on, but Davey has still got to go to school, like Dale did.

"I told Billy France that there ain't but one man who was in Dale Earnhardt's class and he isn't here no more. I am talking about Tim Richmond. He was the next Dale Earnhardt. He was the only man who could race Dale, because Dale could not terminate him. He could not shake him up. If Dale tried to run him high, Tim would stick right in there with him. If Dale chopped him off, he would come right back and do the same thing to

Dale. And Dale knew that, because Tim would take the extra chances that Dale would take."

There is no greater authority on winning the Daytona 500 than Richard Petty, who has collected seven trophies from the race. If anything, Petty had learned that having a superior car is no guarantee of winning, and in 1991 he was one of only a few in the garage area who did not think Earnhardt had a lock on the race.

"I have won this race when I didn't have the best car, and I have lost it when I did have the best car," Petty said as he sat on a tire in the shade during a break in practice. "In 1979 and 1981, there was no way I should have won those races. In '79 Donnie Allison and Cale Yarborough just blowed me away. I was 20 seconds behind with a mile or so to go and still won the race when they wrecked each other. In '81, it was Bobby Allison's week until it came to the race. He sputtered a little bit on gas and I was able to out-pit him, really. He dominated the whole race and I think I led only the last 15 or 20 laps.

"But in 1976, when me and David Pearson wrecked on the last lap, I should have won. And the year before that I had a super, super fast car and busted a radiator and had to keep pitting to put water in it. It takes a while for some of the others to figure out that you don't win this race just on horsepower. You got to have a good handling car, too. Earnhardt is beating everybody now in handling and horsepower. His car really, really handles good because he can run right around the bottom of the track, and he has got more horsepower than anybody else. All it takes is just a little bit in both places. See, we had four races in 1991 with the restricter plate and he dominated all four races.

"He was good enough – and this is where it goes with the power deal – he could start 14th in the Busch Clash and in a lap and half, you know, he is leading the race. That is horsepower. That is not just handling, because all them cats got brand new tires on, and they are sitting there running wide open, too. It is a combination. He's got a good, slick car. It handles good to make him run fast, and he's got power, too. So, it is not just the one thing. He is not doing it just on handling. He's not doing it just on engine. He's not doing in just on driving ability. You need all of that, and he's got it."

There was another part of winning, too, that Petty mentioned – luck.

"You take if someone had pulled out in front of Dale in the Clash, he was going to have to let off the accelerator or run through the infield or through the wall. So, you got to have the breaks. If you ain't careful, the longer the race is, the more breaks become involved, because you have got more chance of good breaks or bad breaks to happen. No matter how good you are, you have got to have a big percentage of luck to go along with it. No matter how dominant you are, there is so much that can happen to keep you from winning.

"Last year, Dale dominated the race and then he runs over something on the track. If he had done that with 20 laps to go, or 50 laps to go, he could have got by with it. He did it on the last lap. Circumstances where there was no chance of him recovering.

"Circumstances just were not going to let him win that race, no matter how dominant he was. He's got to be thinking about that again this year. But if you do it long enough, like I have, you got good days and bad days and they sorta equal out in the middle."

Petty had been both flattered and a little amused to hear Earnhardt giving him credit for showing him how to accept disappointment and defeat more graciously.

"I didn't ever talk to Dale about that specifically, but we have had conversations about different things over a period of time. Dale is just like the rest of us. He's just matured. A lot of that stuff was thrust on him, and it was tough for him to handle it during his early years. Now he's been around long enough that he's learning how to handle it, and he is doing a good job.

"From now to four or five years ago, he's just a different person, as far as what I see. The way I see him handling the media, and how he handles the general public, his whole attitude has changed. I think he has got a good attitude now. I think he's got an attitude now that he can win or he can lose. He can be a good loser, now. Used to, he was a good winner and not a good loser, know what I mean?"

• • •

Dale warmed up for the Daytona 500 on Saturday by driving to his third victory in seven days in the Busch Grand National Goody's 300, the fourth time he had won the race. He led 75 percent of the 300-lap race. Michael Waltrip finished second and Davey Allison third.

Following the Grand National event, the Winston Cup cars took to the speedway for a final round of practice for the big race on Sunday. Dale took only a few laps before returning to the garage area and giving his crew the okay signal.

"Ready to race," he declared.

Dale's crew was looking around the garage area to see which teams might have a chance to beat them. They saw two: those of Davey Allison and Ernie Irvan, who had finished a close second to Earnhardt in the 125-mile qualifier.

Irvan had drawn criticism from Earnhardt for an incident that happened early in the qualifying race. "He bothered me pretty much when he ran into the back of my car at the end of the straightaway and knocked me sideways. It got a little out of control there for a little bit, but I guess he was just trying to do all he could do to get by me," Dale had said.

Irvan's Chevrolet had developed a slight handling problem in the qualifying race, but his crew had made adjustments to give him hope that he could upset Earnhardt in the 500. "I think we have proven we can run with Dale in race conditions, so I feel real good about the 500," Irvan said.

On Sunday morning, with the cars lined up on pit road and more than 100,000 fans packed into the grandstands and infield, the pre-race storyline related by the CBS television crew was short and simple: Could anyone stop Dale Earnhardt from winning his first Daytona 500?

Veteran announcer Ken Squier opened the broadcast by saying, "Throughout this entire week, one name has been on everyone's lips. That is Earnhardt. The Intimidator has been invincible. He has won three races in the past seven days, and the question for my racing colleague David Hobbs is, can anybody beat him?"

"Well, Ken, forecasting racing winners is a chancy business at best," Hobbs replied. "But everybody that should know down in the pit area has really given this race to Dale Earnhardt. But it is a very strong pack. Davey Allison on the pole. Richard Petty, in his 31st start, running incredibly well, and relative newcomers Ernie Irvan and Hut Stricklin, looking good. But the chances of any of these drivers just flat winning this race are, to be quite honest, pretty slim."

Pit road reporter Dave Despain got the final pre-race thoughts from Earnhardt during a quick interview just before the call to start engines. "The car has been working good all week, but it is the Daytona 500 and there is a lot of competitive cars here and it is a long day," Dale said. "You got to run good all day long and you've got to have the luck with you, too. We proved that last year, that you don't win just by car alone. You have to have a little luck to go with it. We just want to get the day behind us and see if we come home to Victory Lane."

Not everyone was as sure as the CBS crowd seemed to be that Earnhardt was finally going to shake the Daytona 500 jinx. Longtime motorsports writer Jack Flowers, waiting for the start of the race in the infield media room, shook his head when asked if Earnhardt was going to do it.

"I have seen this too many times, when a driver is so dominant that it seems there is no way for him to lose and something happens and he loses. Hey, remember last year?"

When the green flag dropped, Dale, who was starting outside on the second row, fell in behind Allison and Ernie Irvan through turns one and two. He wheeled by Irvan heading into the third turn, and by the time the cars had reached the starting line, he was fast after Allison. He passed him going into the first turn and took the lead.

But on the second lap, Dale's car struck a startled seagull, that clogged the left side of his grill, causing concern that it might cause the engine to overheat.

"We will have to bring him in if the engine temperature gets up to 250 degrees," said his crew chief, Kirk Shelmerdine.

The bird never presented a serious problem, however, and its remains were removed without dignity during a pit stop on Lap 32.

Earnhardt continued to race at the front, swapping the lead with Allison, Kyle Petty, Rick Mast, Sterling Marlin, and Joe Ruttman during most of the first 250 miles, 100 of which he led. But Dale was sent to the back of the field, with Ruttman on Lap 81, after both received stop-and-go penalties for crossing above the safety line while exiting pit road.

In the second half of the race, Dale seemed content to play a waiting game, trying to conserve fuel and tires. He did not take the lead again until after a caution period that began when Richard Petty and rookie Robbie Gordan spun on the back-stretch on Lap 184. Rusty Wallace was in the lead on the restart on Lap 194 and Dale drove around him to take the lead for the first time since Lap 64.

Two laps later, Kyle Petty tapped Wallace in the fourth turn. Wallace banged the wall, slid across the track and was struck by Darrell Waltrip. Derrike Cope, Hut Stricklin, and Harry Gant also got caught in the wreck.

The race restarted with only seven laps remaining and Dale at the front, trailed closely by Irvan, Kyle Petty, Joe Ruttman, Sterling Marlin, Rick Mast, and Davey Allison, the final car in the lead lap.

Dale got a good jump off the corner on the restart and

opened a seven-car-length lead over Irvan. But Irvan made a quick recovery and got help from Allison, coming on strong behind him, to pass Dale for the lead on Lap 195. Dale cut in front of Allison to keep him from passing, and the two drivers locked into in a side-by-side duel, with Allison on the outside, for two complete laps.

Into a third lap of no-give racing, Dale's Chevrolet lost traction off the second turn and went into a slide. The rear end of the car slapped into Allison's Ford, sending it out of control into a huge dirt bank that separates the bottom of the track from the infield lake. Earnhardt's car spun backwards and was clipped in the left fender by Kyle Petty, but Dale managed to recover and keep it going to the finish.

Irvan, who had looked in his rear view mirror to see both Earnhardt and Allison sliding out of control, went on to win under a caution flag.

Unlike the previous year, Dale was smiling when he drove the damaged car back to the garage.

"One more year," he shouted as he wiggled through the window to inspect the damage.

"What happened is that I was going for the win," he said. "I was trying to take the car to the front when me and Davey just got hung side-by-side there, trying to get back to Ernie. I lost the air off the spoiler and got sideways. I couldn't get it back under me and spun around. It caused Davey and a couple of them to wreck.

"Davey wouldn't give me any room at all. He was trying to run door-to-door with me, right down against me, and it was taking the air off me pretty bad. You know, Ernie had bumped me in the qualifying race and I was just sitting there wanting to get a shot at him. I wanted to see what I could do with him the last lap. I had something for him on that last lap."

Dale suggested that NASCAR's new pitting rules, which did not permit tire changes during caution periods, had affected the race. "I don't like that rule, and it really makes it hard on the drivers because it puts them on the ragged edge. There were a lot of tore up cars and I think the new pit rules were the big reason for it."

Earnhardt gave a disbelieving look when asked if the finish was as hard to take as the one the previous year. "Nah, hell, no," he shot back. "It just happened, that is the way it goes. That is all I could do. But they will be holding the Daytona 500 again next year, and we'll be back, trying to win it."

Allison, who didn't make it back to the line, finished 15th, and he definitely was not smiling when he arrived back at the garage.

"I got hit. That is all I've got to say. I got hit. I was passing him clean on the outside, and I got hit. I had a shot to win the race. I was making a clean pass and then I got a hard lick in the door that put me in the outside wall. Racing is a business where you got to use your head. I was using mine. But Earnhardt has got everyone so scared of him right now that no one would draft with me, they were trying to go with him, and my car was still strong enough to stay on the outside of them.

"He's 'The Intimidator' and it was intimidation. But I ain't scared of nobody. I will say all of my stuff on the track by beating him, and I am going to beat him more than once this year."

Richard Childress helped his crewmen clear the pits and load the truck. A new season had begun as had so many before – and for the second consecutive year Childress was going back to North Carolina without the trophy everyone had expected his team to win.

"Life goes on after the Daytona 500," he said. "We want to win, and we will win it someday. We just got to go to Richmond now. Put all of that behind us and go to Richmond. I can't blame Dale for what happened out there today. He was just trying to take the car to the front, and that is the reason he is Dale Earnhardt. I wouldn't want him to be any other way. Three-hundred and sixty-five more days, we'll come back and try it again. It will come to us one of these days."

• • •

The Richmond race always has been a good place for Dale to get over the disappointment and frustration of losing another Daytona 500. It was again in 1991.

Sick with a cold, Earnhardt spent little time with the car in practice and qualified for only the 19th starting spot. "Get the car as good as you can, and we'll get them on Sunday," he told his crew chief.

Feeling a little better after a couple of days' rest, Dale was in a racy mood when the Pontiac 400 began. He needed only 27 laps to move into the top 10, and he took the lead for the first time a quarter of the way into the race.

In the late stages, when Sterling Marlin was trying to stay in the lead lap, Dale cleared him out of the way with a shot from his bumper. "I didn't really mean to get into him, but he was a lap down and I was racing for the lead, so it really didn't bother me," Dale said after winning. Then he paused and asked, "Where does this put me in points?"

First place, he was told.

He smiled.

"Good," he said.

• • •

Dale became the the first two-time winner of the season in the Hanes 500 at Martinsville in late April. It was the 50th victory of his career and tied him on the all-time list with Hall-of-Famers Ned Jarrett and Junior Johnson.

"That makes me proud, because those were two of the drivers that my daddy raced against, and I know he would be proud, too," Dale said.

Humpy Wheeler, who had driven up from his Lake Norman home to see the race, knew that Ralph Earnhardt would have been very proud of his son, but not only for the victories and championships he was collecting.

During the 1960s, when Wheeler and his wife Pat were expecting their first child, Humpy and his friend Ralph had got-

287

ten into a conversation before a Thursday night dirt-track race in Columbia.

"You want your children to be race drivers?" Wheeler had asked.

Ralph thought a few seconds and replied, "I want them to grow up to be good people."

Wheeler recalled that conversation as Dale was charging through the field to victory.

"If I had come as far in life as Dale Earnhardt has come," Wheeler said, "I would be President of the United States. I am proud of him as a father, as a husband, as a human being, and, somewhere down the line, as a race driver. He is a good person, and that is what his daddy wanted him to be."

15

The Good, the Bad, the Sad

Dale already had his fifth Winston Cup championship tucked safely in his pocket when he arrived at Atlanta Motor Speedway in November for the final race of the 1991 season. But even though he had not felt pressured by the competition, this had not been a pleasant journey to the title.

His strongest challenge had come from Ricky Rudd, who was in his second year driving a Chevrolet for the rich Rick Hendrick team. Rudd had trailed Dale by 59 points heading into the Holly Farms 400 at North Wilkesboro Speedway, a track where the two had experienced some fierce fender-slamming battles in previous years.

But the championship race was not the hot topic race fans talked about as they lunched on fried chicken and liquid refreshment while awaiting the start of the 400-lap race. The driver commanding their attention was 51-year-old Harry Gant, who owned a steak house in his hometown of Taylorsville, not far away.

Gant was not in contention for the title, but he had created a lot of excitement by reeling off four straight victories in

September. Dale, meanwhile, had not been in Victory Lane since the Diehard 500 at Talladega, Ala., in late July. That win had been his fifth on NASCAR's fastest track and would remain the highlight of this season.

Dale had taken the lead with 75 miles remaining and settled down to watch in his rear view mirror as a flock of Ford drivers battled among themselves to compete with him. But at the finish, Dale had slipped under the checkered flag a car length ahead of Bill Elliott's Ford. Mark Martin, in another Ford, was third. He was followed by Rudd and Sterling Marlin, yet another Ford driver.

At one point, Davey Allison had appeared to be Dale's most serious challenger but he had been shuffled out of the lead draft by his Ford mates. After Allison had pulled alongside Dale with three laps remaining, his drafting partner, Marlin, unexpectedly wheeled in behind Dale.

Allison could do nothing as a string of cars breezed by him. He wound up ninth and had some heated words for his Ford teammates.

"I can't believe that," he said, as he climbed out of his Thunderbird. "If you trust another Ford driver and he hangs you out to dry like that, then that is just plain rotten. If I had gotten just a little help we could have passed Dale and settled it among ourselves. But we were fighting ourselves instead of trying to help each other."

Marlin, who still hadn't won a Winston Cup race, claimed that he had no choice but to duck behind Dale. "Man, you know I did not want that black Chevrolet to win," he said when reporters crowded around him. "But once Davey got up beside Dale, he shot ahead for a second and I got hung out to dry. Earnhardt was blocking me and I couldn't go with Davey. But, I tell you, I didn't see anybody helping anybody out there.

"Everything just got scatter-brained in those final laps. I know the Fords were supposed to help each other, but it didn't seem like anyone was trying to make that work."

Aware that the Fords were trying to team up, the Chevrolet crews of Earnhardt and Rudd also had agreed to try to help each other as much as possible. Their drivers were informed of the strategy by radio. With six laps remaining, Rudd had planted his Chevy on Dale's rear bumper, hoping that they could get far enough ahead to decide the outcome between themselves on the final lap.

"I couldn't hold the Fords back, though," Rudd admitted. "They got underneath me and Dale had to hold them off by himself. He did a great job, too."

Dale had hoped that the dramatic win would give his team the momentum to collect a few more victories before the season ended and merrily celebrate another championship. But that hadn't happened. His best finish in the races leading up to Wilkesboro had been third, his worst 15th. Rudd hadn't done much better, though, and just before the Wilkesboro race he had spoken of how strange the season had been.

"There really has not been anyone dominating all season," he said. "The only thing you can do is keep working and hope that you hit on something that will give you the advantage that you need to break away."

Rudd pointed toward Gant. "He has found something. He hadn't won a race all year, and now he can't seem to lose."

Dale had been puzzled by his team's failure to do better since Talladega. In previous seasons, they had excelled in the championship stretch.

Rudd's team, on the other hand, was in its first championship fight, and Dale knew that their hunger for it could give them an advantage.

Understandably, Dale became upset when reporters kept asking him what was wrong. "I don't know what the problem is, but it is not behind the steering wheel," he snapped. "We haven't been that dominant all year, but maybe you had better ask the car owner and the crew what the problem is. I don't know. What I do know is that the driver is working his ass off."

Dale went on to win the Wilkesboro race to end Gant's streak, but only after Gant had led most of the way and dropped off the pace after experiencing brake problems in the final laps.

Still, the victory did not improve Dale's disposition and rumors soon began spreading of dissension in his once-close team. It didn't help that Dale remained in a grumpy mood, even as Rudd fell further behind in the points battle.

Rudd was also unhappy with his team's failure to try new ideas in the stretch run. He was 157 points behind Dale when the circuit moved to Phoenix for the next-to-last race on the schedule. Both drivers were invited to attend a prerace news conference, but only Rudd appeared to discuss his fading championship hopes.

Dale claimed to have no new answers to the questions he had been hearing for weeks. It was all very simple, he said. "I am going to race the best I can. If there is a car in front of me that I can pass, I am going to pass it. If there is a car behind me that wants to pass and gets under me, I will probably let him by me. At the end of the race, we will add up the points and see where we stand going into the final race at Atlanta."

Rudd knew that his chances were slim. No one ever had come from 157 points down with two races remaining to win the championship. "The only way I can win it now is for Dale to lose it," he admitted. "You know, he has a boiling point and if he loses his temper and does something crazy, he might give me a chance."

Rudd was not counting on that happening. "Dale isn't a fool," he said with a shrug. "He has won four championships already, so he knows how to play the game."

True to form, Dale didn't do anything foolish at Phoenix, and Rudd went to Atlanta two weeks later trying to hold on to second place against the budding challenges of Allison and Gant.

Dale was feeling no pressure. With a 156-point advantage, all he had to do was show up at Atlanta and take one lap to clinch his fifth title. But before that he had some important business to clear up.

Two days before the race, Dale and Richard Childress called a press conference in the infield media building. The rumors that had been circulating had become nasty, involving Dale's personal life, and they had agreed that the best way to stop them was with a strong public denial.

"I don't have any idea how this stuff got started," Dale said, staring straight at the reporters facing him, "but I am going to put an end to it right now. Teresa and I just celebrated our ninth wedding anniversary on Thursday, and we have not had any problems yet."

When Childress spoke, he said that all the rumors were false, and Dale definitely was not leaving his team. "We are going to be together in 1992 and 1993, and I hope long after that," he said. "I am sure there are some in the garage area who would like to see us split up, but it isn't going to happen any time soon."

Dale went on to claim the championship with the same 156-point lead that he had held over Rudd going into the Atlanta race, and he was relieved to put this season behind him. In addition to all the aggravations and rumors he'd had to deal with, he'd also been saddened by the death of veteran driver J.D. McDuffie in the race at Watkins Glen, N.Y., in August.

McDuffie, one of the last of the rugged independents, had been killed instantly when he crashed into a tire barrier on the fifth lap of the race. Once a short-track star in North Carolina, the cigar-chewing McDuffie, 52, hadn't won a single race in 653 starts on the Winston Cup circuit, although he had once claimed the pole position at Dover Downs. But on the night before his death, he had competed in a special 10-lap Late

Model race at a little track in Owego, N.Y., outracing five members of Dale's pit crew to victory.

Dale admired McDuffie's unquenchable love of racing, and after McDuffie had blown his last engine trying to qualify at Daytona in February, Dale had gone to a few other drivers and got enough money to rent J.D. an engine so that he could race.

Dale was still thinking about McDuffie when he went to New York for NASCAR's championship banquet in early December.

"I am looking forward to a happier new year," he said as he received the championship trophy with Teresa at his side.

* * *

Stock car racing was entering another transitional period in 1992, and some in the sport were wondering whether Dale could remain at the top long enough to best Richard Petty's record of seven championships. Could he and his team remain as dominate and intimidating as they had been in previous years?

Dale was well aware that nothing, and no one, lasts forever, and that was clearly evidenced as Petty began the final season of his career as a driver in Daytona in 1992. It had been seven years since Petty had won a race, the 200th of his legendary career, and 12 years since he had won his last championship. Fittingly, Dale had won his first title in 1980, the year after Petty won his last.

During the '80s, Dale's biggest rival had been Darrell Waltrip, but Waltrip hadn't been a serious contender for a championship since leaving Junior Johnson. Now Dale faced a pack of challengers—Davey Allison, Alan Kulwicki, Ernie Irvan, Mark Martin, and old rivals Rusty Wallace and Bill Elliott—all of them younger than he and eager to replace him.

With Elliott leaving his family team to drive for Junior Johnson and Wallace rebuilding with Roger Penske's new operation, the driver who appeared to have the best chance to challenge Dale was Allison. He had the grit to race Dale fender-to-fender without being intimidated and he had a solid team, owned by Robert Yates, behind him.

Dale began 1992 Speedweek activities at Daytona in familiar fashion, by blowing away the competition in preliminary events. He won his 125-mile qualifying race. He won the International Race of Champions, charging from third place in the final quarter-lap. And he won the Goody's 300 Grand National on Saturday, the day before the big race that he still had never won: the Daytona 500.

"I am on the greatest high of my life, so maybe this will be the year," he said with a grin after his Grand National race. "One more time in Victory Lane this week would make everything perfect."

But, as so many times before, only disappointment awaited him the next day. He got swept into a big mid-race crash on the backstretch and limped to a ninth-place finish without leading a single lap.

Davey Allison, who had finished second to his father, Bobby, in the 1988 Daytona 500, became the latest driver to claim the trophy that Dale wanted most.

Davey and Dale had much in common. Davey, too, had grown up in stock car racing, starting out by working in the shop of his famous father. He had run his own short-track operation, gaining first-hand experience and paying his own way, before finally getting a break as a substitute driver on Junior Johnson's team. And as the 1992 season progressed, Davey was about to establish himself as a legendary driver at the Winston All-Star race at Charlotte Motor Speedway, just as Dale once had done.

This was to be the first race held at night under the speedway's new lights, and promoter Humpy Wheeler had promised "One Hot Night." More than 130,000 fans showed up to see if the race delivered on his promise. No one left disappointed, for Davey made the race one of the most exciting in the sport's history.

Kyle Petty sped into a 14-car length lead on the second lap, but the field bunched again after Darrell Waltrip spun through the infield along the front straight to bring out a caution flag.

Dale bolted into the lead on the restart and built a small lead as Petty and Allison hooked up in a duel for second place. Petty took the position and had closed to within two car lengths of Dale when the white flag appeared to signal the start of the final lap. Dale's Chevrolet slipped just enough in the second turn to give Petty the chance he needed to get a good jump on him. Dale drove low to block Petty and suddenly Dale's car bucked and spun back onto the high bank.

Petty momentarily lifted off the throttle to maintain control and that gave Allison an opportunity to pull alongside for a door-to-door battle to the checkered flag. Allison took the inside lane and pulled inches ahead as the two cars bumped fenders at the finish line.

Then Allison's Ford spun and slammed hard into the outside wall. Fans stood watching in stunned silence as Allison's crew and rescue workers rushed to his battered car. Crew member Joey Knuckles, among the first to reach the car, saw Allison's head slumped to the side, his hands still clutching the steering wheel. By the time crew chief Larry McReynolds got there, Allison was beginning to regain consciousness. "He gave me a thumbs up," McReynolds recalled later.

The roof of the car was quickly sliced open, and Davey, still groggy, was pulled out and placed on a stretcher.

"Who won?" he asked his car owner, Robert Yates.

"You did," Yates said with a smile.

"That is great," Davey said.

But after he continued asking the same question over and over, medical personnel decided to have him taken by helicopter to a nearby hospital for observation and treatment.

Allison, who had suffered a slight concussion, remained hospitalized overnight. He was released the next day with permission from doctors to race in the Coca-Cola 600 the following Sunday.

Allison was a sentimental favorite in this race, but the day was to belong to Dale, who got a lightning-quick final pit stop from his crew to record his first victory of the season and end a thirteen-race winning streak by the Ford drivers.

Dale was running third, behind Kyle Petty and Ernie Irvan, when he entered the pits on the 346th lap. Crewmen dumped in a full tank of gasoline and bolted on a pair of outside tires in only 19.4 seconds to put him out front with 54 laps remaining. Irvan, also in a Chevrolet, shadowed Dale through most of the final laps and finished only four-tenths of a second behind him, with Petty and Allison trailing.

"The last pit stop was definitely the key," Dale acknowledged afterward. "The guys just did a fantastic job."

The pit stop was so fantastic that Petty had trouble believing that it was legal. "There is no way a man can be two seconds behind you on a race track and everybody comes down pit road at the same time and he comes out a second ahead," Petty complained. "I know Dale's pit crew is awfully good, but I don't think anyone can be that good."

Apparently, Petty and some others thought the only way that Dale could have come out of the pit stop with the lead was for him to have exceeded NASCAR's pit road speed limit of 55 miles per hour without being caught. "I thought I was going to be racing Kyle for the victory, and then it is Dale after that round of stops," Irvan said, shaking his head. "I don't know how he did that."

Dale was told what the other drivers were saying and asked if his pit stop had been legal.

"Must have," he said with a grin. "I didn't see no black flag."

Actually, there was an explanation for the discrepancy perceived by the other drivers. The three lead drivers had not made their pit stops on the same lap, as Petty claimed. Petty and Irvan stopped one lap before Dale and both had to slow momentarily before entering pit road because of a slow car in front of them. Dale pitted on the next lap and made a clean entry and exit.

Dale also made sure that everyone knew that his championship crew had done a lot more to contribute to the victory than just that final quick stop. He was driving the same Chevrolet that had been badly damaged in The Winston the previous weekend. "They did a week's work in about two days to get the car back together," Dale explained. "The frame was bent and the body was all beat up. They had to work all day Sunday and Monday to fix it, and then they primed and painted it all in one night."

Even so, the car didn't get to Victory Lane by itself. Dale did a fantastic job during the closing laps protecting the lead against Irvan, who had made up two laps that he lost early in the race because of a carburetor problem. Since Irvan had turned quicker laps than Dale most of the afternoon, he had been surprised how effective Dale had been after getting the lead on the final pit stop. "I thought for sure I had him beat, but I couldn't get around him once I got up on the rear bumper," Irvan said.

Even Dale had been surprised at how the final laps had turned out. "He raced me hard, but it was clean," he said of Irvan. "Ernie is coming around. He is getting to be a good race driver."

Dale felt good about stopping the Ford winning streak, too. "I just wish we could have done it sooner," he said.

His pleasure, however, was only momentary. As the season wore on, and the Fords remained superior, his win at Charlotte took on more significance. It would stand as his only win of the season, preventing him from being shut out for the first time since 1981.

That season's championship was to be fought out by Ford drivers. Davey Allison, who suffered bad crashes and lost his younger brother, Clifford, in a racing accident in Michigan in June, was one of the contenders. The other two were Bill Elliott and an underdog named Alan Kulwicki.

A handsome bachelor from Greenfield, Wisc., who held a degree in mechanical engineering, Kulwicki had run on the ASA short-track circuit before entering Winston Cup racing seven years earlier. He had gone on to be rookie of the year in 1986, and had spurned offers from major teams to build his own. Although he had offended some veteran mechanics with his ideas, Dale and his team had taken an immediate liking to Kulwicki.

Kulwicki didn't back off on the track, and he didn't complain if things got a little rough in the turns. Dale admired that. Kulwicki, who was referred to in the garage areas as the "Polish Prince," also seemed to enjoy the friendly kidding that Dale and his group dished out. But everybody had become aware that Kulwicki was no joke on the race track, and despite limited financing, as the 1992 season entered the stretch, Kulwicki was only 47 points behind Bill Elliott, who was leading the race for the championship.

And although Elliott won the final race at Atlanta, Kulwicki took the championship with a 10-point margin by leading more laps and finishing second. He was the first driver-owner to win the title since Richard Petty in 1979.

Allison, with five victories and 15 Top Five finishes, wound up third, 53 points behind Elliott.

Dale finished twelfth in the final standings, his worst championship run since 1982, when he was driving a Ford for Bud Moore.

Richard Petty's final run at Atlanta had ended one era in Winston Cup racing, and after Dale's disappointing season, some couldn't help but wonder if the decline of another era had not also begun.

The future seemed to belong to the two biggest stars of the 1992 season, Davey Allison and Alan Kulwicki. But no one could imagine the tragedies that stock car racing would face in the coming season.

16

Brightness at the end of a dark season

A few minutes before 9:30 p.m. on the night of April 1, 1993, Dale Earnhardt's private airplane was preparing to touch down at Tri-Cities Airport in Blountville, Tenn., where Winston Cup teams fly into for races at Bristol International Speedway. If Dale had looked out the window into the darkness behind him, he might have been able to see the lights of another approaching aircraft, a twin-engine Fairchild Merlin IIIC, that was carrying Winston Cup champion Alan Kulwicki.

Fortunately, though, Dale was not looking. He surely wouldn't have wanted to see what was about to happen.

Three minutes after Kulwicki's plane was cleared for its final approach, it crashed into a hillside a few miles from the airport and exploded in flames, killing Kulwicki, the pilot, Charlie Campbell, and two other passengers.

Mike Colyer, Dale's longtime pilot, was preparing for his landing when he heard a sound come over his radio, as if somebody had suddenly had the air knocked out of him. "I heard the grunt, and a holler, and then the impact," Colyer later told investigators.

Dale's plane was still two miles out at the time, and although shaken by what he had heard, Colyer made a flawless landing before turning to Dale and saying, "Alan's plane went in out there behind us."

Dale was plainly upset by the incident as he disembarked at the small terminal, where several people were waiting for the Kulwicki plane. Most of them were officials of the Hooters restaurant chain, Kulwicki's sponsor. Dale and his pilot turned away as some in the crowd approached them.

"I knew what happened," Colyer recalled. "I knew whose airplane had gone down. But I couldn't tell them who. I didn't want to be the one to tell them."

Kulwicki had been flying from Knoxville, where he had made an appearance for Hooters. The other two passengers on the plane were Mark Brooks, son of Bob Brooks, the company chairman, and Dan Duncan, Hooters' director of sports management.

"I lost a great friend and racing lost a great champion," Dale told reporters after the crash had been discovered. "It doesn't seem fair. Alan worked so hard to get where he was, and he wasn't given time to enjoy being the champion. It is a tragedy that he was taken away so quickly from us."

With heavy hearts, the Winston Cup family went through with the Bristol race three days later. Rusty Wallace took the checkered flag and then wheeled his Pontiac in an arc on the track's high bank and circled it in a "Polish Victory Lap," as Kulwicki had done when he won his first Winston Cup race at Phoenix in 1988 and again after winning the 1992 championship.

Only three months and five days after Kulwicki was buried on April 7 in Milwaukee, the Winston Cup circuit was struck by yet another tragedy.

On July 12, the day after finishing third in the Winston Cup race at New Hampshire International Speedway, Davey Allison piloted his helicopter from his home near Hueytown, Ala., to watch Neil Bonnett's son, David, practice at Talladega. With him was Red Farmer, a longtime racer and Allison family friend. The helicopter was only a few inches from touching down in the infield of the track when it suddenly went out of control, shot some 25 feet into the air, and crashed back to the ground, critically injuring Allison, who died the following day at Carraway Methodist Hospital in Birmingham at the age of 32. Farmer, who also was hurt, recovered enough to attend Allison's funeral on July 15.

Once again, after tearful goodbyes, the Winston Cup crews and drivers steeled themselves and went back racing.

"It is not easy," Dale said. "We are all saddened by this latest tragedy, but we have to go on."

At Pocono International Raceway on the Sunday following Allison's death, only one team was missing: that of Robert Yates, who said he knew Davey would want them to race but that neither he nor his crewmen were up to it.

Allison remained in everyone's prayers and thoughts during the Pocono weekend. On the track, Dale locked up in a battle with Rusty Wallace and broke away in the final 17 laps to get the victory that gave him the opportunity to pay tribute to both of the racing buddies he had lost.

Dale parked his car near the finish line and waited for his crewmen to join him. They kneeled around the car and passed Dale a flag bearing Allison's familiar number 28. Dale held the flag out the window as he took the "Polish Victory Lap."

"That was as emotional as I have ever seen Dale," crewman David Smith said afterwards. "I have seen Dale cry, and not many people can say that."

Dale fought back more tears in victory lane as he dedicated the victory to Allison. "I would have been glad to run second to Davey today," he said. "To win it and to have the death of Davey hanging in your mind, well, it was just an emotional moment."

Aside from the heart-wrenching sorrows off the track, Dale had come back strong from the disappointing season he had in 1992. The Childress team was forced to regroup during the winter after longtime crew chief Kirk Shelmerdine resigned at the end of the season to pursue his own racing dream.

"Richard and I both tried talking Kirk out of leaving us," Dale said. "I told him to take a few days off and think about it. But Kirk had made up his mind. He was honest enough with us to say he had lost some interest and he wanted to pursue his own racing career."

Shelmerdine, who had helped Dale to win four of his Winston Cup titles, predicted that his departure would benefit the team. Dale didn't agree immediately with that assessment because he knew how dedicated Shelmerdine had been and how well they worked together.

The key was finding the right person to replace Shelmerdine. Several candidates were interviewed by both Childress and Dale before they settled on Andy Petree, who had crewed for Harry Gant the previous year.

"I think the main thing that convinced us Andy was the right person for the job was that when we talked to him, he never mentioned money or what changes he thought needed to be made to the team," Dale said. "The only thing he wanted to do was win races and championships. He knew that we were still a good team, despite the kind of season we'd had the previous year, and he didn't see the need to come in and change everything around."

The relationship between Petree and Dale got off to a bruising start, but gave the team something to laugh about as they prepared for the 1993 season with a new leader. "Andy bloodied my nose in one of the first tests we went to during the winter," Dale recalled. "I guess he wanted to show me who was boss."

What really happened was that Dale had been trying to adjust the steering wheel and had removed the pin that held it in place. Petree leaned through the driver's window and thought Dale was trying to remove the steering wheel. Trying to be helpful, he gave the wheel a mighty tug and it flew back into Dale's face.

"I learned right then that I wasn't going to give him any back talk," Dale said with a laugh.

Dale had another strong run in the season-opening Daytona 500, but once again came up a little short in his never-ending quest to win the big race. He led 107 of the 200 laps and took the white flag before being passed on the final lap by Dale Jarrett, driving a Chevrolet owned by former Washington Redskins coach Joe Gibbs. Jarrett got the drafting boost he needed to get around Dale from Geoff Bodine, and with his father, Ned, calling the race for CBS, held on for the victory.

"Jarrett had the strongest engine and there was nothing I could do," Dale explained after finishing second, about two car lengths behind. "I have lost this race about every way possible. I have been out-run, out-gassed, out-tired, and out-everything. The only thing you can do is keep coming back and try again."

Dale's first victory with Petree came at Darlington in late March, ending almost a 10-month dry spell. After dropping almost a lap down early in the race, Dale charged back to lead 212 of the 367 laps for his 54th victory, tying him on the all-time list with Hall-of-Famer Lee Petty.

Dale acknowledged that Petree had helped to bring new life to his team. "It is just a different atmosphere," he said. "It is more exciting, or something. I know I feel different than I did last year. Andy has done a great job of fitting in, and making things easy for me. I feel as comfortable as I did while working with Kirk. I think Andy and I can have the same kind of trust that I had with Kirk."

One victory in 10 months was not enough to convince everyone that Dale had returned to being the intimidating force he had been while rolling to five national championships. But the possibility would become easier to accept a few weeks later after he had swept to victory in both The Winston and the

Coca-Cola 600 in back-to-back weekends. As was so often the case, though, those wins did not come without controversy.

Dale left fans, media, and competitors howling foul following his cagey victory over Mark Martin in The Winston. Martin dominated the first eight laps of the final 10-lap segment before a caution flag appeared to set up a two-lap shootout. On the lap leading to the restart, Dale pulled alongside Martin's Ford and took off down the backstretch before the green flag waved.

NASCAR officials quickly aborted the restart, but instead of placing Dale at the rear of the field, as would be the case in a regular Winston Cup event, they allowed him to return to his front-row position alongside the now jittery Martin for another restart.

Dale slyly played his accelerator and grinned at Martin as they again paraded into the backstretch. This time, Dale waited until he saw the green flag drop before gunning the throttle and leaping ahead of Martin, where he stayed to win a whopping $225,500.

Martin was thoroughly disgusted by the way the race ended, but he was not as outspoken in his criticism of NASCAR for not punishing Dale for jumping the first restart as were some other drivers who hadn't lost nearly as much.

"That was like someone taking a gun and stealing the money," fumed Ernie Irvan. "To jump the restart and then give him another try at it is like giving a bank robber a second chance to do the job." Irvan recalled that he had jumped a green flag the previous year during a regular season race and was sent to the rear of the field.

NASCAR officials explained to Irvan that this was not a regular tour event. It was an all-star race with its own set of rules, designed to maximize competition and excitement for the fans. There was no rule that stated a driver would be penalized for jumping a restart.

Dale seemed to enjoy being the center of controversy again. He laughed during his postrace interview when told that other drivers were angry about what had happened. "They didn't like that first restart?" he asked, teasingly. "If they are that mad, I'm glad I am up here (in the press box) instead of down there in the garage."

Dale confessed that he intentionally had jumped the first restart, just to see what would happen. "I didn't think I would get away with it," he said with a shrug, "but I thought I would try it anyway."

In the Coca-Cola 600 a week later, it was Dale's time to complain, but the results were the same. He wound up in Victory Lane again despite being penalized twice during the race by NASCAR.

In the first incident, Dale was penalized 15 seconds for speeding down pit road during a caution period. Later in the race, he was penalized a full lap for rough driving and causing Greg Sacks to spin out. Dale claimed he was innocent on both accounts. But, unable to convince NASCAR officials to change their minds, he stuck his foot on the accelerator a little harder and overcame both penalties to beat rookie Jeff Gordon to the finish line by four seconds.

The incident with Sacks left Dale a lap down with less than 75 laps remaining. He passed leader Dale Jarrett to get back in the same lap and moved up to eighth place when Rusty Wallace spun and brought out a caution period. Six laps after the final restart, Dale drove by Irvan and began pulling away to the victory.

"I swear I never touched Sacks," Dale said. "He just got loose in front of me and spun. I didn't touch him. NASCAR tried to make this victory tougher than it should have been. But it makes this win more satisfying, coming back after two penalties like that. That says a lot about the strength of my car and my team. You just can't keep a good man down."

In the race for the Winston Cup championship, the same could be said for Rusty Wallace, who had overcome early-season misfortunes to emerge a strong challenger for Dale in the final half of the season. Wallace had experienced two spectacular wrecks during the opening months, first in the Daytona 500 when he suffered only a cut chin, and again in the Winston 500 at Talladega when he and Dale tangled while racing for the checkered flag on the final lap.

Wallace had come into the Talladega race looking for his fourth straight victory and was in contention following a rain shower that briefly halted the race four laps from the end. After a 12-minute delay and a couple of warm-up laps, the race resumed under green with two laps remaining. A crowd of drivers, including Dale, Wallace, and Ernie Irvan took off in hot pursuit of the victory.

Irvan, who had moved from fourth place to lead at the start of the final lap, was about to take the checkered flag when Wallace dropped low in front of Dale. Their cars made slight contact and Wallace was sent rocketing down the track into a series of rolls and flips. Dale saw the terrible crash as he crossed the finish line, and instead of going to the garage, he drove to Wallace's car and climbed out to make sure he was all right.

After getting a thumbs up from Wallace, who was later air-lifted to a Birmingham hospital where he was treated for a broken left wrist and a concussion, Dale was visibly shaken and apologized for the accident.

Nonetheless, Wallace's fans angrily demanded that NASCAR take action against Earnhardt, who they claimed was trying to be the bully of the race tracks again.

A few days later, Wallace cooled the situation by saying he did not blame Dale for what happened. The accident, he said, was caused more by circumstances than by Dale. "We were all racing for the win, to finish as well as we could," he explained.

"I was looking for a hole and I came down the track in front of Dale. I can't blame him for what happened."

Wallace held an 86-point lead over Dale following the Talladega race, but with his injured wrist and a series of mechanical problems he had dropped 251 points behind after Dale won at Daytona in early July. Dale went on to win two more races that month, at Pocono and Talladega, but then the victories ended, and Wallace began to gain in the points battle.

Wallace turned the heat up during a string of eight races in which he finished fourth or better, including victories at Michigan, Dover, and North Wilkesboro. That left him 75 points behind Dale going into the Mello Yello 500 at Charlotte in early October, with four races remaining.

Ironically, that was the same number of points by which Wallace had trailed Dale in 1989 when he rallied to win his only title by a 12-point margin. "I am thinking that it could happen again, and I bet that Dale and his guys are thinking the same thing, too," Wallace said a couple of days before the Charlotte race.

Asked to explain how he had sliced 212 points off Dale's lead in the last three races, and 269 in the last seven, Wallace replied that he thought Dale's team had begun celebrating too soon. "I think they just kind of pulled the throttles back and started running on cruise control. I am sure they never thought in a million years that they would lose 200 points in two weeks."

But Wallace had seen a different attitude on Dale's part the previous week at North Wilkesboro, where they finished 1-2. "He was driving like the ol' Dale again," Wallace said. "He stormed from tenth right up to the front and it was a heckuva race. I think you are going to see that same kind of shootout right to the end, too."

Dale wasn't buying Wallace's theory that history was about to repeat itself. "No two races are alike and no two seasons are alike," he explained. "There really is no pattern to it. What happened in 1989 has absolutely no bearing on what is going to happen this year."

Dale proved his theory was correct in the Charlotte race. In 1989, he had encountered a mechanical failure in the early laps and finished 42nd. Wallace had finished eighth to take the points lead and never relinquished it.

This time, Dale finished third behind Ernie Irvan, who had taken over Davey Allison's ride, and picked up 10 points on fourth-place Wallace, who failed to lead a lap. Wallace regained the 10 points by finishing ahead of Dale at Rockingham the next week, but for all practical purposes the title was decided at Phoenix a week later, when Dale finished fourth behind winner Mark Martin, and Wallace, who was experimenting with tire pressures, had problems and finished 19th.

Dale took a 126-point lead into the final race at Atlanta. He needed only to finish 34th or better to wrap up his sixth championship that would bring him within one of tying Petty's record.

"I know that basically all Dale has to do to win the title is show up in Atlanta," Wallace said. "I don't know what I have to do to catch up, but you can bet I am not going to give up. I'll go there and try to win the race and just see what happens."

Wallace did win the final race, his 10th victory of the season, but Dale did more than just show up. He finished 10th and was assured of the championship just before the midway point when T.W. Taylor crashed his Ford and became the eighth driver to fall out of the race.

When the race was over, both Dale and Wallace paid a fitting tribute to the two friends they had lost during the long, emotional season. Side-by-side, they did a Polish Victory Lap, with Dale holding a banner bearing Alan Kulwicki's No. 7 and Wallace waving a banner with Davey Allison's No. 28.

* * *

While Dale's return to the top of the Winston Cup standings during the 1993 season had been clouded by the deaths of Kulwicki and Allison, he'd had several emotionally uplifting moments as well.

One of those came on October 5, just as Dale was getting read to buckle into the stretch run against Wallace. His hometown of Kannapolis, N.C., gave him a day of his own, and some 20,000 fans turned out to honor him. Dale received many gifts, including a letter jacket, cap and football jersey with No. 3 on it from A.L. Brown High School, which he had attended.

"I never graduated from high school, and it was one of the worst mistakes I ever made," Dale told Brown students. "I want all of you to realize how important it is to stay in school and get an education."

One tribute that brought a big smile was the renaming of Earnhardt Road, which intersects with Interstate 85, to Dale Earnhardt Boulevard. Although it already bore his family name, it had not originally been named with him in mind.

"I have got a lot of memories from that old road," Dale said with a laugh. "I have been bird-hunting along there many times, and I can remember driving my '56 Chevy down there sideways a time or two."

Checkered flags decorated this cotton mill town where Dale had grown up, and a large black No. 3 flag flew at the center of Cannon Village downtown, where Dale took the stage with his mother, Martha, his wife, Teresa, and his daughters, Kelley and Taylor Nicole.

"It is pretty neat for your hometown to recognize you for what you have done in racing, but on the other hand, I am just Dale Earnhardt," he reminded. "I am from Kannapolis, just like everyone else here. And I am really proud to be from Kannapolis."

Later in the evening, Dale was honored again with a black-tie reception and dinner at the Kannapolis Country Club. In a video shown during the event, Dale remembered the help he received from his family and hometown friends early in his career. He recalled that his sister, Kathy, once pried him out of a crash in a race at Asheville, and used three rolls of duct tape to secure his rib-cage so he could drive. "You just did what you had to do," Dale recalled of those early days. "I remember driving a car for Bud Moore with my leg broke. I knew if I didn't drive it, someone else would."

Dale also remembered the help he received from friends who worked at Cannon Mills. "They would make us parts we needed for the car in the machine shop and then sneak them out in their lunch boxes. It is like I said, you just did what you had to do to keep racing, because we loved it so much."

Kathy Earnhardt perhaps paid the most meaningful tribute to her brother, when she said, "You have taken us places we would never have gone if not for you and Daddy. You have taken something Daddy started and made it into a legacy that has embedded us in the life we love."

The Earnhardt family tradition was being continued by another generation in 1993. Dale's two sons, Kerry and Dale Jr., and daughter, Kelley, all were starting their own racing careers.

Kerry, the eldest of Dale's sons, separated from his father at the age of three when his mother, Latane, and Dale divorced. Although Kerry grew up not far from where Dale lived, he did not see his father again until he was 16 years old and got his driver's license.

"We have become pretty close during the last four years," Kerry said. "I know he is special to a lot of fans as a driver, but the only thing that makes him special to me is being my father."

Both Dale Jr. and Kerry began racing on their own, receiving only encouragement and some words of advice from their father.

"Dad told us he wanted us to do it ourselves so we could learn," Kerry explained, "and that was fine with me because I wanted to make it myself instead of having people say the only way I made it was off my daddy's money. Daddy did get out in the garage and help us work on the cars, just as my granddaddy helped him. I guess it brought back some of the old memories for him."

A few oldtimers told Kerry that he reminded them of his father when he was starting out. If so, he said, it was unintentional. "I drive my own style. I am not sitting in the car wondering what Dad might do," he said. Yet Kerry wasn't offended by the comparison, no more than Dale had been when people told him that he had the same style in a race car as did his father, Ralph.

17

Farewell to Neil

An unwritten rule in auto racing is that you do not form close friendships with other drivers. You tolerate those you seek to defeat. Some, of course, you tolerate more enjoyably than others, but you just don't form close friendships until careers are finished.

Dale had followed this rule carefully through most of his career. There were a few drivers he admired, a few he liked, and a few he respected, but until Neil Bonnett came along, Dale did not have a close friend on the race track.

He and Bonnett, however, shared the same racing philosophies and had the same love for hunting and fishing. And while Dale was drawing harsh criticism on his bumpy ride to the top, Bonnett had become one of his strongest defenders. "It is a race car," Bonnett would remind critics. "You don't just drive it, you race it."

Dale and Neil had begun racing against each other on short tracks, and as much as they had enjoyed it, they really hadn't cemented their friendship until Bonnett's bad crash at Darlington in 1990 had threatened to end his career. Neil suffered amnesia following the crash and could not recognize members of his family for several days. Slowly, his memory began returning, and one of the first signs of his recovery came when he pointed to a deer head on the wall of his den and told his wife, Susan, that he'd gotten the trophy while on a hunting trip with Dale.

Bonnett eventually regained full memory, but it took many more months of physical therapy before he regained his balance and the self-confidence needed to begin thinking about returning to racing. Doctors were pleased with Bonnett's progress, but they advised him not to race again. Another severe blow to the head might bring permanent loss of memory, they warned.

But Bonnett couldn't slip away from racing so easily, although he tried. At first, he contented himself by helping his son, David, launch a racing career. Then he employed his keen wit and vast knowledge of the sport to become a successful radio and television commentator. He narrated one of the best racing series ever produced for television, "Winners," which documented the careers of drivers in many forms of motorsports and was seen weekly on The Nashville Network.

Bonnett later admitted, however, that he was doing this to to stay close enough to the business to seize the opportunity to race again, should it present itself. "The television people were using me for what they wanted, and I was using them for what I wanted," Neil recalled with a chuckle.

Only a few people knew how determined Neil was to get back behind the steering wheel of a race car. One of them was Dale, who talked many hours with his friend while on hunting and fishing trips about his need to race. "I didn't quit racing because I was ready to give it up," Bonnett said. "I had to quit because I was hurt and couldn't drive a race car. So, if I am healthy again, why shouldn't I resume racing?"

Dale and his car owner, Richard Childress, eventually provided the opportunity that Neil had been seeking. Bonnett tested Grand National cars for Dale and tested Dale's Winston

Cup Chevrolet for Childress. But Dale could see that his friend was not ready to return to racing. "You got to get your confidence back," he told Bonnett. "You can't go racing until you feel comfortable in that car again."

Dale continued to give Bonnett the tough support he needed, however. At times, Neil's thoughts seemed like blurs and he would stumble vocally when trying to express himself. Frustrated, he would blurt out, "I'm crazy, Dale."

"No, you are not," Dale would reply. "If I hear you say that again, I am going to kick your butt."

"People joke about Dale and myself," Bonnett said. "But I don't care how much therapy you do, what he did for me was incredible. He stuck by me more than anyone when I was down. My best rehabilitation was when Dale asked me to climb into his race car."

Bonnett tested for the Childress team for most of the 1993 season and Dale credited him with helping to develop a superspeedway car that carried him to that year's championship. In appreciation, Childress had provided Bonnett a car to drive in the Diehard 500 at Talladega in July.

It was Bonnett's first race since the accident at Darlington three years earlier, and he wanted to show car owners who might be seeking a driver for next season that he could still do the job. "Do whatever is comfortable to you," Dale advised. "But, remember, you don't have anything to prove to me. I know you are a helluva race car driver."

Bonnett settled into a steady, smooth pace, but as so often happens on the race track, it isn't what you do but what others do that dictates circumstances. On Lap 132 of the 188-lap race, Bonnett was coming off the fourth turn when his black No. 31 Chevrolet was tapped in the rear, sending the car into a wild flight. The car slammed, wheel-first, into the grandstand wire fence on the frontstretch. Bonnett did not suffer anything more than a few cuts and bruises, but the wreck was spectacular and damaging enough that the race had to be stopped for 70 minutes for repairs to be made to the fence.

"I'll bet Richard Childress won't be loaning me any more race cars," Bonnett quipped afterward. "This might end my comeback."

A lot of Bonnett's family and friends hoped the accident would cause him finally to quit racing. But they knew that the wreck hadn't been his fault. Anyone, even Dale Earnhardt, could get hit from behind and put into the wall. And Bonnett still couldn't relinquish his compulsion to race.

"I wish I could get in a race car and feel that I wasn't comfortable and just walk away from it," he said. "But I know that isn't going to happen. The wreck at Talladega was just racing. It may have looked negative to a lot of people, but I had a real positive attitude when everything was over. I got out of the car and said to myself, 'Hey, I can drive one of those things again.'"

Bonnett was back in a Childress team Chevrolet for the final race of the season in Atlanta, but this time his job was not to race, as it had been at Talladega. His mission was to serve as an insurance policy for Dale clinching the championship. He qualified a backup car for the 35th starting position, so it would be available for Dale to drive in case something happened to his No. 3 car before the start of the race. Once Dale took the green flag, Bonnett's job was over. He parked the car at the end of the third lap, claiming engine failure as the reason for quitting.

Dale mentioned the role Bonnett played in his sixth Winston Cup championship at the NASCAR banquet in New York, where Bonnett was made to feel like part of the team. Bonnett also was still a television commentator, and one of his assignments was an informal interview with Dale about his season.

The interviews Bonnett conducted with Dale were always open and interesting, more like a couple of friends sitting down to chat than a formal question-and-answer session, and that was the format for the interview following the championship banquet.

"When we started racing, we ran all over the country," Bonnett reminded his friend. "You said when you won that first championship that you didn't realize what you had done. But this is number six. You got to realize what is happening now."

"Well, it is hard to believe, isn't it?" Dale said. "It came around, and me and you been hunting and talked about winning races and championships and stuff, and still you are just Dale Earnhardt and Neil Bonnett doing what you enjoy doing, and then—boom—you are champion and then six-time champion. You didn't really set out to do that. You set out to race and win races, and you win a championship, and you win another one. You know, this life takes you to great places sometimes."

Dale told Bonnett that he hoped to race until the year 2000, when he would be 48 years old, and that he hoped to win a couple more championships to break Richard Petty's record. "You know yourself, Neil, your health is what slows you down. And if my health stays good, we don't get in any big accidents or anything, if my health stays good, I think I can race that long. If you stay healthy and sharp, you can race that long."

Bonnett mentioned in the interview that one of the things that impressed him about Dale was his ability to take a 10th-place car and finish second. "You are so competitive. What is it that keeps driving you?"

"You can answer that," Dale replied. "You are wanting to get back into a race car as bad as I'm wanting to be in one tomorrow. But it is something that is born and bred into you. I grew up in racing and I love racing to the point I am comfortable with it. I am more relaxed in a race car than I am on TV or whatever. But you know yourself, it is the most important thing in life to you and me. Racing is what we live for. It is our life, our profession, our fun. People say, 'Well, it is your job.' It is not your job. It is fun. When you are in a race car and getting after it, you are having a good time, and making a living, too."

Not only was Bonnett wanting to get back in a race car, both he and Dale were excited about his plans for the 1994 season. Bonnett was going to drive a limited schedule, only six races, for James Finch, a longtime friend from Panama City, Fla. Initially, the deal was for Bonnett to drive only four races and the Daytona 500 was not among them. But the team sponsor, Country Time drink mix, decided it wanted the exposure from NASCAR's most prestigious—and publicized—race.

"It took about two seconds for them to talk me into it," Bonnett said.

When Daytona International Speedway opened for Winston Cup practice on February 11, those who saw Bonnett working around the neon pink and yellow No. 51 Chevrolet say they had never seen him happier. He was doing what he wanted to do, doing what he was compelled to do. Doing what he lived to do.

But, in a matter of hours, Neil Bonnett was dead at the age of 47.

He was making a routine practice run about 12:45 p.m. when the Chevrolet broke loose in the third turn, bucked sideways and struck the outside wall. The car skidded down onto the grassy apron, then shot back across the track to slam into the outside retaining wall with violent force.

Rescue workers had to cut Bonnett from the car. He had only a faint pulse when he was placed on a stretcher, and less than an hour later, at 1:17 p.m., he was pronounced dead.

Dale was in the garage when he realized there had been an accident. At first, he did not know it was Bonnett, and he had no idea how serious it was until someone quietly broke the news to him as he walked between the garage and his truck. He dropped his head, closed his eyes, and felt a swelling in his throat.

It would be awhile before Dale could talk about his feelings, and team owner Richard Childress spoke briefly to only a few close friends in the media. "I just lost a great friend, and racing has lost a great driver," Childress told Mike Mulhern of the Winston-Salem (N.C.) *Journal.* "We have been so close for several years, hunting together and all. Neil came up to our team Christmas party this year.

But every morning you wake up you don't know what life will deal you. The first time Neil got back in a race car for us, for a test two years ago at Rockingham, he told me, 'This is the happiest I've ever been.' When he told me about the deal for him to drive this year, he said, 'I would rather be doing this than anything in the world.' So, he died doing what he wanted to do. We've all got to keep on going. That is what Neil would want us to do."

A day after Bonnett's death, the first round of Daytona 500 qualifying was run as scheduled. Dale won a front-row starting position and later shook off reporters who wanted to talk to him about his friend's death. "I will talk about it, just let me get through the next couple of days," he asked.

He and Childress, though, did issue a statement that expressed their feelings. It read:

"We really don't know what to say. Yesterday we went on with the job we had in front of us because we were in shock. You don't feel anything when you are in shock. You're numb. But after a night to think about it, you remember the racing and the hunting trips and fishing trips and the things that make people good friends. Then, when it is gone, and you realize all you have left are those memories, it all comes crashing down. It hits you. That's what has happened. We have lost one of our best friends, and it has hit us hard."

Bonnett was buried on Monday near his home in

Hueytown, Ala. Ironically, a short time before the funeral began, tragedy struck again on the Daytona high banks. Thirty-one-year-old Rodney Orr, who had won the Dash Series championship in 1993, was killed in a single-car crash while practicing for his first Daytona 500.

No firm conclusions were reached about the cause of either fatal accident. Some said a hard wind may have been responsible. Some said Bonnett's car may have skidded on a patch of oil. But no would could say for sure.

On Tuesday, the day after attending Bonnett's funeral, Dale walked into the Daytona media center, pulled up a chair and began expressing his feelings in greater depth.

"Why did it have to happen to Neil Bonnett? Why did it have to happen now?" he asked. "Neil was as happy as I had seen him in three years. He hadn't been this happy back when he was winning. Who would have thought this could have happened? One of the ARCA drivers had a crash the day before that seemed a lot worse than Neil's and the driver was not seriously hurt. You wonder why one guy crashes and walks away and one guy crashes and there is no hope he will make it."

Dale recalled the spectacular crash Michael Waltrip had in a Grand National race at Bristol. His car was demolished. But he walked away. "Why not Neil?" he asked again.

The question Dale didn't have to ask, but that others were asking throughout the garage, was why Neil had wanted to race again when there were so many other opportunities for him. Dale knew the answer to that question better than anyone. "He wanted to drive a race car," he said. "He never wanted to stop."

The deaths of Bonnett and Orr cast a dark shadow over the racing fraternity, and put drivers and their families on edge for the Twin 125-mile qualifying races on Thursday. Rusty Wallace, after conferring with Dale and Ken Schrader, attempted to ease the situation with an emotional plea at the prerace drivers' meeting. "Please respect each other," he began. "These cars don't just drive straight into the wall by themselves, or flip over by themselves, or go flying through the grass by themselves. That shouldn't happen. If you don't fit a hole, don't try it. If the car doesn't handle, bring it in for a pit stop. Harry Houdini couldn't drive a car that doesn't handle here."

Wallace recalled his wrecks the previous season at Daytona and Talladega. "I have been upside down at Daytona, and I have been upside down at Talladega. It hurts like hell. I am tired of losing my friends, and I am tired of seeing my friends get hurt. Everyone is running a little scared, and my wife is damn scared. So, everyone, please. Let's use our heads."

Dale walked away from the meeting nodding his head. "Rusty is right," he said. "I am glad he spoke out and said the things he did. I hope it does some good."

Dale, who had finished third in the Busch Clash two days after Bonnett's death, got his first victory of the week in his 125-mile qualifying race. He led 34 of the 50 laps and crossed the finish line about two car lengths ahead of Sterling Marlin's Chevrolet.

During the postrace interview, Dale again spoke eloquently about Bonnett. "He was with us today and will be in our hearts forever," Dale said. "I can't say enough good things about him. He was an important part of our team the past couple of years, doing so much testing for us. But more than that, he was my best friend."

Someone asked Dale if he would dedicate the Daytona 500 to Bonnett if he won it.

"Dedicate a race to him? I am going to dedicate my life to him," Dale said solemnly.

Dale had another victory to celebrate the next day after the International Race of Champions. He started on pole position, by luck of the draw, and slapped back a series of challenges by Indy driver Al Unser Jr., on the final lap to protect the victory.

"I just flat blocked him," Dale said. "I blocked him in one and two. I blocked him three or four times on the backstretch. He would go high and I would go high. He would go low and I'd go low. My car was wide on the backstretch, and it grew even wider as we neared the finish line."

Dale made it three victories in as many days on Saturday as he surprised even himself by driving out of a pack on the final lap to win the Goody's 300 Grand National race for a fifth consecutive year. The finish came down between Dale and Terry Labonte after a bunch of fast Fords experienced problems in the stretch run. Labonte twice blocked Dale on the backstretch of the last lap before Dale sneaked low in the third turn and came through with a winning pass. He was smiling so broadly as he sped under the checkered flag that it could be spotted from the Goodyear blimp.

"Unbelievable," Dale shouted while climbing out of his car. "I can't believe I won this race. That has to be one of the most unbelievable finishes I've ever had in a race at this track. I didn't think I had a chance when those Fords began pulling away. Then they started falling out, and that left Ernie Irvan by himself up there."

Labonte had passed Irvan with about five laps left and held on to the lead until Dale pulled under him.

The Goody's victory was the 23rd of Dale's career at Daytona. No one had won more races there. But none of the victories had been in the Daytona 500, and Dale was still trying to understand why he had done so well at the big track in other events, and had led so many laps in the 500 without ever winning it.

"I am having trouble figuring out what it takes to win that race," he said. "Haven't I done enough to qualify as a winner of that race? I really, really want to do it this time. When you come as close to winning as many times as I have, and still haven't won it, it begins weighing on you. It weighs on the team. You think about it. You have bad memories about it."

Dale had never felt better about his chances for winning, though, and because of his avowed determination to win this one for Neil, a lot of people were pulling for him this time. "I get damn emotional about this race every year," he said, "but my emotions are on an even higher level this time. I am going to take Neil along with me on this ride. He'll be right here in my heart."

As mightily as Dale wanted to win this Daytona 500, for so many reasons, it again was not to be. Rookie pole-sitter Loy Allen, Jr., gave way on the first lap to Ernie Irvan in a Ford, and Dale pushed his Chevrolet into the lead on the 11th lap. He led nine other times as well, for a total of 114 miles before his car began to wiggle and skate on the high banks. Dale could feel the car getting looser and looser. He dropped back to seventh place, and kept hoping for a caution flag that would allow him to pit for new tires and a chassis adjustment to allow him a strong charge down the stretch.

The caution flag never came, and Dale was the sixth driver to follow winner Sterling Marlin under the checkered flag. It was Marlin's first victory in 279 Winston Cup races, and it had come in the Daytona 500.

Dale shook his head and tried his best to grin after climbing from his car. He started the long walk back to his team truck. Turning to the crowd of reporters following closely on his heels, he said, "I've got the rest of the year to race. It wasn't my day. I've won 23 Daytona races and no Daytona 500s. What the hell. This isn't the end of the world. We will come back next year and try again. I am not giving up. I am going to win this race some day."

Others believed just as firmly that Dale would eventually get the Daytona 500 victory he wanted so badly. But if he did, or if he didn't, it was not going to matter in the way his career would be remembered.

He was The Intimidator, the greatest stock car driver of his era.